SDN and NFV
Simplified

A Visual Guide to Understanding Software Defined
Networks and Network Function Virtualization

Jim Doherty

SDN and NFV Simplified

Jim Doherty

ISBN-13: 978-0-13-430640-7
ISBN-10: 0-13-430640-6

Library of Congress Control Number: 2015956324

Text printed in the United States on recycled paper at RR Donnelley in Kendallville, Indiana.

First printing: March 2016

Many of the designations used by manufacturers and sellers to distinguish their products are claimed as trademarks. Where those designations appear in this book, and the publisher was aware of a trademark claim, the designations have been printed with initial capital letters or in all capitals.

The author and publisher have taken care in the preparation of this book, but make no expressed or implied warranty of any kind and assume no responsibility for errors or omissions. No liability is assumed for incidental or consequential damages in connection with or arising out of the use of the information or programs contained herein.

For information about buying this title in bulk quantities, or for special sales opportunities (which may include electronic versions; custom cover designs; and content particular to your business, training goals, marketing focus, or branding interests), please contact our corporate sales department at corpsales@pearsoned.com or (800) 382-3419.

For government sales inquiries, please contact governmentsales@pearsoned.com.

For questions about sales outside the U.S., please contact intlcs@pearson.com.

Visit us on the Web: informit.com/aw

Editor-in-Chief
Dave Dusthimer

Executive Editor
Mary Beth Ray

Development Editor
Jeff Riley

Managing Editor
Sandra Schroeder

Project Editor
Mandie Frank

Copy Editor
Keith Cline

Indexer
Tim Wright

Proofreader
Debbie Williams

Technical Reviewer
Brian Gracely

Editorial Assistant
Vanessa Evans

Designer
Mark Shirar

Compositor
Studio Galou

To Katie, Samantha, and Conor

SaaS   Software
IaaS   Infrastructure
PaaS   Platform

Hypervisor
Bare Metal   Type 1
Hosted   Type 2

Contents

Acknowledgments

I would like to thank the following people.

First and foremost, I want to thank my researcher and writing assistant, Alasdair Gilchrist. This book simply could not have happened without his hard work and dedication.

This book has been in the works for quite a while, and over the course of a few years, it has morphed from what was originally called *Cloud Networking Simplified*. For a variety of reasons, there were stops and starts, do overs, and evolutions, and in a couple of cases, potential co-authors were brought in. Among them were Dave Asprey, who was a very knowledgeable tech guy before becoming the "Bullet Proof Coffee" guy, and Brian Gracely, who is still a very knowledgeable tech guy who ended up being the technical reviewer of this version of the book. While this book is its own thing, several of their original contributions influenced this version.

Brian Gracely also gets his own thank you for being the technical reviewer of this book. He kept me on my toes and spent a lot of time reading, reviewing, and verifying my work. This book is much better than it would have been without his efforts.

Finally, I want to thank the great team at Pearson. Always the consummate professionals, they make my job much easier, and they are all a pleasure to work with. Specifically, I'd like to thank Executive Editor Mary Beth Ray, who had the patience to keep this project alive through all the iterations. Development Editor Jeff Riley for being a great "man behind the curtain." Line Artist Laura Robbins for helping with the whiteboard layouts and line art. And last but not least, the editing team, including Project Editor Mandie Frank, Development Editors Drew Cupp and Jeff Riley, and Copy Editor Keith Cline, who I'm sure I drove crazy with my many spelling errors, typing errors, run-on sentences, and use of passive voice. This is my sixth book with Pearson, and every crew I've worked with has been outstanding. This one is no exception. Thank you all.

Jim Doherty

About the Author

Jim Doherty has more than 17 years of engineering and marketing experience across a broad range of networking, security, and technology companies. Focusing on technology strategy, product positioning, and marketing execution, Jim has held leadership positions for Cisco Systems, Certes Networks, Ixia, and Ericsson Mobile. Currently, he is the SVP of Sales and Marketing for Percona.

Doherty is also the creator and co-author of the *Networking Simplified* series of books, which includes *Cisco Networking Simplified*, *Home Networking Simplified*, and several other titles. He has also written books on mobile security and other networking topics.

Jim is a former U.S. Marine Corps Sergeant and holds a Bachelor of Science degree in electrical engineering from North Carolina State University and an MBA from Duke University. Jim lives in Raleigh, North Carolina, with his wife and two children.

Introduction

Dear Reader,

Thank you for buying (or considering) this book. By way of background, this book is the latest in a series of *Networking Simplified* books that have covered topics such as basic networking with *Cisco Networking Simplified*, and other titles that have taken a "simplified" approach to Voice over IP (VoIP), security, and home networking.

If you are not familiar with the approach of the *Networking Simplified* books, the idea is to explain networking concepts and technologies to people who are not intending to become technical experts, but want to know what underlying networking technologies are and how they work at a high level. This includes business and marketing folks, salespeople, investors, people who work in technical companies but in nontechnical roles, and even technical people from different vocations who want a cursory introduction to networking.

In others words, I wanted to write a book that explains how all this stuff works, and why it matters, without assuming people needed to configure a router or set up a wireless network, and without assuming the readers were dummies. The aim is to not go too deep but not be too light either.

To that end, I've now written (with the help of many people listed in the acknowledgments) a book on the next big wave in networking: software-defined networking (SDN) and network functions virtualization (NFV). My approach to this book is similar to the previous books in that I start with some foundational topics, which in this case is virtualization. In fact, the first several sections of the book focus on this because 1) it's really important and 2) I did not think that there was a good resource out there that took the same simplified approach. The book then moves into SDN and NFV, and through it all are parts about cloud networks, virtualized data centers, and network virtualization.

Whiteboards

Also throughout this book, typically at the end of chapters, are "whiteboard" diagrams. These hand-drawn (and then digitized) whiteboards are meant to capture key aspects of the chapter topics and present those ideas as if they were drawn on a whiteboard.

In keeping with the at-a-glance feature of the previous *Networking Simplified* books, the whiteboards are meant as enhancements to the text, and it is hoped that they will help aid in your understanding of the topics they cover.

Who Is This Book For, and What Will You Get Out of It?

This book is mostly meant for nontechnical people who want to know what SDN, NFV, virtualization, and cloud networking are about: what they are, how they all work, and why they are important. You won't walk away from this book knowing how to configure an SDN controller, but you will know what one is and what it does. If you are a technical person with no exposure to these topics, this book can serve as a high-level introduction.

How This Book is Organized

I've broken the book into ten sections, each covering a central theme. This allows you to bounce around and pick one topic at time. If this is all brand new to you, tackling the topics in order is recommended, because they tend to build on each other.

Part 1: Virtualization 101: The Basics of Virtualization

As the name implies, Part I provides a primer on virtualization and virtual machines (VMs): what they are, how they work, and why they were adopted so quickly.

Part 2: Virtualization 201: Virtualizing the Data Center (a.k.a. Clouds)

Once you understand what VMs are, you need to know how they work together and what happens when you have an entire data center of them. This part focuses on the particulars of how clouds work and how they are managed.

Part 3: Network Functions Virtualized: Why Stop With Servers?

Servers aren't the only thing you can virtualize. In fact, many of the traditional applications such as firewalls can be virtualized, too. NFV is a key aspect of modern networking. This part explores not only the technology, but also the impact on how the networks work as a result.

Part 4: Modern Networking Approaches to Virtualization

Understanding how virtualization works is a great start, but unless you can connect to them over a network, a VM is not very useful. It turns out, however, that connecting to VMs requires some changes to networking before you can leverage their full power. This part explores some of the ways modern networks are managed.

Part 5: Software Defined Networks: Virtualizing the Network

SDN represent a pivot point in how networks are built and who manages them. The technology is analogous to the virtualization of data centers, and in fact, the shift to SDN is in large part an attempt to leverage the most value out of virtualized data centers and clouds. This part covers the basics of SDN technology and the economic impact of its adoption.

Part 6: SDN Controllers

Furthering the SDN discussion, this part goes into depth about SDN controllers. There's a lot of competition among many companies to be among the leaders in this technology, and given the economic benefits of being among the leaders, the stakes are high. In addition to looking at specific controllers, this part also looks at the economics of the technology.

Part 7: Virtualized Networks: Connecting It All Together

With an understanding of the pieces, this part puts virtualization, SDN, and NFV together. More than just how it works, the chapters here explore building and managing virtualized networks.

Part 8: Security: The Security Thing

Security is an ever-present part of networking these days, and in virtualized networks, where you don't always know where your data assets are, security is always an interesting topic. The chapters in this part deal with the unique security aspects of virtualization and virtualized networks.

Part 9: Visibility

You can only manage and control what you see, and this is no different in virtualized networks. The problem is that the very nature of virtualization creates blind spots in the network because data and information can move in a way that traditional network monitoring cannot detect. This part looks at how virtual networks are monitored.

Part 10: The Big Picture

In the last part of the book, all the topics previously mentioned come together for a view of how it all works together. Here we also look at how this technology will affect the way people work and communicate, and we take a peek into what might be coming next.

In the end, I'm hopeful that you will find this book to be useful, informative, and interesting. I sincerely appreciate having the opportunity to share this information with you.

—Jim Doherty

Virtualization 101:
The Basics of Virtualization

Primer on Virtualization

Over the past decade, we have witnessed a revolution in the way information technology (IT) works from an infrastructure perspective. Gone are the days of purchasing and deploying a new server for each new application. Instead, IT has become much more adept at sharing existent underutilized resources across a catalog of IT applications, and this technique is called *virtualization*.

Of course, sharing of resources is nothing new. Back in the days of mainframe computers, IT would segment processing capacity to provide many smaller logical central processing units (CPUs). Similarly, networks have used virtualization for years to create segregated logical networks that share the same wire (for example, virtual local-area networks [VLANs]). Even in desktop computing, IT has logically partitioned large hard disks to create several smaller independent drives, each with a dedicated label and capacity that is capable of storing its own data and applications.

Therefore, we can see that the technique of virtualization has existed in processing, storage, and networking for several decades. What has made virtualization in the past decade different is the concept and development of the virtual machine (VM).

If you look up the definition of a VM, you'll find one such as the one found on the VMware website: "A VM is a tightly isolated software container that runs its own operating system and applications as if it were a physical computer."

Obviously, this is correct, but it does not really give you the "a-ha" you were probably hoping for, nor does it give you an understanding of why or how these things have transformed servers, storage, and networking.

To help get to that a-ha, let's start with the big problem that VMs fix.

Server Proliferation, Massive Power Bills, and Other IT Nightmares

Over the past 30 years, we have become a data-driven society that relies on computers (in their many forms) to help run both our daily lives and businesses. In fact, businesses have become so reliant on computers, servers, and networking that the absence of these things (due to an outage, virus, attack, or some other calamity) even for a short period of time can have a significant financial impact on a company.

As a result of living in this data-centric world, enterprises need to run applications for nearly every facet of their business, and all these applications have to run on servers. In fact, not only do these applications need to run on servers, but *each* application often requires its *own* server to run on even when the server is not used to its fullest capacity by the application. In fact, that turns out to be the case most of the time. This has led to a phenomenon known as *server proliferation*, which is as bad as it sounds. It refers to the ever-increasing need to buy more and more single-use servers to account for increasing data and application usage.

Data proliferation is compounded by the need for businesses to always have their computing resources available (meaning that you have to have a backup for every server and sometimes the backups need backups), effectively doubling or tripling the number of servers that a company needs, and that number was already big and getting bigger.

Figure 1-1 shows a single physical server, running a single operating system, which runs a single application.

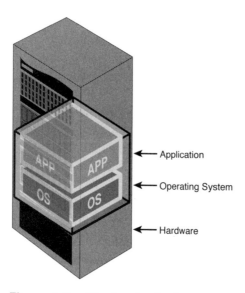

Figure 1-1   *Single physical server, running a single operating system, which runs a single application*

So, at this point you may be asking, "What's so bad about server proliferation?" The answer is that it wastes a lot of money, and it requires a lot of resources (power, cooling, and personnel to manage it all), and it's all very inefficient. How inefficient? Well, numerous studies have shown that on average nonvirtualized enterprise servers are only running at about 5% to 10% utilization. This is partly due to advancements in chip density (they can just do more stuff in less time), but it's mostly because almost every server only supports just one application. Multiple applications can be supported on a single server as long as they are all supported by the same version of the operating system (OS), but for the purposes of this chapter, however, we will assume that servers have a 1:1 OS to application ratio. This means that when a new application is needed, you can't just load it on an existing underutilized server; you have to buy a new one.

Figure 1-2 shows three servers, each with different operating systems. Although each is underutilized, any new application would require its own server.

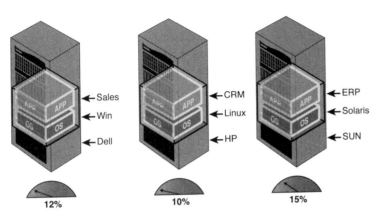

Figure 1-2 *Three servers, each with different operating systems*

So, now you have two servers, each running at about 10% to 15%. Unfortunately, you have to have these servers backed up in case a power outage or some other disaster occurs. Now you have four servers, two here, two somewhere else, and all four have about 90% of their computing resources idle. Making matters worse is that these servers have to be powered on all the time, and that takes a good amount of power. Still, it gets worse, because even idle servers generate a lot of heat; so, wherever they are, you need to keep them cool, and that takes a lot more power. (Servers are often more expensive to cool than they are to keep on.) There's also a matter of real estate. If your business is growing, chances are that your server farm is growing really quickly , and now you may have a space-planning issue on top of everything else.

Now let's say that you are up to 100 or so of these servers and there's a need for a new application. As a result, your IT team has to go through the process of spec'ing out the server(s), getting them ordered through procurement, getting them installed, making sure they are replicated, loading the application…you get the picture. It's a lot of work and a lot of expense, and we can't lose site of the fact that these servers are mostly underutilized and that many are just running on idle.

To put this in perspective, imagine if you had to buy a new car for every location you had to visit, and even when you were not going anywhere you had to leave all the cars running. Oh yeah, you also need two of each car in case one of them breaks down, and all of those backup cars have to be running all the time too.

You don't have to have an MBA to figure out that server proliferation and all the associated cost is a bad deal for business. That is, of course, unless you're in the business of selling the servers, but more on that later.

This problem is exactly what VMs fix. Before we get to them, however, let's look first at why servers are so inefficient.

How Servers Work

A server, like most computers, is a collection of specialized hardware resources that are accessed by a software OS through a series of specialized drivers. These resources can be many things, but commonly consist of the following:

- **CPU processor:** Does the computing part

- **RAM (or memory):** Stores and stacks short-term instructions and information

- **Storage:** Keeps long-term data

- **Network interface card (NIC):** (Pronounced "nick") Allows the machine to connect to other computers or devices via a network

The OS communicates with the drivers to access these resources, and a one-to-one relationship exists between them such that they comprise a set (hardware, drivers, and OS). Once the OS and drivers are loaded, the hardware is locked in. (Technically, you could reformat it and start over, but this is the equivalent of throwing out the old one and buying a new one.)

Now comes the application. The application is loaded onto the OS, thus becoming locked in to the OS, drivers, and hardware. Once loaded, you are all set, and you've defined that server's job. Running that application is what the server does, or more accurately that's all it does. Now this might be confusing to you if your only experience with applications is what you load onto your phone or tablet. After all, those things hold tons of apps, and they're really little; so why can't these big honkin' servers do more than one thing? Well, the reason is twofold:

- The applications running on servers are not the "angry birds" variety of application. They are much more complicated and do things such as run email systems for large enterprises.

- The operating systems are dedicated to the application and are the link to the drivers, which enable access to the hardware resources (CPU, RAM, and disk). Also, it turns out that operating systems are not good at sharing.

Figure 1-3 shows the relationship between the hardware resources, the OS, and the application running on a server.

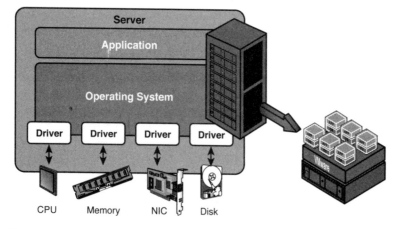

Figure 1-3 *Relationship between the hardware resources, the OS, and the application running on a server*

At this point, you might be saying to yourself, "That's dumb. Given all of those excess resources, why would they ever design it that way?" It turns out that when all this computing stuff got started it made perfect sense, because back then the computing capabilities were much lower (so utilizations rates were much higher per server) and there were many, many fewer business applications. The problems that exist today did not exist back then, but rather developed over time. Basically, no one thought that the slow-moving tide was a big issue until they found themselves neck deep in the surf. All of a sudden (seemingly), it's a problem.

How VMs Fix the Underutilized Server Problem

At a high level, a VM creates a software version of a server that runs within the hardware server. This VM is an exact copy of the physical server. Many VMs can run on the same physical server, and they can all be customized to the application needs. A physical server can now mix together Windows and Linux applications on the same piece of hardware.

In addition, because VMs are software, not only can you run them on any server but you can also suspend or freeze a VM and then you can move it to a different server any time you want. And it's all quick and easy. You can also make a copy of a VM or even a whole bunch of copies and spin them up on multiple servers.

Figure 1-4 illustrates the concept of a self-contained application – OS bundle (called a VM) that is not bound to the server or the hardware on that server.

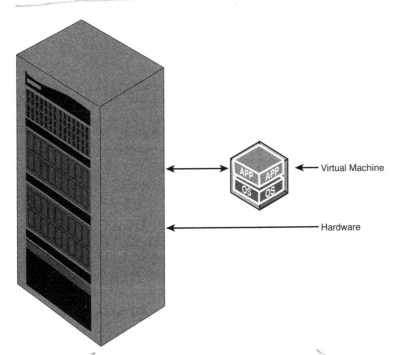

← Virtual Machine

← Hardware

Figure 1-4 *Self-contained application—OS bundle*

Note in that description that the application and OS are still tied together, but they have now been decoupled from the server hardware. In the old way of doing things, you could not just up and move an operating system without considerable effort. As you learned earlier, the reason why the OS was so tightly coupled to the server was because it could only access the server's resources through drivers that allowed access to the hardware. Because those drivers were written for specific operating systems, the servers were able to run only a single application. Well, we still need to access those resources, and we still need to do it through the drivers, so how does that work with a VM?

Enter the Hypervisor

A hypervisor is piece of software that sits between the OS and the server's specialized hardware resources. When in place, it's the hypervisor, rather than the OS, that manages the connections between the drivers and the server's resources.

At this point, you might be asking yourself, "They added a layer in; so, how can this lead to greater efficiencies?" That's a good question.

The answer is that a hypervisor can present a *virtual connection* to the server's resources for a VM's OS. What's significant, though, is that it can do it for a lot of VMs all running on the same server, even if those VMs all have different operating systems and unrelated applications.

Figure 1-5 shows a hypervisor acting as the interface to the hardware resources of a server for multiple operating systems.

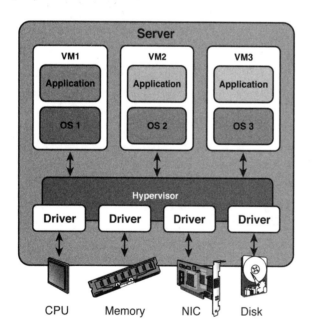

Figure 1-5 *Hypervisor acting as the interface to the hardware resources of a server for multiple operating systems*

From an efficiency standpoint, this is huge. In fact, it's transformational, and it has changed the IT, storage, server and networking industries in profound ways. Chapter 3, "Hypervisors (VMware, KVM, and Others)," discusses hypervisors in more detail.

With the availability of VMs and hypervisors, we can achieve server consolidation on a very large scale. Remember that most servers are only running at 5% to 10% capacity. Even being cautious to keep the CPU below 80%, we can still achieve anywhere from a 6x to 15x reduction in the number of physical servers a company would need by combining multiple applications onto a single server. There are other efficiencies as well. With a 10x reduction in the number of servers, companies enjoy a massive reduction in energy costs for server power and cooling.

The other big benefit of virtualization is flexibility: With this technology, it's relatively easy to migrate the servers within an entire data center to another data center in a matter of hours with little or no disruption in service. Without virtualization, a data center migration would take weeks or months and would almost surely result in widely felt service disruptions. Virtualization also results in a much better disaster recovery capability and nets a huge decrease in the time it takes to provision new applications.

For example, with virtualization, when a department wants to use a new application, the IT department can order the software and spin up a VM. In just a few hours, it's up and running. Once that's done, the IT group can easily replicate the VM (configurations and all) over to the disaster recovery site, and it's all ready to go.

Figure 1-6 shows the benefits of server consolidation made possible through virtualization.

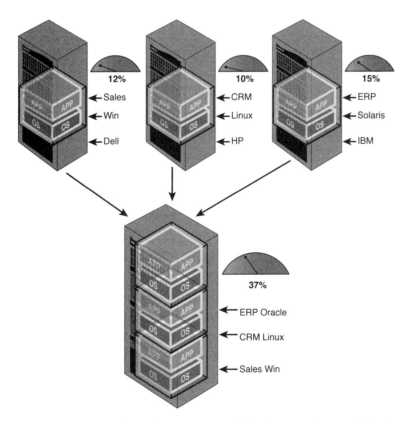

Figure 1-6 *Benefits of server consolidation made possible through virtualization*

Why Are Virtual Machines Such a Big Deal?

The net of all this is nothing less than a transformation in how enterprises provision, deploy, operate, manage, and back up computing resources. In other words, it's kind of a big deal. Using virtualization tools, enterprises can eliminate a great deal of inefficiency. But that's not all. You see, even with all these efficiencies that were eliminated, it turns out that there were still a lot of inefficiencies in the system. For example, what if there is a lot of volatility in the amount of computing resources you need? This is a common issue for ecommerce vendors during the holidays, when there is a big spike in computing activity.

There's also the matter of designing, tuning, or modifying the network to accommodate changing needs in usage, availability, security, or other factors. It turns out that for all the benefits of virtualization with respect to server operating systems and applications, there are still massive gains to be had by virtualizing the entire network infrastructure.

This concept of *virtualizing the network* leads us to the thrust of this book: software-defined networking (SDN). This concept is every bit as profound as server virtualization. We'll spend most of this book discussing SDN, but first we have to lay the foundation by going a little deeper into virtualization, which will lead up to "the cloud," and from there to SDN.

Benefits of Virtual Machines

When we consider the benefits that virtualization brings, it is good to recap on why virtual machines (VMs) are necessary in the modern information technology (IT) infrastructure. The fundamental problem with the traditional IT infrastructure model is that the x86 server architecture (the way modern servers are designed and built) supports only one operating system at a time, and each operating system is typically dedicated to a single application. It would be great if we could run lots of applications on one standard server, but that's not the way they work most of the time.

Despite the inefficiencies, there were a few benefits of the one-server/application model. Not only does this model minimize resource competition and system maintenance on any given server, but it also isolates application failures. For example, if there is a problem with an application, a common solution is to reboot the system. If there is more than one application running on the same server, the process of rebooting the operating system (OS) takes all the applications on that server out of service.

The good news is that with a VM running on a server you can reboot the VM (the app and the OS) without impacting the other VMs on the server. Further, if the server needs to be reset, it's a simple matter to suspend the VMs, move them to other servers, and then reactivate them or to even *live migrate* them using *vMotion* (described later). In addition, advances in hardware and chip performance have greatly mitigated the negative impact of resource sharing.

Irrespective of this, the benefits of VMs are so significant that their broad adoption was almost inevitable. There's just too much to gain for companies not to go this route. The major benefits are discussed throughout this chapter.

Reduced Cost

As discussed in Chapter 1, "Primer on Virtualization," the most obvious benefit of VMs is that they greatly reduce the runaway expenses from server proliferation. These costs are compounded by the extremely inefficient usage and the costs associated with 24/7 power and energy consumption, which contribute to the rising temperature of the data centers and consequently the high costs of cooling the environment.

This is wasteful and inefficient; thankfully, VM virtualization technology is the solution to these environmental and business problems. VM technology provides a way to consolidate the large number of small and medium-sized servers with a much smaller number of more efficient and larger servers. VMs solve this problem by enabling several operating systems and applications to run on one physical server. This in itself solves the problems of server inefficiency and addresses the wasted power and cooling costs. In addition, VM technology solves the IT best practice dilemma of one application per server/OS, because each VM is isolated from any other VM hosted on the same server and therefore uses only the amount of server resources it requires. It manages this by sandboxing (strictly isolating) applications from one another so that for all intents and purposes these are isolated, individual machines. For example, should one VM fail due to OS problems or application error, the other VMs are unaffected and continue working away as normal.

VMs are the foundation technology of server virtualization. Virtualization provides the method to run several instances of an OS or different operating systems on the same physical server. As a result, VMs cut costs, reduce risk, and allow IT to build architectures more aligned with agile business requirements. Figure 2-1 shows how VM technology allows for much greater utilization of server hardware.

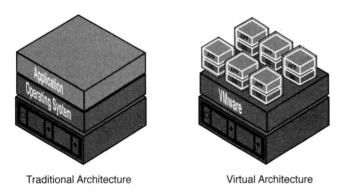

Traditional Architecture   Virtual Architecture

Figure 2-1   *VM technology allows for much greater utilization of server hardware.*

VMs cut costs by addressing the twin problems of underutilization of each server and over usage of power due to supporting server proliferation or server spread in the data center. A typical server today is extremely powerful and is severely underutilized if dedicated to running only one application, running perhaps as low as 5% to 10 %. VMs allow for server consolidation because several VMs can be installed and operate on a single server. Therefore, server consolidation can not only reduce the number of servers in the data center by a factor as high as ten but also increase the efficiency of each server by as much as 80%. Fewer servers and more densely deployed VMs per server provides for the largest cost savings.

Less Space (Even More Cost Savings)

In the large data centers, where server farms live, the cost of the actual hardware is only a fraction of the total cost of the data center. Other costs include real estate (land), buildings, power, racks, and cables. It's also important to remember that companies have to have at least two of everything; so at a minimum, the cost of a data center is roughly double depending on the cost of land and power.

One of the biggest considerations with spacing is the rate of growth. For example, a company that is building a data center must attempt to accurately gauge growth to avoid underutilized space or worse, underestimating server growth that would require yet another data center.

There is also the cost of power, which is a major financial consideration. All of these servers generate an enormous amount of heat, and the servers need to be kept cool. Interestingly, though, the temperatures that data centers are cooled to are more about human consideration than server consideration. It turns out that servers can operate efficiently at much higher temperatures than humans can tolerate over a sustained period of time. In fact, in some cases, robots are being used within the data centers left at higher temperatures (80+ F). The robots are controlled by people in command rooms where the temperature is set for humans.

Another consideration in the cost of data centers (especially single-use server data centers) is cabling. Connecting servers together (to each other and to the network) requires a lot of cabling, including power cables, direct connection cables between ports, and the massive data center networks that connect all the servers to the network and monitoring tools.

With VMs, all of these costs are significantly reduced by factors of 3x to 10x in a virtuous cycle of cascading benefit. Fewer servers, less space, lower power costs, fewer cables… the savings go on and on.

Availability and Flexibility

Cost savings through server consolidation may be the most obvious benefit to server virtualization, but there are others, such as application availability, fault tolerance, and flexibility. Traditionally in nonvirtualized environments, servers running mission-critical applications had to be hosted on clustered or fault-tolerant hardware with complex failover protocols and configurations. With VMs, that is no longer an issue. This is because if a server hosting several VMs were to fail, all the VMs would continue to run or restart on another server without any downtime or data loss. The centralized controller manages this by monitoring each VM's state using a heartbeat function (a periodic signal that tells the controller the VM is still operating) and can relaunch or move a VM in case of a failure.

As shown in Figure 2-2, this seamless shift from one server to another provides all the benefits of costly and complex server clustering but without any of the intricate configuration and deployment problems. To a system administrator or a support engineer, this is the biggest benefit to server virtualization: the ability to seamlessly fail over to another VM instance on another server without any manual intervention or horribly complex configuration changes.

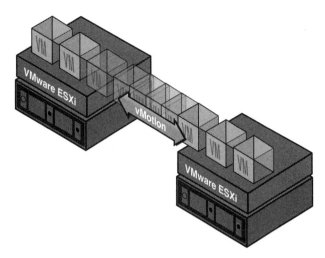

Figure 2-2 *vMotion allows for the movement of VMs from one server to another, even for active applications.*

Similarly, server virtualization using VMs has an important role in disaster recovery and business continuity. IT can move a VM from one server to another as simply as if copying a file. What that means is that in a disaster recovery scenario, IT can quickly move business-critical applications seamlessly from one location to another without downtime or data loss. Now, consider that for a moment: IT can move an entire virtual server from one data center to another without shutting it down or even taking it offline!

The ability to move VMs around without having to take the applications offline or incurring downtime makes responding to business requirements a trivial task. For example, if a traditionally deployed application requires more resources because it is exhausting those available to it, IT has to reinstall the application on a new server and configure links for it to databases and other external services, which is a time-consuming and difficult task. However, with an application running on a VM, it is simply a case of either shrinking other VMs and expanding the VM in question to provide the necessary resources or, more likely, moving the VM (like a file) to another server with sufficient available resources, which is a quick and trivial task.

Faster Application Spin-Up and Provisioning

The benefits VM technology brings to systems and operations (SysOps) and development operations (DevOps) are almost magical. Previously, building, testing, developing, and publishing servers for application developers was a tedious, difficult, and expensive task because of the different test environments required for every development project. Test servers had to be installed and configured with a specific OS, a set of development tools, languages, and libraries, and this was very time-consuming and difficult to maintain. Furthermore, due to the shortage of physical servers, these test environments had to be recycled between projects. This entailed formatting the server and reconfiguring it for another OS, development environment, and libraries.

Virtualization 201

How Virtualization Works

DEDICATED SERVER

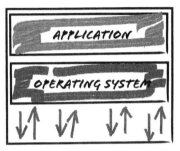

APPLICATION

OPERATING SYSTEM

Applications accesses HW resources through the OS, which links to various device drivers.

CPU   MEMORY   NETWORK   STORAGE

VIRTUALIZED SERVER

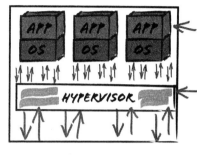

APP   APP   APP
OS   OS   OS

HYPERVISOR

These are called "virtual machines".

This is where virtualization takes place! The hypervisor manages HW resources for multiple OS's.

CPU   MEMORY   NETWORK   STORAGE

SW applications must have access to HW resources to execute their code. Resources include:

-CPU (compute)
-RAM (memory)
-Network Access
-Storage

The operating system (OS) provides access to the drivers that provide information to flow between the application and the resources.

The OS also provides the human interface and it's what makes Windows look and act like WIndows and Mac look and act like Mac.

In a virtualized server there is an added layer called the hypervisor.

The hypervisor sits between the operating systems of the virtual machines and the HW Drivers.

Because the hypervisor does for VMs what operating systems do for apps, some refer to hypervisors as an operating system for other operating systems.

The hypervisor provides "virtual" access to and control of the drivers so that each OS thinks it's on its own server.

This is key, because it keeps SW and OS providers from having to change their code to support virtualization.

Hypervisors (VMWare, KVM, and Others)

Most of the conversation about virtualization usually centers on virtual machines (VMs). This is perfectly reasonable because VMs are the things you "see and touch." However, when you pull back the covers on virtualization, you'll find that the hypervisor does much of the important work. In fact, the hypervisor is the thing that is doing the virtualization and pulling the strings for each VM.

A hypervisor is

- An operating system for operating systems
- A Virtual Machine (VM) Monitor

That's pretty much it—nice and simple. Now let's take a deeper look at each of these parts, as well as hypervisor vendors and how to choose a hypervisor.

An Operating System for Operating Systems

Chapter 1, "Primer on Virtualization," described VMs as self-contained operating systems that run applications. As a result of them being "abstracted" from the hardware, VMs could be replicated, suspended, saved, and moved around just like a file. This abstraction, however, is problematic, because it's the operating system that provides the application with access to the server's resources. The OS manages this interaction with the computer's hardware and services via drivers (compute, memory, disk, and network access).

The hypervisor is a piece of software that allows the computer's hardware devices to share their resource between VMs running as guests and sitting atop the physical hardware. In one type of hypervisor, the software sits directly on top of the hardware—no server OS is loaded—and the hypervisor interacts directly with the guest VMs.

From this perspective, it's easy to see why we can consider the hypervisor as an operating system for operating systems. For example, the hypervisor has replaced the server's own OS and as such has taken responsibility for interacting between the hardware devices and the

VM's internal OS. It's doing for the operating system portion of a VM just what the server's own operating system would do for applications on a dedicated machine.

A Virtual Machine Monitor

The second part of our working definition of hypervisors takes into account the fact that multiple VMs can run on a single server. To do this, the hypervisor must also provide a monitoring function for each VM to manage the access requests and information flows from the VMs to the computing resources and vice versa.

Although this might seem simple, the VM functionality that a hypervisor plays is critical. Not only must the hypervisor successfully allow multi-VM access to the hardware via a process called *multiplexing*, but it must do this in a way that is transparent to the VMs. Incidentally, multiplexing used to be a core function solely of operating systems—the fact that hypervisors do it too supports the idea that a hypervisor is an operating system for operating systems.

The VM function of hypervisors is what makes transparency of operation possible. Transparency of operation is really important because one of the inherent promises of virtualization is that when you go virtual, you can not only do all the things you used to do, and use all the programs you already use, but that you can do these things without any noticeable difference in how the applications and programs work. In others words, we do not want (and typically will not tolerate) significant changes in performance or usability.

Not surprisingly, there are different types of hypervisors for different operating systems, and all of the major OS providers all have their own version of a hypervisor, as do several other vendors who specialize in cloud and virtualization. Several of these are discussed later in this chapter.

Hypervisor History

Hypervisors are not new; they are actually quite old. In fact, they've been around since the mid-1960s. (I'd like to apologize to those readers who have also been around since the mid-1960s and do not consider themselves to be "quite old." Suffice to say that technology time is kind of like dog years, so a 50-year-old technology is close to ancient.)

The very first hypervisors ran on IBM mainframes, but these were quite a bit different from the hypervisors in use today. Programmers used an emulator, which is a close cousin of the modern hypervisor, to aid in the development of operating systems. This should make sense given the definition of a hypervisor being an operating system for operating systems.

Types of Hypervisors

There are two types of hypervisors, denoted as Type 1 and Type 2. A Type 1 hypervisor (see Figure 3-1) is called a *bare-metal* hypervisor in reference to the fact that the hypervisor runs directly on the server hardware without any native operating system. The hypervisor is the operating system of the server providing direct access to the hardware resources for the guest VMs riding on top of it. Most of the servers in production today are using Type 1 hypervisors.

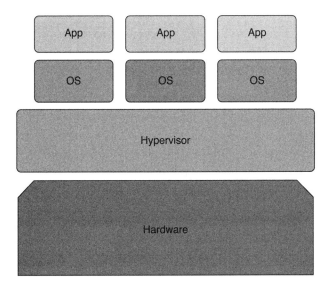

Figure 3-1 *A Type 1 hypervisor interfaces directly with the hardware resources.*

Type 2 hypervisors (see Figure 3-2), called *hosted hypervisors,* run on top of a native OS. In this use case, the hypervisor is a shim that sits between the OS of the VM above and the OS of the server or computer below.

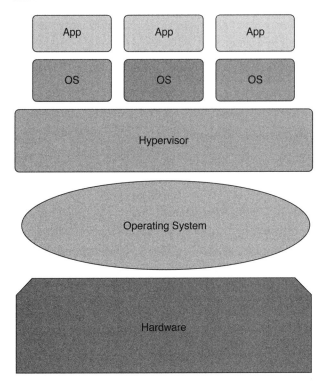

Figure 3-2 *Type 2 hypervisors interface with the native OS running on the server.*

The hypervisor is the bridge between the operating systems and the server hardware. It carries the input/output (I/O) commands and interrupt commands from the virtualized OS to the hardware. The I/O commands are the normal program functions for the applications, and the interrupts are just what they sound like—interruptions that halt a process. A keystroke (such as pressing the Escape key) is a common interrupt function. This command has to be accounted for and in some cases may override the various I/O commands.

One of the most important functions of the hypervisor is to manage all of these I/O commands and interrupts and make sure that they are kept separate. Furthermore, there are "traps" that must be set to ensure that errors in a guest VM (such as those that would lock up an application or crash an OS) do not impact the other VMs running on the same server, the hypervisor, or the underlying hardware. If the hypervisor were a Type 2 hypervisor, this would include the underlying OS as well.

The other main function of the hypervisor is that it also manages both the metering (usage) of the various resources as well as the network access.

Hypervisor Vendors

As data centers proliferated, the battleground for mind share and market share was around the operating systems. Big players such as Sun (now Oracle), Microsoft, and various Linux providers (such as Red Hat) fought hard to get their operating systems purchased and installed on as many servers as they could. Once they were installed, they became entrenched, and if the sales rep (and the product) was good enough, you could get an entire enterprise to standardize on your OS. The ultimate goal was to have IT departments calling themselves your "shop," as in "We are a Microsoft shop." Once that happened, the account manager could play lots of golf and collect a nice commission check. All kidding aside, this was a fiercely fought battle that went on for years and accounted for tens of billions of dollars in licensing and support revenue over the span of a couple of decades.

Today, a similar fight for market share is being waged, this one on hypervisors. The main versions of hypervisors are discussed in the following subsections.

KVM

KVM (acquired by Red Hat) is an acronym that stands for Kernel-based Virtual Machine. A kernel is the part of the OS that interfaces directly with the hardware. Think of the kernel as the main part of the OS—when you strip away all the code that makes Windows look and act like Windows and Mac OS look and act like Mac OS, what's left is the base code that accesses the CPU, memory, and disk. That's the kernel.

KVM (see Figure 3-3) is a part of Linux and is a *Type 2*, or *hosted hypervisor*. Type 2 hypervisors are a little easier to install and operate. However, because there is an added layer, the performance is not always as good as hypervisors that run on bare metal.

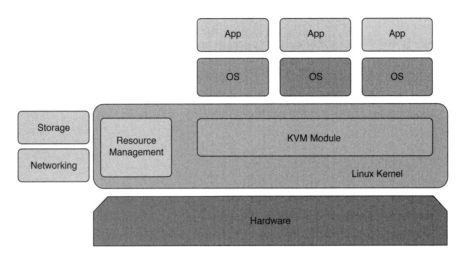

Figure 3-3   *KVM VM hypervisor*

Xen   ⊂ ↑ X ∫

Pronounced as "zen," Xen is a Type 1 hypervisor based on open source code. Xen has been acquired by Citrix. Typically, the open source community (a large group of independent coders contributing to the code development) will develop base code for an open source package, and then companies will form based on a business model where they stabilize, test, package, and support their version of the open source software. Red Hat is the most notable company to have done this. (They did it with the Linux code base mentioned in the previous section back in the 1990s.)

Xen (see Figure 3-4) uses *para-virtualization*, which means that the guest operating systems are made aware of the fact that they are not running on their own dedicated hardware. This requires some modification of the guest OS, but this disadvantage is made up for with increased performance as the OS modification essentially "tunes" the guest to operate more efficiently in a virtualized environment.

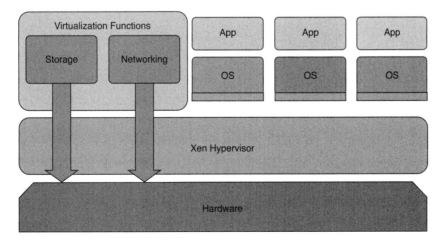

Figure 3-4   *Xen hypervisor*

VMware ESXi

As of the writing of this book, VMware leads the hypervisor market in both revenue and total share. VMware offers both a Type 1 hypervisor called ESXi (their main server-based hypervisor) and a popular Type 2 (hosted) hypervisor called VMware Fusion, which runs on desktops and laptops.

vSphere 5.1 (ESXi) is a bare-metal hypervisor, meaning that it installs directly on top of the physical server and partitions it into multiple VMs that can run simultaneously, sharing the physical resources of the underlying server. This is shown in Figure 3-5 as a series of individual VMs within the hypervisor block.

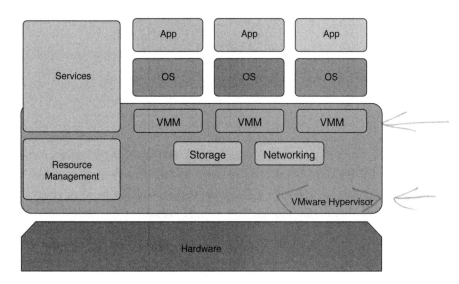

Figure 3-5   *VMware hypervisor*

As the "most mature" of the commercial hypervisors, the ESXi version of the VMware hypervisor is based on the original ESX hypervisor. VMware claims that this version is less than 5% of the size of the original ESX. This is a good thing because it allows the guest operating systems to access the hardware resources without a lot of intermediate functions and wasted CPU cycles.

Microsoft Hyper-V

It's no surprise that Microsoft, the largest OS provider, is also a major player in the hypervisor market. Their virtualization platform, now called Hyper-V (originally it was called Windows Server Virtualization), was originally released in 2008, and now has versions for several of the server platform operating systems.

Choosing a Hypervisor

The first consideration in choosing a hypervisor is whether you want a hosted or bare-metal hypervisor.

Hosted hypervisors are easier to install, but they do tend to run at less than full capacity due to the extra layer. They do have greater flexibility, though, and if you already have servers running a specific operating system, the transition to virtualization is easier.

Native hypervisors typically offer better performance for the VMs running on them because they are directly connected to the hardware. This improved latency response is an important factor, especially in a service model where there may be service level agreements (SLAs) that specify server and application performance.

Summary

Hypervisors are the foundation of virtualization, providing the bridge between VMs and the server hardware and native operating system. Without this crucial piece, we would not be able to abstract VMs from the servers they run on.

What's more is the hypervisor is a precursor to what is referred to as an SDN controller, a foundational component of software-defined networks. You'll learn more about that later in the book and will continue to read about the role of hypervisors in cloud networks and the virtualization of networking functions.

Hypervisors
How Server Consolidation Drove Virtual Switching

VIRTUALIZED SERVERS

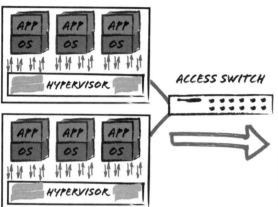

LARGE VIRTUALIZED SERVER

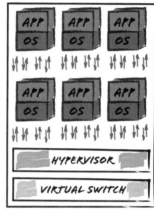

Hypervisors not only allowed virtualization but they also drove server consolidation of underutilized server CPUs—before the whole cloud thing came along combining a few virtual machines on one server was a big driver of virtualization.

As server manufacturers put more and more powerful CPUs into larger servers with more memory, users could put as many as 20-50 virtual machines onto a single server. This drove the need to put the first "layer" of switching (the access layer) inside the switch to better allow traffic within the server (from VM to VM) to run at high efficiency. This Virtual Switch or VSwitch is part of the overall switching fabric of the data center, but embedding the server greatly enhances the speed of "east-west" or VM to VM switching.

TOP OF RACK (TOR) SWITCH

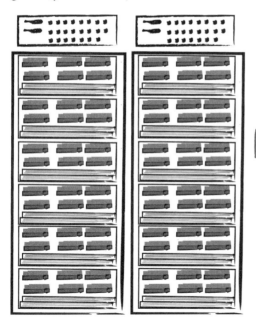

This consolidation replaces racks of servers, with single servers that run many VMs. These servers are then racked up, achieving the consolidation everyone was hoping to achieve. This drove the first tier of switching into SW. Now the first physical server is the second tier switch. Often placed on top of the rack housing all of the virtual servers, it is called the Top of Rack or TOR Switch.

Managing Virtual Resources

When considering the benefits derived from virtualization, one of the top benefits is the improved administration and management of the virtual machines. Virtualization provides the tools and opportunities to create, configure, and manage virtual machines (VMs) in a way administrators could never have previously imagined. Examples of the virtual resources that can be managed through common administrative tasks include the following:

- Creating VMs, from scratch or from templates
- Starting, suspending, and migrating VMs
- Using snapshots to back up and restore VMs
- Importing or exporting VMs
- Converting VMs from foreign hypervisors

A recurring theme in virtualization is the ease with which an administrator can spin up on-demand instances of a virtual server. This administrative and operational ability is what makes server virtualization so hugely attractive in DevOps environments as it decreases the time to implement new services and applications. In addition, the ability to spin up a VM hosting an application greatly enhances the administrator's time to restore service after a failure. However, what does it take, in terms of knowledge, effort, and time to create these VM instances?

Vendors have developed their VM application software to such an extent that it is an almost trivial task to spin up a virtual server. All the knowledge that an administrator requires for most vendors' 'wizard' driven applications is to know some key parameters in order to create the VM. These key parameters are as follows:

- The physical server's hostname
- A VM name
- The defined memory allocation assigned to the VM
- The number of cores and CPU sockets being assigned to the VM
- A default display type, and remote access protocol
- The type and version of OS

An administrator can manage most tasks on the VM console, such as running, pausing, and stopping the VM. However, other more complex tasks (such as the migration of a VM to another machine) may require other management objects to be loaded. Consequently, managing VM resources are typically limited to editing the VM configuration; starting, pausing, or stopping the VM; managing snapshots; and exporting, importing, and finally deleting a VM.

As you can see, creating and configuring a VM is not a difficult process; all you have to do is configure the parameters of the VM's resources. As long as you know what memory size is and the hard drive space that you want to assign to the VM, configuration is very easy. Once it's all configured, you have what is commonly referred to as a *workload*.

Irrespective of this, the benefits of VMs are so significant that their broad adoption was almost inevitable. There's just too much to gain for companies not to go this route. The major benefits are discussed throughout this chapter.

What Is a Workload?

One of the simplest ways to explain a workload is to think of it as a collection of computing "stuff" you need to run an application. A lot of people get hung up on the idea that a workload is a program or an application, but that's only part of it. More than just the application, the workload also includes resources needed to run it, including operating system burden, compute cycles, memory, storage, and network connectivity. In the VM environment, the workload can even include the load on the components apart from the server itself, such as network or storage components that are not permanently attached to a server.

One common description of a workload uses the concept of a *container*, which offers a good conceptual model because a workload is often viewed as being the complete set of resources needed for the task, which is independent of other elements. Using the container definition, it's easy to conceptualize that when we define a workload we piece together all the components we need to run the application, task, or program. In most cases, the required resources are drawn from different resource pools, and these pools can be (and often are) in different locations.

In the virtualization model, these workloads are able to be spun up and torn down very quickly, and in some cases require that another workload be spun up to complete a subtask. Furthermore, all this could be happening to thousands of workloads at any given time. Virtualization is what allows us to break up all the various resources into pools so that we can create very efficient workloads (such that the containers all have the resources they need, and no more), but it's what we commonly know as cloud networking that allows us to stitch these workloads together quickly and reliably.

NOTE   One note on the idea of containers: The earlier description uses the word *container* as a conceptual aid rather than as a name or description. This is important because there is such a thing as a "Linux container," which is an isolated virtual environment. If you hear someone talking about a container in a virtualized context, this is probably what is being referred to.

Managing Virtual Resources in the Hypervisor

Once the VM is up and running, the task of controlling and managing the virtual resources belongs to the hypervisor. For example, the hypervisor will control the multiplexing of VM requests between other VMs and handle the control of I/O interrupts and the information flow between the guest OS and the hardware.

However, one of the goals of going down the virtualization route was to improve server utilization and efficiency. The aim was to get those servers from sitting idle to working at a reasonable utilization level—let's say 80% of the physical server's resources (CPU, memory, disk, and network bandwidth). The secondary idea behind this goal of higher utilization is that it goes hand in hand with faster return on investment (ROI), which makes accountants and CFOs very happy.

Unfortunately, our efforts to bring a smile to the CFO's face may rebound badly on us if we push the utilization thresholds too far. After all, our VMs are using virtual resources, created and supplied by the hypervisor, such as virtual CPU, virtual RAM, virtual disk, and virtual network. Therefore, we must understand the correlation between virtual and real resources, because the virtual resources are being taken from very real and finite physical resources, such as the physical RAM and physical CPU.

So even if the goal is to push our average utilization up to approximately 70% to 80% and then sit back and let the hypervisor manage the VM's virtual resources, we must ensure it is managing the resources properly, because it "thinks" it has infinite resources available. It is therefore essential that we remember to manage both physical and virtual resources.

This is especially important given the fact that VMs get moved from physical host to physical host even while being utilized. Managing resources under these constantly changing conditions is more than even the most diligent and talented tech team can manage and is therefore automated, as shown in Figure 4-1.

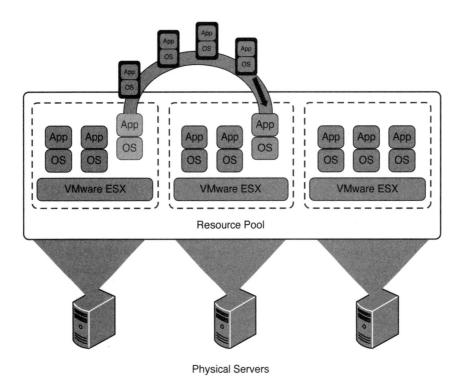

Figure 4-1 *Changes in the physical location of VMs require network-wide updates that must be made with the same speed and ease of provisioning as the VMs. Manual configuration does not scale in this environment.*

In any virtualized environment, the key resources you must manage are as follows:

- CPU

- Memory

- Storage

- Network

- Power

The first four resources are probably expected, but power might come as a surprise.

The reason that power is included is that even power is a finite resource in the data center, which means it must be monitored and managed. For that reason, hypervisors can manage the utilization of power distribution through power distribution management (PDM), which can consolidate VMs when utilization is low on fewer hosts and even put some hosts to sleep.

Virtual Resource Providers and Consumers

In a virtualized environment, physical resources are provided by physical hosts, which is a little different than traditional data centers. In traditional data centers, all required resources were supplied by a single host. In virtualized data centers, you'll find resource clusters, which are groups of physical resources. Resource clusters can include the following:

- Storage

- Memory

- Data stores (storage)

- Hosts (physical servers with VMs loaded on them)

It is from clusters of hosts that large virtual infrastructures typically draw their virtual resources. In most large data centers, these clusters providing resources are distributed via distributed resource scheduler (DRS). In the case of storage, it is the data stores that are grouped into clusters, and then the I/O utilization and capacity can be balanced as required using the storage distributed resource scheduler (SDRS). Figure 4-2 shows an example of resource pooling.

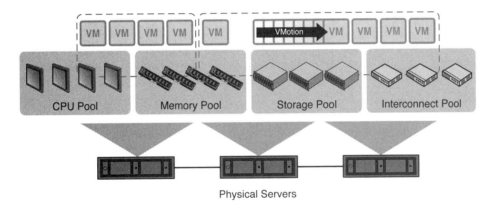

Figure 4-2   *VMs often draw their resources from dedicated pools or clusters of resources that are shared among many VMs and hosts.*

Whereas clusters are the sources for the virtual resource providers, the VMs are the consumers. Recall from the earlier discussion the need for admins to configure resource requirements. Because there are many consumers and fixed resources (at least in the near term), the resource limits for VMs must be set correctly such that the total virtual consumption does not exceed the physical resources available. If it does, applications will run slowly before they eventually crash.

So How Do You Manage Virtual Resources?

The reason that virtual resource management is so important is that performance isolation must be maintained. In other words, applications must run with a high level of performance consistency day in and day out. Further, the applications must have predictable performance even if virtual resources are a shared resource. To achieve this, it is necessary to ensure active VMs do not monopolize system resources, hog the CPU, crash the applications, and bring a world of pain down upon us.

Efficient utilization is another goal of virtualization, and it's important to ensure that VM density is neither too high nor too low on a physical server. In addition, the resources of individual VMs must also be managed; this is especially true if created via a standard template. It's also important to ensure VMs that require resources have not been set too low and that those idle VMs are not set too high, which only creates waste.

In summary, virtual resources can be managed through both administrative controls and through automated hypervisor virtual management. However, both have to be configured as preset VM resource allocations, which if not predicted carefully can create resource starvation in busy or active VMs and resource waste in less-intensive or idle VMs. However, by utilizing good management and oversight, you can enable dynamic stretching and shrinking of resource pools, which allows applications to demand and consume resources on an as-needed basis without impacting performance.

Flexible Workflows

New Requirements for Cloud Networks

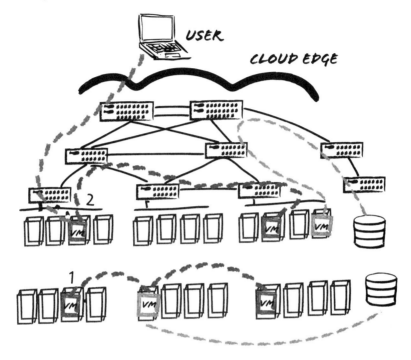

At Time 1 a user spins up a VM. The VM calls up another application VM, which stores

user data. If demand rises, another VM can be called up and the network has to keep track

of all the connections—but that's not all.

At Time 2, the same user spins up a VM, but it might be on a different physical server, and the

2nd application might VM be on a different server, as well. Regardless of which servers they reside on,

it all has to connect just like it did before with the right data from without the user having to

do anything to manage the new connections.

The biggest differences between a traditional data center and a cloud are that
1) In a cloud there is a lot of east-west traffic (from vm to vm) and less north-south
   (client to server) traffic.
2) The location and address changes that occur in a cloud happen much faster and much more
   often than in a DC.

The cloud network must be designed to accommodate the different ways traffic moves around in a cloud.

Virtualization 201
Virtualizing the Data Center (a.k.a. Clouds)

Virtualized Data Centers (Some Call Them Clouds)

The previous chapters discussed virtualization and virtual machines (VMs) in particular as a general concept of technology. These chapters showed how virtualization could bring the business benefits through cost saving, increased efficiency, flexible deployment that aligned with business goals, faster server deployment, and importantly, recovery of service. This chapter puts these concepts into a practical scenario, to derive the benefits of virtualization by applying the techniques in a modern data center.

As with any project, even a theoretical one like this, the operations team will have to present justifications for spending money and creating risk. In short, the CFO or the financial management team will want to know why they should invest money in the project, because that is actually what they are doing, they are investing rather than just spending. Further, they are expecting that money back based on some return on investment (ROI) calculations. As part of this, they want to see what benefits they are likely to realize, and what risks they are likely to incur. This exercise is known as a cost/benefit exercise.

Benefits of Virtualizing the Data Center

Therefore, in this section, let's first look at what benefits virtualizing the data center will bring in practical terms.

Less Heat Buildup

Less wasted energy leads to considerable savings in operation costs. The more servers there are, the greater the heat buildup and consequently the greater the amount of energy expended cooling the data center. The answer to this is simply to reduce the number of servers. By just consolidating servers by as little as one-tenth, considerable savings can be made.

This is a tricky one for IT departments within an organization because usually IT does not have direct responsibility for facility costs such as power. In these cases, the finance team has to estimate the data center's power consumption costs relative to the rest of the organization. For a hosting company, it's much easier because most of the facilities are used specifically to run the servers.

Reduced Hardware Spend

Another benefit of reducing the number of servers in the data center is the reduction in server sprawl, which results in less spend on new and replacement hardware. Fewer servers require less electricity and a reduction in rack space. Reducing the number of servers reduces capital and operational costs as maintenance and support costs drop.

This cost saving can be limited, however, because these servers are often replaced with much larger (more expensive) servers, and they also require more bandwidth, which increases networking costs and storage costs. All things being equal, though, these costs have to be considered in terms of what the same output would cost with the old model versus the new model. One assumes that the changes are growth driven and that replacements or upgrades are needed.

Faster Deployment

Installing new servers is a time-consuming business, because suitable hardware has to be locally sourced or brought in. Rack space has to be found, and cables have to be run. These are not trivial tasks; indeed, they require mini projects of their own just to get consensus and permission simply to install things in the racks. Server virtualization removes many of these headaches because VMs can be deployed quickly onto an existing server in a matter of minutes.

Testing and Development

In a data center, development operations (DevOps) teams are always looking for test and development servers to play with and try out new ideas. There is a constant struggle to meet their requirements when using physical servers, as time after time the IT team will need to rebuild the environment they have just messed up. However, with VMs, the problem no longer exists, because VM test server environments for any OS can be stored as a file and then when required started, paused, and shut down in a matter of minutes. This makes provisioning and recovering a test environment a trivial task.

Faster Redeploy

Servers fail, and even expensive physical servers will fail sooner or later, and it can be time-consuming and stressful to replace them and restore service. VMs, however, can fail over gracefully to another existing server without any loss of data or downtime, even if the physical server they are running on fails, because they can be easily moved to another server. An administrator can configure VMs to start automatically, start manually, or can copy them over to a new location in a matter of seconds; this makes fast service recovery a key benefit.

Easier Backups

Backing up physical servers often requires a full-time administration team. However, with VMs, backing up using full and snapshot backups makes life much easier, and restoring from backups is also easier.

Disaster Recovery

VMs provide the ability to ensure business continuity in a disaster scenario, because operational VMs can be migrated live across WAN links to another location without any downtime or loss of data. Furthermore, VMs in secondary sites can monitor the heartbeats of VMs in the primary site and fail over automatically should the primary VM fail. Having this level of flexibility makes disaster recovery planning so much easier. Note that setting a fully capable failover site is not trivial in terms of cost or complexity. However, once set up, virtualization makes failing over much, much easier

Server Standardization

VMs don't really care what hardware they run on, as the level of abstraction removes that dependence on individual hardware specifications. This allows companies to avoid vendor lock in because the VMs will run on any make of server. Many large hosting providers even go so far as to specify their own servers from hardware manufacturers to avoid vendors altogether.

Separation of Services

Some data center applications have their backend database reside on the same server. Although not ideal, this is sometimes done to reduce latency and costs. With VMs, the administrator can create separate VMs for the application and the database and host them on the same physical server, remediating any performance or cost issues.

Interestingly, though, virtualization can actually create issues with regard to separation of services between the networking, IT, and security teams, given the ease with which new services and applications can be deployed in a cloud environment. This topic is covered in later chapters.

Easier Migration to the Cloud

Virtualization in the data center prepares the mindset for eventual migration to an all-cloud environment. This can be a big shift for companies because migrating to a third-party cloud can offer significant cost savings. This is especially the case for companies whose usage is "bursty" (for example, retail companies that have a massive jump in server utilization during the holidays). It makes little sense for them to invest in the resources that can handle that load but would otherwise be idle for 10 to 11 months out of the year. By virtualizing their data center, a company such as this could use a third-party cloud provider to handle the peaks during the holidays for a fraction of what it would cost them to set up their own environment.

Is It a Cloud Yet?

Virtualizing the data center does not make it a cloud environment, but it does get it a few steps closer. So, what is a cloud environment, and how does virtualization differ? Well, this is where the confusion arises, because virtualization is the foundation of cloud computing, which could not exist without it. However, virtualization is based on software (it is a technology), whereas a cloud refers to all the services built upon a virtualized infrastructure. Simply put, a cloud is the delivery of shared computing resources, whether that be data, software, or infrastructure as a service. Most confuse virtualization and cloud computing, which is easy to do, but they deliver different types of services. They are so, so tightly integrated that it is sometimes difficult to tell them apart.

To help distinguish between virtualization and a cloud, it helps to understand what constitutes a cloud, and that is best done by examining the attributes of cloud services.

The Five Cloud Attributes

The hard part of defining a cloud is that the word has been overused and even abused during the hype cycle that accompanied the investment and build-out of data center virtualization. Rather than go with a strict definition, it's more instructive to instead focus on the attributes.

The five attributes of clouds were originally outlined by the National Institute for Science and Technology (NIST) and have largely been adopted (or at least recognized) by the rest of the industry. The five attributes are as follows:

1. On-demand self-service
2. Ubiquitous network access
3. Pay per use (metered usage)
4. Rapid elasticity
5. Location-independent resource pooling

These attributes are shown in Figure 5-1 and are outlined in the following subsections in greater detail.

Cloud computing is defined by the presence of 5 features

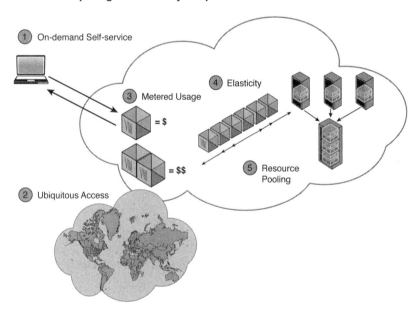

Figure 5-1 *If the cloud you are using does not have all five characteristics, it may not actually be a cloud.*

On-Demand Self-Service

With on-demand self-service, a client (which can be a person or a company) can provision computing resources from the cloud without having to interact with IT or service provider personnel. In other words, you can order it online by clicking buttons (without a salesperson trying to meet you for lunch).

Now, obviously, this breaks down if a major corporation wants to provision massive amounts of computing power. In this case, they would need to understand availability, and would likely negotiate on price, service levels, and uptime with the provider personnel, and there might be a few meals in there as well. But the actual service they provision could be on-demand at the scale at which most users would consume it.

Ubiquitous Network Access

Simply put, you should be able to connect to the cloud from wherever you are with whatever you have. In other words, you should be able to use standard platforms that provide simple connectivity without having to put down dedicated cables or systems and without having to buy custom hardware for access.

In many cases, network access to the cloud can be done over the Internet, but this is not really a requirement. It simply means that you should not have to build out a separate or specialized network to gain access to a cloud.

Pay Per Use

The cloud is, generally speaking, a pay per use model. This attribute is a bit hard to pin down because some clients may want or need a fully private cloud (as explained later). Private clouds require a fixed monthly payment because, by definition, another client could not use the same resources even if they were idle.

That said, even this model allows the client to outsource ownership of the computing assets, eliminating both the large capital expense and the management expense of maintaining servers and storage devices.

Rapid Elasticity

Elasticity is probably the one characteristic that most people refer to when describing a cloud. Accomplished via automation and application programming interfaces (APIs), elasticity is the ability to very rapidly (or even instantly) "spin up" computing resources for a short while or to accommodate an event and then spin it all back down (just as easily) when you no longer need it.

This capability is where most of the efficiencies of the cloud come from. For example, this feature could allow a small biomedical firm to perform computationally intensive research analysis on a per-project basis rivaling what a large public company or university could do, all without any of the massive upfront costs and at a small fraction of the cost per CPU. The cloud in a very real way allows small clients to bring enterprise-class computing resources to bear at an affordable rate. At the same time, it provides an enormous reduction in operational costs for large enterprises whose businesses require them to maintain large data centers based mostly on the concept of rapid elasticity.

Location-Independent Resource Pooling

Resource pooling is where many of the advantages of cloud networking are derived from. As the name suggests, the cloud provider has different types of grouped resources, including storage, memory, computer processing, and bandwidth (just to name a few), which instead of being dedicated to any one client are allocated to clients as they need them. Rather than having a dedicated resource allocated to a user, the cloud model allows clients to draw resources from functional pools as needed.

This pooling (and allocating) of resources allows what is commonly known as a *multitenant* model, where the provider is able to maximize the utilization and efficiency of its resources by sharing them among many customers. Users no longer have to pay for resources they are not using, and it allows the providers to gain efficiencies by having a common set of tools to draw from rather than replicating them for every customer.

In some cases, such as a private cloud (described later in this chapter), a client might want their own dedicated resource pool, but even within that model, the resource pool is shared among the individual users from that single client.

Types of Clouds

The attributes described earlier define the characteristics of clouds, but there are different ways that providers can offer the resources within in a cloud to their clients. Because this is a pay-as-you-go model, IT resources are offered as a service (that you rent) as opposed to a product (that you purchase), and there are three different ways to carve out services for users in an "as a service" model:

■ **Software as a service (SaaS):** The provider offers an application that clients connect to over the network.

■ **Infrastructure as a service (IaaS):** The provider offers processing, storage, and other computing resources in a manner that has the attributes listed earlier.

■ **Platform as a service (PaaS):** The provider offers the ability to run applications that they have created themselves.

Software as a Service

When people think of cloud computing, it is usually software as a service that comes to mind. Most individuals who connect to a cloud infrastructure (and many are doing this without even realizing it) are taking advantage of the SaaS model. With SaaS, a user can access an application that is hosted by the provider, rather than installing that application on their own machines. The application software is run out of one or more data centers, where the user's data is also stored. Typically, access to the application is made via a web browser, installed software, or a "thin client" that connects to the cloud application over the Internet.

The technical definition of a thin client is a usage model where the program running on the user's machine (or machines) is very simple and requires only a small amount of computing power. The web browser meets this definition, but in practice, thin client usually refers to remote desktop architectures like Citrix or VMware VDI. In both web browsers and remote desktops, the real computing is actually on the servers running in the cloud, and the user is presented with the results through a user interface (such as a web page or thin client software).

SaaS offers a lot of advantages for the clients, including the following:

- The ability to connect to the application from anywhere and from multiple devices, as opposed to having a dedicated machine to which you must have physical access

- Not having to manage stored data, software upgrades, operating systems, or really anything else

- The reduction in management resources and technical personnel for companies

SaaS also has some downsides, including:

- The requirement to have network connectivity to access an application. This is becoming less and less of a problem because it is now possible to get network connectivity from almost anywhere, including planes in flight, but it reduces the reliability and predictability of the user experience.

- The loss of 100% control of your data, which might make it difficult to switch from one application provider to another. This is also becoming less of an issue because many application providers now have relatively easy methods of exporting and importing data from other services, something that was driven by user demand.

Figure 5-2 illustrates the span of control between providers and clients within a SaaS model. As shown in the diagram, in a SaaS application the client gets some control of the application (usually interface customization), while the provider maintains full control of the rest of the stack as well as some control over the application.

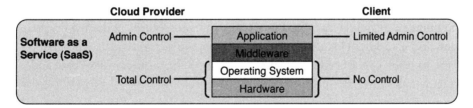

Figure 5-2 *With SaaS, the user has access to their data and some admin control, but the provider maintains complete control of the environment.*

Infrastructure as a Service

In an infrastructure as a service (IaaS) model, the client rents compute resources that enable them to run their own software programs, including both operating systems and applications.

With IaaS, the client is renting the infrastructure (which the provider retains control of) but is still able to control the applications and operating system software. The client is also able to control storage of their data and has some control over network functions and security (such as firewalls). Basically, the client rents a server (or servers) that they can then install their own programs on.

This model is most common with enterprise-class clients, who can enjoy significant reductions in IT operational costs, especially if they only need these resources on a part-time basis (or when there is a big disparity between peak use and average use).

Smaller organizations can also benefit because this model eliminates what was often an overwhelming startup cost for access to enterprise-class computing resources.

IaaS offers a lot of advantages for the clients, including the following:

■ A significant reduction (or complete elimination) of startup and ongoing costs for IT infrastructure

■ The ability to use multiple operating systems without losing flexibility to switch between them

IaaS does have some downsides, though, including:

■ Some security concerns with outsourcing the infrastructure, especially when using a shared or multitenant cloud for sensitive or regulated data.

■ Loss of physical control of your data. With the traditional infrastructure, you know exactly where your data is. However, when your data is "in the cloud," it could be in any number of places, so you can't walk into a room and tell someone "our data is here." In the grand scheme of things, this has no real value, but there are a lot of people who derive comfort (or reduce anxiety) by being able to point to the exact location of their information resources. Giving up that feeling of ownership can be a difficult thing for some, and one of the byproducts of cloud adoption is that you lose the ability to point to your stuff.

■ Lack of visibility into cloud network traffic.

Figure 5-3 illustrates the span of control between providers and clients within an IaaS model. As shown in the diagram, in an IaaS application, the client gets some control over the applications and middleware, while the cloud provider maintains control of the hypervisor operating systems and hardware. This service, however, is able to accommodate multiple operating systems; so if the client needs to change or use more than one, it's very easy and cost-effective. Figure 5-3 shows the span of control.

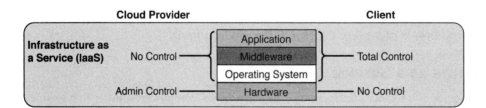

Figure 5-3 *With IaaS, the user has control over their applications and operating systems, but the provider maintains control of the hardware (and the location of the user's software and data).*

Platform as a Service

In a platform as a service (PaaS) model, the client is provided a computing platform upon which they can develop and run their own applications or programs.

In a PaaS model, to ensure that the proper resources are allocated, the client must usually let the service provider know what programming tools they will be using (such as Java or .NET). The underlying network infrastructure (servers, storage, networking) is managed by the provider, while the client maintains control of the computing/development environment. Figure 5-4 shows the span of PaaS control.

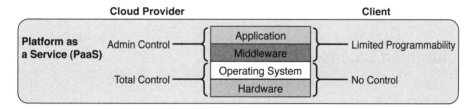

Figure 5-4 *With PaaS, the user has control over their applications and configuration settings, and the provider delivers programming libraries and maintains control of the hardware.*

PaaS offers the following advantages for clients:

- It eliminates the need to maintain an IT team for the development environment. Usually developers and IT support teams have to exist in parallel, or (and probably more often) coders are forced to spend time building and maintaining their own infrastructures. With PaaS, developers can just code. Developers love that.

- This system makes it very cost-effective to port programs or systems to new platforms. With most programs, the vast majority of work goes into the initial coding and testing of a program. If there is a need or desire to port that program to a new platform, much of the expense goes into building out the development and test beds of the new platform. The porting part usually is not that hard, but the build-out can be prohibitively expensive. PaaS basically makes this is a non-issue.

PaaS does have some downsides, though, including:

- With a PaaS model, your code is located elsewhere. In many cases (especially for developers), your source code is your biggest and most important asset. Typically, you will keep your code in a private or public repository such as GitHub. You then link your code to the PaaS platform via a framework that will build your applications. Although there are secure methods for doing this, having it outside "your four walls" can be too much of a risk for some organizations. This issue of "physically having your stuff," whether it's user data, applications, or codes, is a big hump to get over, and it's a required shift for cloud usage. This topic is explored in depth in Chapter 31, "Where's My Data, Exactly?"

- Another potential issue is security and secrecy. There are many cases where you not only want to keep your data secure, but you also don't want anyone to even know what you are working on. This can be a bit of risk with PaaS because there are "outsiders" who will know what platforms you are renting.

Cloud Deployment Models

With the attributes of a cloud service and the types of services defined, it makes sense to look at how cloud services are deployed. Clouds have four basic deployment models: private clouds, multitenant clouds, public clouds, and hybrid clouds.

Private Clouds

The first step that most enterprises take toward cloud adoption is the virtualization of their existing data centers. A private cloud is created when an enterprise data center is reconfigured in such a way as to provide the five attributes described earlier in this chapter. In this case, the enterprise owns the cloud, so it's both the provider and the client.

Shared Multitenant Clouds

For our purposes, a multitenant cloud is run by a service provider that hosts services for a select group of customers, almost always businesses (as opposed to individuals). The various tenants are likely sharing common resources, but the service is not public in the sense that just anyone can access these cloud resources any time they want. Providers of this type of cloud often cater to business clients, and there are usually contract service agreements that are entered into. Not that all public clouds (addressed in the following section) are by definition multitenant clouds. In this case, however, we are referring primarily to hosted services that cater to select business clients.

Public Clouds

A public cloud is just what the name implies. It's open to anyone and everyone who has connectivity and a credit card (or some remote method of payment). Public clouds are the means by which enterprise-class computing is made available to the masses. This is great for start-ups and individuals, but it might not be the best service option for an existing enterprise looking to reduce their infrastructure overhead. It is less available (99.9%) than traditional enterprises IT apps (99.999%.)

Hybrid Clouds

Okay, this category is an obvious catchall, but the reality is that all of this technology is changing very rapidly, and new technologies and services are being introduced all the time. Virtualization and cloud technologies also lend themselves to mixing and mashups; it's one of the things that makes it so interesting from an innovation standpoint. In fact, some providers offer administrative control over multiple cloud platforms (private or public) that can be managed through a single interface. This allows seamless access to both cloud environments.

Software as a Service (SaaS)

The Cloud is an Application

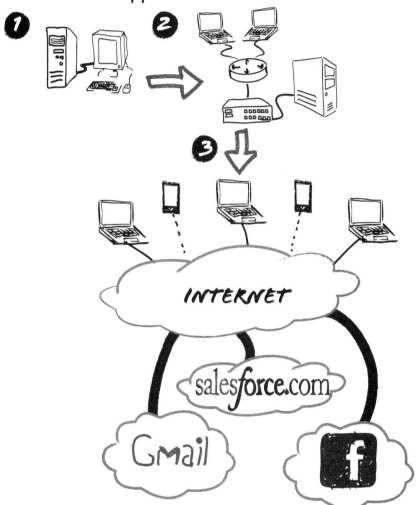

1. Applications used to be contained on a single machine for a single user.

2. The apps migrated to data centers where dedicated servers host apps for multiple users.

3. Software as a service clouds takes this one step further running scalable apps on virtual servers that can be accessed by many users and on multiple devices from pretty much anywhere.

Benefits include:
* Device and location independence
* Easy collaboration and massive scalability
* No software to manage for user IT staffs
* Only one "live" version to manage for APP developers, which is much easier (and cheaper) to manage

SaaS gives us more apps, from more places, that are easier to use, share, and grow.

Infrastructure as a Service (IaaS)

The Cloud is Your Data Center

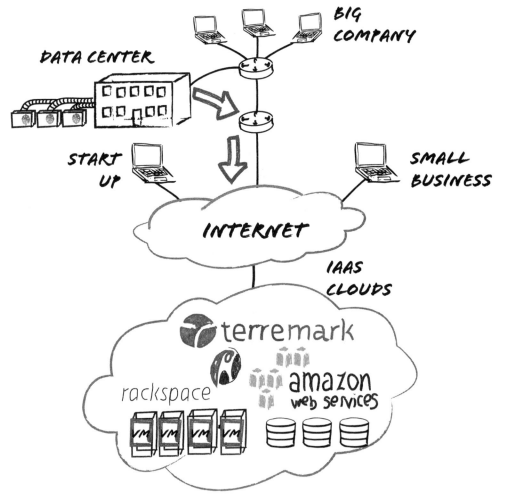

1. Infrastructure as a service is a way to outsource or expand expensive data centers to third-party providers to take advantage of the costs/ efficiency benefits of virtualization and cloud networking.

2. IaaS allows for cost effective "bursting" where companies keep a data center that is sized for day-to-day usage, and then "burst" to the IaaS cloud to make peak workloads.

3. IaaS allows small companies and startups to take advantage of enterprise class computing without having to pay a lot of cash (which they tend not to have).

4. This allows for more innovation as more companies get access to high performance computing resources. This benefits the entire economy!

Platform as a Service (PaaS)

The Cloud is a Development Environment and Service Library

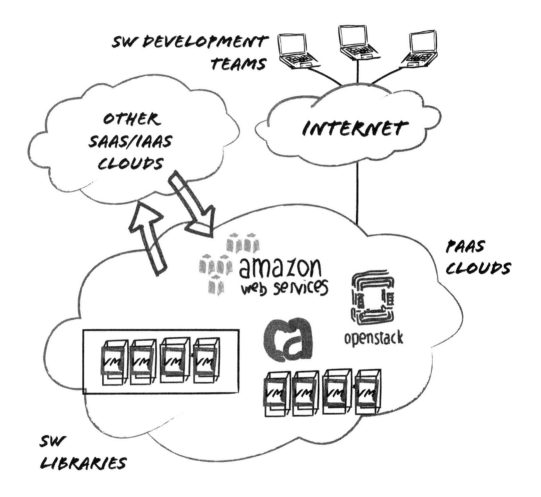

1. Platform as a service is a virtualized SW development environment with all of the tools and libraries required to code programs.

2. PaaS clouds can sometimes offer services to other clouds—for example, if a SaaS application uses a function that requires frequent data updates (such as an anti-virus tool), it can access it in a PaaS cloud.

3. PaaS makes software development very affordable and makes collaboration very easy, too. This is a big deal for small companies, startups, and techie entrepreneurs.

Virtual Machine Connectivity

Up until now, this book has considered virtualization purely as a method to consolidate servers and leverage efficiency from hosting VMs on fewer servers in the data center. Indeed, the approach has been completely server and application centric. Perhaps you have the impression that all that needs to be done to virtualize the data center infrastructure is to start deploying a vendor's hypervisor software. Once done, you can simply go about creating and deploying virtual machines (VMs) to your heart's content, while simultaneously ripping out servers that are now surplus to requirements.

Unfortunately, there is a rather large problem that prevents you from charging ahead with data center virtualization that way. First you must solve some connectivity problems, or more precisely you have to tackle data center networking. The issue is that because of the nature of virtualization, everything has changed. You no longer have one OS and its applications along with all the memory and storage residing on a single server. In a virtualized data center, you have many instances of OS/applications residing on a single host. Further, the memory and storage may not be (and often are not) on the same server. Further still, where all that stuff is right now might not be the same as where it is later. And, therein lies the problem: How do you figure out how to connect all the pieces, especially when they are in a near constant state of flux?

Networking in Traditional Data Centers

To understand this problem, let's take a quick look at how traditional data center networking handled data flow between client and server applications. When a user wants to use an application, the machine that they are using (called the client) initiates an application call. This is a request that goes from the small application connection program running on the user's machine or more likely today over an HTTP request from the user's browser.

The user's application call will point to an address associated with the server where the application resides. Data centers were traditionally designed in a hierarchical network model that consists of a core, an aggregation layer, and an access layer, which ensures that data is collected, aggregated, and then transported at high speed to its final destination. This is shown in Figure 6-1. However, at this point, we are dealing with an incoming request so that the application call's IP packets, which are destined for our application server, will arrive via a router connected to the core. The incoming packets will be fast routed through the core, to the high-port-density access switches via the aggregation layer. At the access layer, the packets will be examined for the destination address, and they will be fast switched across the wire to the required server (based on that server's unique address) where the destination application is running.

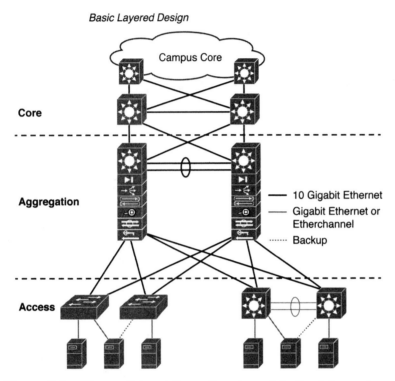

Figure 6-1   *The traditional three-tiered model of a data center network that was optimized for client-host traffic*

The key to all of this is the addressing scheme. The Layer 3 or IP address is used to get the packet across the wide-area network to the right data center location, and once there, the Layer 2 address tells all the switches in the data center which server the traffic should be sent to.

In the preceding scenario, the following was true:

- The application was associated with a single server, and all the application-based addressing and programming of the network was based on where that physical server was located, starting with the access switch that the physical server connected to.

- The addresses assigned to the server were dependent on a Layer 3 routing subnet, which is location dependent. Therefore, regardless of where the user was connecting from, the server's IP address would always find its way to the correct data center and the core routers.

- After the IP packets arrive at the core routers, they will again automatically route to the correct subnet on the aggregation routers before they in turn route or switch the packets to the access switches.

- The access switch will look up the packets, destination MAC address (the address of the server's network interface adapter) and fire them down the wire via the correct VLAN to the destination.

- After the packets arrive at the server's network interface card (NIC), the TCP port will determine which application to send the packets to.

It's worth noting here that data center designs were based on these factors, and the three-layer design was implemented specifically to optimize "north-south" traffic flows. That is to say there was very little traffic from server to server. Most traffic was from a server to a client outside of the data center (or vice versa), so data center networks were designed to optimize that traffic flow.

You have probably already figured out the problem that VMs cause based on the network addresses. With virtualization, the application (and the operating system) is not associated with any particular server. In fact, that is a key aspect of our working definition of what virtualization is. Not only does this method support more than one app-OS combo running on a particular server, but it also means that the servers and the VMs are all interchangeable; think back to how easy it was to move and copy VMs to other servers, without downtime or loss of data. Further, the different parts for one application (the compute power for the app, memory, and storage) may all be in different places. Consequently, network addressing is a huge concern with virtualization, and the old scheme simply does not work. So how on earth do we get around this network address conundrum?

Virtualized Data Center Design

First, for the sake of simplicity, imagine that each VM is running one application on an OS. Second, on any given server, there can be multiple VMs. These VMs will need to communicate with one of three entities.

1. Another VM on the same host (or server).

2. Another VM on a different host. This could be any virtual resource within the data center (such as disk storage for example)

3. A remote host, which resides outside of the data center. This would most often be back to the client (user) machine but it could be anything. For the sake of this description it's a "don't care." The important part is that the communication is leaving the data center.

There are two key pieces to making this all work. The first is figuring out how to establish and maintain addressing when the VMs are both sharing common physical devices yet are prone to moving from session to session; and the second is changing the physical layout and performance characteristics of the data center networking devices to better accommodate the new requirements.

Addressing with Virtual Machines

As a quick recap, let's remember how Layer 3 and Layer 2 communications work. In a Layer 3 routed network, we assign IP addresses to devices, and then divide IP domains into IP subnets for security and performance reasons. Communication between subnets or IP domains requires Layer 3 routing. When a router receives a packet with an IP address corresponding to a known subnet (router interface), it knows which interface to send the packet out.

Within a Layer 2 network (for example, within a data center), when hosts are communicating across the LAN (through switches), routers are not needed, and the hosts IP addresses are only used to look up the host's MAC address via Address Resolution Protocol (ARP).

The key point here is that each host needs both a MAC (Layer 2) address and an IP (Layer 3 address). For physical devices, unique MAC address are assigned by manufacturers as devices come off the assembly line. This makes Layer 2 addresses easy for the network engineer. Layer 3 addresses, however, are assigned by network engineers, which can be cumbersome when done all at once, but generally they do not change.

NOTE   With Dynamic Host Configuration Protocol (DHCP), IP addresses can and do change often, but it is all automated. We conveniently ignore DHCP for now.

You can probably see some obvious problems. First is that VMs do not roll off a factory line. They get "created out of thin air." Second, although VM machines do not often move from one data center to another, they move a lot within the data center. As a result, we have some new problems to solve. First, who or what creates MAC addresses, and second, how do we account for all this moving around because the rest of the network has to know where to send traffic flows to ensure uninterrupted connectivity.

In the absence of factory assigned MAC address allocation, VM software such as VMSphere or Citrix provides a unique MAC address for each VM created. These VM managers also assign a virtual NIC (vNIC) or multiple vNICs; you'll recall that the NIC is a specific piece of equipment within a device that uses the MAC address. For what it's worth, most of these VM managers enable you to manually configure the MAC address, but leaving the software to manage dynamic MAC addresses is much simpler, so there is no compelling reason (for most situations) to manually configure VMs.

By assigning each individual VM its own MAC, you can then address that VM individually on the network; this is an important concept when it comes to mobility of individual VMs from one host physical server to another. The point being that the VM MAC address is inherent to that VM and is independent of the physical server's network card. Therefore, it is capable and free to migrate over to another server without any restrictions. The trick then is to let the rest of the data center know where that VM is located at any given time.

Once a VM has a MAC address, it can then be assigned an IP address. This is the same as with any other virtual or physical server in that you assign the OS (not the VM itself) an IP address either through DHCP or by manually configuring static IP addresses to each OS.

The key point here is that it is the OS that is assigned an IP address, the VM is identified by its MAC, so when the VM migrates away from the physical host to another location on the network, the IP address will remain the same rather than changing each time the VM moves to a new physical host. If not for this, the mobility of a VM would be restricted to a LAN segment, and consequently VMs would not be able to migrate across a Layer 3 network.

Note that VMs moving within a data center is much, much simpler than moving across data centers. In fact, the regularity of intra-data center moves, along with the huge increase in east-west traffic, is the driving force behind the change in data center architecture.

When is comes to enabling migration across Layer 3 boundaries, the solution is network virtualization, a topic covered in detail later. By extending the network as a Layer 2 LAN, as an overlay, which is the purpose of network virtualization, IP addresses are no longer a concern because they are in the same broadcast domain. Consequently, VMs can communicate by ARP to obtain the MAC address of other hosts across the shared broadcast domain (which can span data centers) as if it was on a real LAN.

Network virtualization takes the extended LAN principle a step further by building a virtual LAN as an overlay on top of the physical Layer 2/3 network. This virtual LAN overlay enables VMs to migrate across the data center as if they were on a LAN segment. They can do this even though they might eventually be in different subnets. However, the VMs don't see it that way because they are connected by the virtual overlay that operates at Layer 2 and is effectively a LAN.

Virtual Machine Connectivity

From Idea to Productivity

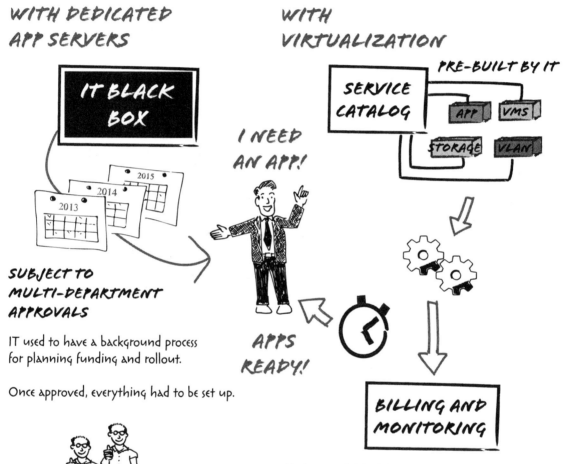

WITH DEDICATED APP SERVERS

IT BLACK BOX

2013 2014 2015

SUBJECT TO MULTI-DEPARTMENT APPROVALS

IT used to have a background process for planning funding and rollout.

Once approved, everything had to be set up.

I NEED AN APP!

APPS READY!

WITH VIRTUALIZATION

PRE-BUILT BY IT

SERVICE CATALOG

APP VMS

STORAGE VLAN

BILLING AND MONITORING

MANUAL PROCESS

After the process was completed, the user would finally get access to the app—hopefully there was still a need.

AUTOMATED PROCESS

With virtualization the user simply looks up the app from a service catalog—the apps and services are pre-built by IT, and they can be provisioned and rolled out within hours (or minutes), via an automated process. Users are productive almost in real time.

Virtual Machine Connectivity

Abstracting the Physical Connections

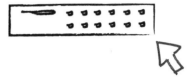

In a fixed server, the MAC address is assigned to the Network Interface Card (NIC). This address is permanently assigned to the physical NIC at the factory during the manufacturing process.

Physical IP addresses are not permanent like MAC addresses but they tend not to change often within a network.

MAC ADDRESSES

In a virtual machine, the MAC address is a logical assignment. On the physical server where the VMs reside, there is a permanent MAC address assigned to the NIC—the Virtual Controllers in the network associate the virtual MAC and physical MAC on the server.

IP ADDRESSES ON 1ST LEVEL SWITCHES

In a virtual environment, the first switch is actually the hypervisor and the IP addressing system is much more flexible with regards to address assignments.

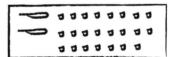

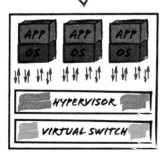

2ND LEVEL SWITCHING

For the most part, after traffic gets to the second level of switching, the addressing methods and schemes are nearly identical to what they were in pre-virtualized data centers despite the fact the traffic behaves a bit differently.

The big difference is that in a virtual environment there is a supervisory controller that manages the MAC/IP associations.

Networking Gear in Virtualized Data Centers

As you have just learned in the previous chapter, virtualization within the data center had a considerable impact on network addressing and how individual virtual machines (VMs) were uniquely identified within the switched network. You learned that the hypervisor took the role of a virtual switch within the hypervisor software layer and interacted with the network controller to assign and manage Layer 2 switching identifiers. The data center access switches were oblivious to these new networking elements, and they continued to operate as before using the standard Address Resolution Protocol (ARP) to update their switching tables.

The Evolution of Data Center Switching

In addition to the need for location-independent addressing, which is enabled by the network controller, there is also a need for a new generation of data center switches to handle both the increased volume of intra–data center (cloud) traffic and changes in the nature of the traffic.

The need for a new generation of switches is a result of two significant changes in network traffic that occur when a data center is virtualized (or when a cloud infrastructure is created), as compared to the traditional fixed-server data center.

The first change is that as a result of several VMs running on a single server, the traffic density has significantly increased. This is compounded by the fact that servers now have multicore processors, which means you can increase the number of VMs running on them. In short, the amount of traffic generated within a single server now equals or exceeds what used to be generated by a full rack of servers.

There is also the fact that the hypervisor is itself a switch, albeit a virtual one. These virtual switches are now serving as the access layer of switches in the classic N-tiered model of networking, as shown in Figure 7-1, but they are largely absent from many network monitoring and management platforms. This means that the first physical layer of switches now sees a much higher traffic rate and therefore must also have a much greater port density.

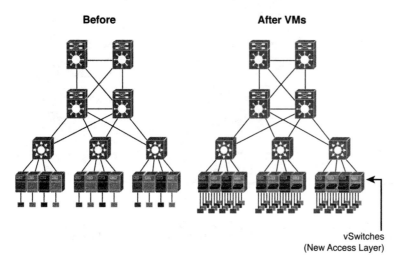

Before **After VMs**

vSwitches
(New Access Layer)

Figure 7-1 *In virtualized data centers and clouds, the vSwitch is the new access layer.*

On the left is the classic N-tiered model where access switches connected to servers. On the right is a virtualized data center or cloud model where the virtual switches (hypervisors) take over that role.

The other impact of virtualization is that traffic patterns have shifted from being predominantly client to server (from inside the data center to outside and vice versa) to being predominantly server to server (within the data center) as workflows from VM to VM increase and the prevalence of independent resource pools increases. In other words, instead of a having a server that does it all, there are clusters of specialized resources that an application will draw from within the cloud (that is, the virtualized data center).

This traffic shift from client to server to server to server is often referred to as a shift from north-south traffic to east-west traffic. The directional traffic reference is based on the common practice of diagramming data center networks with the servers on the bottom running left to right (or east-west) and then stacking the access, aggregation, and core layers on top such that the edge of the data center (or cloud) is on the top, as shown in Figure 7-2.

Data centers and clouds still need to efficiently handle north-south traffic, but the increase in east-west traffic has increased the need for uniform bandwidth and latency between servers, especially given that the physical location of VMs may change mid-session (during VM migrations [vMotion]). Virtual data center design must account for this to ensure performance is not impacted.

In the old model, traffic between two servers would go up a level (or two) in the hierarchy and then go back down to another switch. Called *hair pinning*, this method of server-to-server communication is not too bad as long as the servers are fixed (so that the performance is predictable) and it is not too frequent. As already discussed, neither of these is the case in virtual environments and clouds.

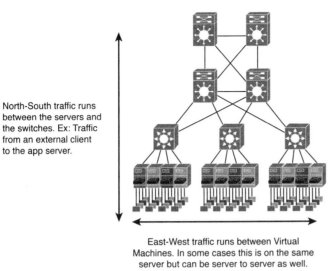

North-South traffic runs between the servers and the switches. Ex: Traffic from an external client to the app server.

East-West traffic runs between Virtual Machines. In some cases this is on the same server but can be server to server as well.

Figure 7-2 *In a virtual environment, VM-to-VM traffic (referred to as east-west traffic) makes up a significant portion of the overall traffic.*

The other issue is political. Because we need to accommodate all the changes in location and addressing that occur in virtualized data centers, teams that control the management of the VMs and teams that control and manage switches are often at odds. There was already a traditional rift between "network teams" and "IT (server) teams," but virtualization creates the need for a virtualization management team, which is a hybrid of the two. In some cases, one team would end up reporting to the other, and the perceived loss of control or autonomy was problematic.

One of the big changes in data center networking is the emergence of *virtualization-aware* switches that allow for dynamic configuration of the switches in response to the creation, suspension, or movement of a VM. In time, IT organizations will decide whether this is a server function, a network function, or whether the distinction between the two is not really that important anyway when it comes to cloud networking and virtualized environments.

Cloud and Data Center Layout and Architecture

The N-tiered model is still used on virtualized data centers and clouds, but as a result of the traffic changes, there are some new ways to put it all together.

As before, the first access switch is now the hypervisor, which is itself a virtualized switch (and, because it supports virtual LANs [VLANs], it is also a virtual switch). The first physical switch, however, now typically sits on top of the physical server rack, serving as the access switch for multiple VMs that operate on that machine. This switch is referred to as a *top of rack* (TOR) switch (see Figure 7-3), which in turn connects to one or more 10Gbps *end of row* (EOR) switches. The EOR switches (see Figure 7-4) connect traffic to physical servers and aggregate traffic up to the core switches. This new model is referred to as a *leaf-and-spine* architecture, and it works well primarily because it scales well horizontally (east-west) without giving up vertical (north-south) performance.

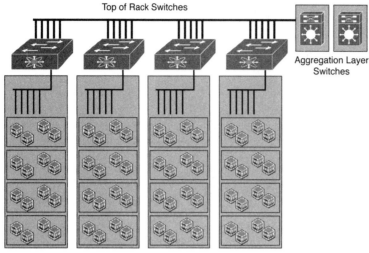

Figure 7-3 *TOR switches aggregate traffic from several servers (in a single rack), which can be hosting many VMs.*

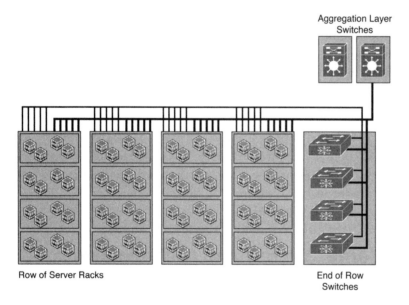

Figure 7-4 *EOR switches aggregate traffic from an entire row of server racks.*

The last change in the data center to examine in this chapter is the rate of change, which of course is increasing. A number of factors are driving this, but the main one (at least at the time of writing this) is the increasing processing power on the servers. The increasing numbers of very fast multicore processors (following Moore's law) means that a single server or host can handle more and more VMs. The traffic impact of this is an exponential response as more VMs on a server communicate with more VMs on adjacent servers. This drives the need for faster switches with greater port densities located closer to the servers.

One aspect of Moore's law is that it predicts processors growing much faster than networking speeds have the potential to grow. This could become a major weakness for modern cloud networking as the I/O functions within virtualized environments become the chokepoint on performance rather than processing speed.

We're already seeing the need for 10Gbps switching at the TOR level and 40Gbps and 100Gbps switching at the higher levels. The need for greater speeds beyond the data center may not exceed 100Gbps for some time, but we are likely to see the homogenization of switching speeds within the data center near the 100Gbps range and VM-aware switches, resulting in flat, virtually aware, blazing fast data centers and clouds.

Virtualized Aware Network Switches

The hypervisor vSwitch was a good idea, and it solved many of the basic Layer 2 addressing problems; however, it was not without some drawbacks. For example, the vSwitch having no control plane to speak of was unable to update the physical switch with the VLAN information that was required to support VM mobility and vMotion (the VMware product that manages the orchestration of VMs moving around in a data center). Therefore, to facilitate VM mobility and vMotion between physical hosts, many VLANs had to be configured on the physical switches' server-facing ports. This caused unnecessary and indiscriminate flooding of broadcasts, multicasts, and unknown unicasts (garbage traffic), which increased uplink utilization and CPU cycles, which resulted in dropped packets. This might not be a problem if the data center uses just a few large flat domains. However, in situations where there are many small broadcast domains, having to configure VLANs on every switch port can become an increasing burden.

The solution is VM-aware switching that can learn the VM network topology typically by using a discovery protocol to interact with the vSwitches and build a map of the virtualized network.

VM-aware switches also provide the visibility to vSwitches that are usually hidden from view on network monitoring tools. This allows administrators to measure and troubleshoot network traffic per VM. VM-aware switches also enable administrators to configure the network parameters of VMs and track them as they migrate within the network and reduce complexity by requiring no additional server software or changes to hypervisors or VMs.

The takeaway from this chapter is that one of the biggest impacts of virtualization is that it has driven a significant change in the physical makeup of data centers. This was not something that was designed from the start, but rather a consequence of the fact that it was the best way to extract maximum value out of virtualizing servers. The impacts have been so profound that it has often been worth the money for companies to overhaul data centers even though they had already invested billions of dollars over the years. This also foreshadowed the virtualizations of networks that we cover in the rest of this book.

Layers 1 and 2
What's Driving the Changes in How Networks Are Built

We talk a lot about the fact that virtualization is driving changes in the network, but in many ways virtualization is one of the solutions rather than the cause.

The reality is that the explosion of connected devices and the growing expectation of instantaneous connectivity from any place at any time (or even while moving) is forcing changes in the way networks are built. The transformation from traditional networks to cloud networks is a result of the changes in the amount, type, and usage of these new devices.

Networks were initially built at a time when there were relativity few device types, which tended to stay put.

Today, there is an ever increasing number of connected devices and many of them are mobile.

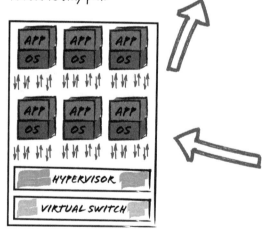

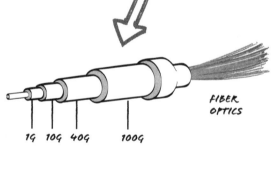

FIBER OPTICS

1G 10G 40G 100G

The modern increase in devices, bandwidth, and app usage has driven a massive increase in the use of data centers. This has paved the way for virtualization, which makes better use of server HW and supporting resources—making it easier to use more apps and add more resources.

As the number of devices increases, the required bandwidth explodes—this has driven the race to 100Gbps speeds but the size (and weight) of these cables, as well as the limited distances they can be used for, has driven the use of fiber optic cables.

VMware, VSphere, VMotion, and VXLAN

In the previous chapters, we looked at virtualization in the data center, from both a server and network perspective, but from a software-agnostic viewpoint. This was fine when dealing with high-level overviews of the theory behind the technology and its operation. However, now we need to move forward to discuss lower-level details, and that will require looking at specific hypervisors rather than generic examples. To simplify matters, this chapter takes a deep look at the leading hypervisor vendor, VMware, and their products, such as VSphere, VMotion, and VXLAN and others.

VMware Product Design

VMware is probably the most well-known virtualization vendor around. Indeed, many technical people were first introduced to virtualization back in the early 2000s when playing around with VMware workstation and later the GSX freeware products such as VM Player.

VMware has been producing their hypervisors aimed at the server market since 2001 with the launch of the VMware GSX server (type 2) and the ESX Server (type 1) hypervisor products. VM hypervisors provide a virtualized set of hardware for a video adapter, a network adapter, and a disk adapter, with pass-through drivers to support guest USB, serial, and parallel devices. As a result, VMware virtual machines (VMs) are highly portable and are able to run on just about any hardware because every host looks practically identical to the VM.

One of the early features that captured the imagination of network and server administrators, or those playing with the products, was the ability to pause operations running on a VM guest, and then move that VM file to another physical location, before resuming operation at the same point that service had been suspended. This seemed almost unbelievable back at the turn of the millennium, and even now it still doesn't fail to amaze those witnessing it for the first time. This is a huge departure from traditional server-OS-application combinations that were semipermanent.

VMware has an extensive product line, but this chapter covers only the enterprise VMware vSphere product. This enterprise-class product, sometimes known as ESXi, is a higher-performance hypervisor that easily outmuscles its sibling, the freeware version VMware Server. VSphere's increased performance level is due to it being a type 1 bare-metal product, which runs directly on the host server with no native OS installed. This bare-metal configuration permits the guest VMs to (almost) directly access the host hardware devices, giving it higher performance than the VMware Server product, which is a type 2 product. VMware Server (GSX) runs on top of a native OS running on the host server. This makes it easier to install and configure for the beginner, and for that reason, it is very popular in test and evaluation scenarios. Unfortunately it all too often creeps into production deployments, which it should never really do. As a virtualization best practice, VMware ESXi should be the production build.

VMware also has advanced cloud management software, such as vCloud Director, which was a software-defined networking and security solution. vCloud Director has since been superseded by vRealize Suite (via an acquisition).

vSphere

VSphere is designed as a data center server product, and it leverages the power of virtualization to transform conventional computing architectures into simplified virtualized infrastructures or private clouds. The vCenter Server product (part of the VSphere family) provides a single point of control and management for data centers. VMware vSphere is best understood as a product if we think back to an earlier definition of a hypervisor as an operating system for an operating system. Being a bare-metal hypervisor, it is an operating system that manages a dynamic operating environment such as a data center.

The components that comprise vSphere are as follows:

- Infrastructure services, which provide abstraction, aggregation, and they allocate hardware resources, through the component, vCompute, vStorage, and vNetwork services.

- Application services, which are high-availability and fault-tolerance services that provide availability, security, and scalability to applications.

- Clients, in which IT administrative users access vSphere through clients such as a vSphere client or a web access through a browser.

As shown in Figure 8-1 VMware vSphere consists of several functional components, such as ESX and ESXi, which is the virtualization layer run on physical servers that abstract processor, memory, storage, and resources into multiple VMs.

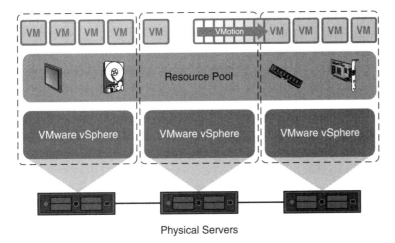

Figure 8-1 *VSphere is an operating system for cloud computing environments.*

The difference between the ESX and ESXi is that the former has a built-in service console, whereas ESXi comes in either an installable or an embedded version. Other important components of vSphere include the following:

- Virtual Machine File System (VMFS), which is a high-performance cluster file system

- Virtual SMP, which allows a single VM to use multiple physical CPUs simultaneously

- VMotion, which enables live migration of a running virtual machine

- Distributed resource scheduler, which allocates and balances computing capacity across the hardware resources for VMs

- Consolidated backup, which is a facility that provides agent free back up of VMs

- Fault tolerance, which is a secondary copy of the original VM that is created and all actions applied to the primary are also applied to the secondary VM

- vNetwork Distributed Switch, which is a distributed virtual switch (DVS) that spans ESx/ESXi hosts, enabling significant reduction of ongoing network maintenance and increasing network capacity

- Pluggable Storage Array, which is a storage plug-in framework that can provide multipath load-balancing to enhance storage performance

VMotion

A stunning feature of vSphere is vMotion, which permits an active VM to be migrated live across a network to another physical server in a way that is completely transparent to the users. This feature is absolutely incredible to watch, and it is pretty amazing how VMware manages this feat (but it does, and it looks so simple). What VMware manages to do is migrate a running VM from one physical server to another with zero downtime, continuous services availability, and complete transaction integrity. The only slight caveat is that vMotion can only migrate VMs within the same data center. That is, it does not support migration of VMs from one data center to another. Even so, this is an amazing property that allows maximum flexibility and agility within the data center in a way that was hard to imagine not that long ago.

VMotion (see Figure 8-2) also supports storage vMotion moving virtual disks or configuration files of a powered up VM to a new data store. Migration using vMotion storage allows an administrator to move a VM's storage without any interruption in the availability of the VM. It is important to note that a frozen or suspended VM can be moved across data centers, but an active VM can only be moved within a data center.

There is a key nuance here. VMotion and Storage vMotion are two different functions. VMotion works because of shared storage; that is, a VM can be moved because the data (storage) is shared. Storage VMotion is a storage admin function that allows the data to be moved.

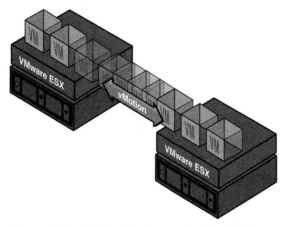

Figure 8-2 *With vMotion, an active VM can be migrated across a network to another physical server in a way that is completely transparent to users.*

VMotion provides impressive agility and flexibility, especially when you consider these are running VMs, and there is absolute transactional integrity and continuous service availability while this amazing feat takes place.

VXLAN

As you might guess from the name, VXLAN is a close relative of the humble VLAN, which is itself a virtualization protocol used to create virtual Layer 2 LAN segments across the common physical network media, such as Ethernet or air interface. VXLAN provides the same services and purpose as VLANs, but it has been given extensions to enable it to address some common VLAN failings.

One of VLAN's biggest failings is that when the protocol was created the VLAN ID was only assigned 8 bits, which meant it could only address 4096 unique VLANs. This seemed like a huge number years ago before IP/MPLS core networks hosted Layer 3 virtual private network (VPN) services that use other techniques to alleviate the address capacity problem. Consequently, when redesigning protocols for virtualization, the VXLAN addressing scheme has been given 24 address bits, giving it a possible identifier range of up to 16 million VXLAN identifiers (which should be enough for even the largest of data centers).

VXLAN also provides better utilization of available network paths in the underlying infrastructure. VLANs need to use a protocol called Spanning Tree Protocol to prevent loops by shutting down redundant paths in the network. Without this feature, seemingly harmless administrative messages can loop and multiply to create what is known as a broadcast storm, which can quickly take a network down. Spanning Tree Protocol, however, has the undesirable effect of shutting down a lot of ports to prevent them forwarding messages over paths that could form a potential loop. In contrast, VXLAN uses a Layer 3 header, which also means it can be routed and take advantage of equal-cost multipath routing and link-aggregation protocols to make the best use of all available paths without the potential for broadcast storms.

Although this might to sound horribly complicated, the main point to remember is that VXLAN is effectively tunneling (Layer 2) Ethernet frames across the (Layer 3) IP network. In effect, VXLAN is a Layer 2 overlay scheme over a Layer 3 network. It uses a technique to encapsulate MAC address in User Datagram Protocol (MAC-UDP) to tunnel through IP. In doing so, VXLAN is a solution for large-scale multitenant environments using a shared common physical infrastructure. VXLAN works by attaching a Layer 3 header to the standard Layer 2 frame and then encapsulating it within a UDP-IP packet. As a result, VXLAN tunnels Layer 2 frames through a Layer 3 network allowing for massive Layer 2 data center networks that are easy to manage and allow for the efficient movement of information.

VXLAN Tunnel Endpoints

VXLAN uses VTEP (VXLAN Tunnel EndPoints) devices to map tenants and end devices to VXLAN segments and to perform encapsulation/decapsulation. As shown in Figure 8-3, each VTEP has two interfaces: a switch port on the local LAN network and an interface on the transport IP network.

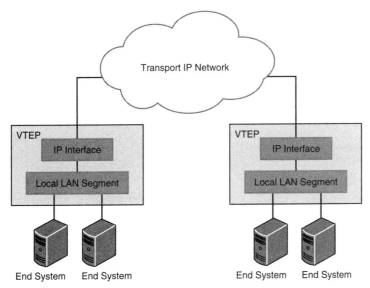

Figure 8-3 *VXLAN Tunnel EndPoints (VTEP) map tenants and end devices over VXLAN segments.*

The IP interface has a unique IP address that identifies the VTEP device on the transport IP network, also known as the infrastructure VLAN. The VTEP uses this IP address to encapsulate Ethernet frames and transmit them through the IP interface and over the IP transport network. Furthermore, a VTEP device discovers remote VTEPs for its VXLAN segment and learns the remote MAC Address to VTEP mappings.

NOTE VTEPs are used on physical switches to bridge together virtual network and physical network segments.

Summary

VMware has brought a number of products to market that help manage very large-scale virtualized environments, and that's the real takeaway here. These products are interesting and well designed, but they were all borne out of necessity due to the explosive scaling of virtualized data centers and clouds. Whereas early data centers were predicated on efficient movement of traffic, modern data centers must also account for orchestration on a grand scale.

Multitenancy and the Problems of Communal Living

Multitenancy is an important concept in virtualization, and getting customers comfortable with the concept of "communal living" requires a shift in how enterprises view data security. The "book" definition of multitenancy is a computing or networking model where several clients use the same resources on a shared infrastructure. In the cloud, multitenancy is used in both software as a service (SaaS) and infrastructure as a service (IaaS) environments. In fact, multitenancy is pretty much the norm for both of these, and it's one of the things that makes the business model work. This chapter looks at an example of each model and explains how multitenancy works in different types of virtualized environments.

SaaS Multitenancy

There are a lot of multitenant software as a service applications (for example most, if not every, online email system), but the customer resource management (CRM) company named SalesForce.com is often held up as the poster child of multitenant SaaS because the value of the data it stores is high and is considered very confidential.

SF allows companies to track information on all of their sales prospects, leads, and customers and measure the progress through the sales cycle and into a support cycle once they become a paying customer. What made SF different is that instead of asking their customers to purchase, install, and maintain CRM software, they host it all, including the customer data. In fact, their slogan even has the word *software* with a circle and line through it. In other words, they point out that the "no software" approach (as in their customers don't have any software to buy, install, or manage when using their service) is an advantage worth bragging about, and they were doing this before most people knew what software as a service was. Turns out they were really on to something..

One big advantage with this model, now commonplace in CRM and other enterprise applications, is that users can access their information from anywhere because it is web based. This is ideal for a customer/lead-tracking tool if your sales team happens to be mobile and geographically dispersed (which, of course, is usually the case).

When SF was founded, multitenancy was easy to implement by using separate physical servers for each different customer. This was state of the art back when they got started. SF chose a new multitenancy model based on the application itself being designed to support hundreds of thousands of users. This is one of the first examples of very large-scale application-level multitenancy.

Like many SaaS providers, SF uses a single instance of the hosted software application. This is more than making sure that all of their customers are on the same version; it literally means that SF runs one big application and all of their customers are using that same software at the same time. What separates customers from each other is how the data for each customer is partitioned and accessed, and how the application itself addresses multitenancy and partitioning of accounts.

As shown in Figure 9-1, each tenant (which amounts to hundreds or thousands of users per client) logs in to one big application (running on many servers), and those servers access one large data pool. This, of course, is a bit of a simplification; in fact, SaaS providers will have several data centers that are load balanced, as well as disaster recovery sites, but logically it's all one big resource pool.

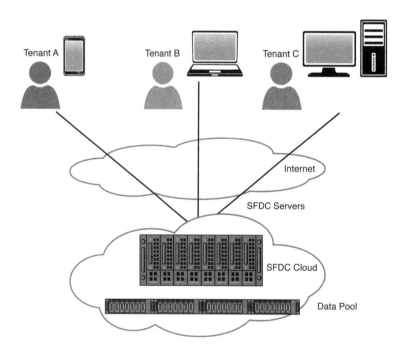

Figure 9-1   *Salesforce.com is a typical enterprise-scale SaaS application where all clients access a single live application that presents each client with their own data.*

Each customer is able to customize their interface to a small degree, but these options are presented to the tenants by the provider, who may offer more customization options with higher service tiers. For example, the basic tier may allow a small number of interface options or add-on options. At higher payment tiers, the client may have some additional options. It's important to make the distinction that these are not fully customizable interfaces, but rather menu-driven options presented to the client by the provider.

Pros and Cons of SaaS Multitenancy

The biggest advantage of multitenancy in this model is cost savings both for the provider (landlord) and the clients (tenants) over what they would pay in a single-use model.

On the provider side, there is a massive reduction in support costs, and SF was one of the first companies to "get this." In fact, they adopted this business model before virtualization allowed customers to build clouds the way we build them today. Let's take a look at what a provider goes through in building a commercial (enterprise) software program to illustrate the differences.

First, the software company has to develop some software and to design it to work on any number of hardware systems (especially if the software is not delivered as a virtual appliance, which ties the software to a single operating system). The company also has to figure out packaging, piracy protection, and exporting laws—a lot of extra work (time and money) to do things not directly related to the software. But it does not end there. The development team will likely continue to add features, resulting in software updates. New customers will get the newest versions, but existing customers may or may not adopt them. Or maybe they do, but some skip an update here and there. And all of these customers require some level of support and revision control.

What the software developer ends up with is a huge matrix of software versions mapped to supported hardware devices, which changes over time as upgrades are made. This ends up being a really, really expensive part of the business, and it drives costs up for the provider, who then passes on those costs to the users. It also dramatically slows the software development lifecycle, resulting in major releases for an older software vendor coming out every 18 months to 2 years. That is centuries in cloud time.

Salesforce.com, and the companies that adopted a similar multitenancy model, has basically eliminated most of these costs from their businesses. This is good for them, but it's also good for their customers. With multitenant SaaS models, the software developer (who is also a service provider) has one live software version at any given time. There are no shipping costs, no licensing issues, almost no issues with software piracy (at least not in the typical way), and no worries about supporting matrixed combinations of hardware to software and migrations of software versions over the various hardware platforms.

Instead, the provider develops the software, which they install on the hardware of their choice (which is often customized for the provider). When a new software release comes out, there is a single migration path (because there is only one version in production at any given time). There are some new considerations, of course. The provider has to maintain at least two big data centers, and they have to ensure reliable access, but these costs are much less than the costs that this model eliminates. Best of all, it reduces the typical software release window to once a month versus once every two years for larger enterprise vendors. And it provides detailed analytics about how end users actually use the application. That kind of usage info is something traditional software companies salivate over but rarely get.

The tenants get in on the cost savings, too. There is no need to install, maintain, or upgrade software on hundreds or thousands of computers out in the field, and no need to create and maintain big data storage facilities. In fact, there is no capital expenditure at all, just a monthly bill that comes out of operational expenses.

The biggest downsides to this model are often said to be the security risks of a shared service and the potential for a disaster of some sort to take down access. These are real risks, of course, but they are largely the same risks that any company would have if they physically owned and installed the application on their own systems. In fact, you can make the argument that in a multitenant model the provider's level of sophistication with regards to security and data resilience is superior to what most client companies could achieve. The provider's entire business depends on their ability to ensure security, and availably issues rarely occur.

The bigger issue is the potential for either a software bug or a configuration error that inadvertently allows one customer to see, access, or even modify another client's data. This is a risk that is unique to the multitenant SaaS model because of the shared database of customer data. Life seems safer when you know you have your own operating system and your own virtual machine (VM) protecting your data. With multitenant SaaS, all that stands between your data and others is the competency of the software developers at the SaaS provider.

Another commonly cited concern with SaaS multitenancy is that the provider typically holds all of the customer's data. Over years, this data could become a significant asset for a company, and access to this asset is controlled by a third party. Third-party control of your assets is a risk, of course, but most of the companies in this space have mechanisms to easily export client data, and there are many third-party tools and services that enable customers to back up and download copies of their data. This not only mitigates the risk, but it also lowers the barrier to switching from one provider to another, which incents the providers to provide high-value service.

IaaS Multitenancy

The other kind of multitenancy occurs when multiple users share physical and network infrastructures rather than a single instance of an application. Technically in a SaaS multitenant model, clients share both the application and the hardware, but they only have access to the application through which they access data. With IaaS, tenants share the hardware, but each tenant is able to install and run their own applications and operating systems.

IaaS multitenancy is a much less-restrictive form of resource pooling because each cloud user can run their own VMs, which could lead to thousands of resource allocation combinations from CPU, RAM, disk, and network functions.

For example, in Figure 9-2, Tenant A could have a CPU-intensive application that requires a lot of RAM but little in the way of disk storage and network access. Tenant B could have low CPU requirements, some RAM, a lot of storage, and medium network access requirements; and Tenant C could need high CPU, low RAM and disk, and frequent network access. These could all be large or small or somewhere in the middle, and they could all be static or dynamic (to varying degrees) in their application of those resource models.

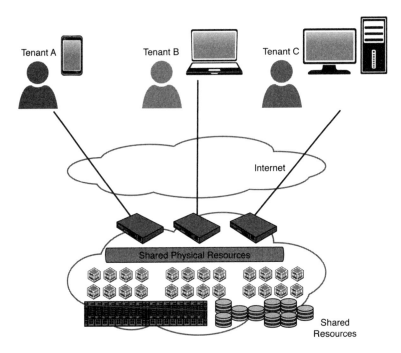

Figure 9-2   *In IaaS multitenancy, the clients load their own applications, which can all have different resource requirements. IaaS providers must therefore plan their resource availability accordingly.*

From the provider's perspective, this can be quite tricky to manage because they have to allocate their resources according to their forecasts and they have a strong incentive to always be in the "Goldilocks zone" of capacity. Which is to say that if they have too little resource allocation, they lose customers, and if they have too much resource allocation, they lose money on unused resources. Having (and by extension forecasting) the "just right" amount of resources is a big advantage. In fact, this is why tools such as vCenter exist; they provide visibility to all workloads and balance them across all available resources.

Pros and Cons of IaaS Multitenancy

The benefits of this model are the same for a third party as they are for a company that virtualizes its data center. In fact, a company that virtualizes a data center, changing from dedicated servers to VMs that use shared resources, is, in fact, a private IaaS cloud. Both the landlord (provider) and tenant (client) reap the advantages of the efficiency, cost savings, and flexibility that cloud and cloud networking enable.

On the down side (for a public IaaS cloud), the provider has to implement and maintain a virtualized infrastructure and cloud network, and this can be a complicated endeavor, given the need to meet the needs of somewhat unpredictable client behaviors without wasting money on excessive capacity.

In this model, security is also a much bigger concern than in the SaaS model. Unlike a SaaS application, which is single purpose and tightly controlled by the provider, IaaS clients can put any manner of applications or data on the same servers and networks as you (you being the concerned party).

As a client, you should be concerned about who your neighbors are and what they are doing. Of course, you can't know this, and the provider will not tell you (they might not have full visibility into this themselves), but if they are doing something illicit or inherently unsecure, it may end up affecting you. This makes sense from a tenant perspective: If you are a law-abiding tenant in an apartment building, you would likely have cause for concern if you found out your neighboring tenants were operating a meth lab, running a gambling den, or harboring dangerous fugitives. Security is discussed in depth in Part 8, "Security: The Security Thing." So for now, the takeaway is that with greater tenant flexibility comes greater concern for all the other tenants.

The sad truth of the matter is that virtualization-based multitenancy, the very foundation of infrastructure as a service clouds, only arose because some application developers didn't do their jobs well enough. Except in the case of carefully designed multitenant SaaS infrastructure, IT designers rarely trust applications to maintain multitenancy. All it takes is a single bug to mix two different customers' data sets together. With virtualization, you can rely on the hypervisor to achieve multitenancy, which lets you run applications you might not trust to be multitenant aware. That said, when application-level multitenancy is achieved, it provides powerful cost savings and efficiency effects.

Multitenancy
Sharing Computing Resources With Other Users

YOUR APARTMENT

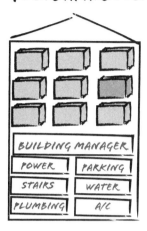

BUILDING MANAGER
POWER | PARKING
STAIRS | WATER
PLUMBING | A/C

The concept of multitenancy in a cloud or data center is analogous to an apartment building where there are...multiple tenants. Like the idea of an apartment, the user of a cloud has their own space (a VM or a set of servers). Most of the other services are shared, and there is often a manager of some sort that handles billing and ensures the proper allocation of services.

YOUR VM

CLOUD MANAGER
POWER | SERVERS
NETWORK | OS IMAGE
STORAGE | COOLING

KNOWNS

UNKNOWNS

Who the other users are Infrastructure Details HW types used Outage Procedures Shared Security Performance

Although there is a lot of cost savings and efficiency in using a multitenant environment, there is, by definition, some loss of control and certainty with regards to procedures and control of critical assets (especially when there is an outage). There are some knowns and unknowns that have to be understood to minimize misunderstandings.

Two Ways to Implement Multitenancy

DATABASE

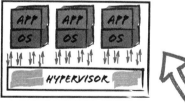

HYPERVISOR

In the database version of multi-tenancy you rent, a "VM" that often shares a server with other users.

In this version of multi-tenancy you rent time/resources for your virtual machines to operate on.

- Typically used in SaaS databases.

- VMs are partitioned for different customers.

- This is a fully shared infrastructure.

INFRASTRUCTURE

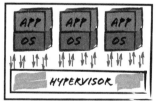

HYPERVISOR

In the infrastructure version of multitenancy you rent, the servers that your VMs run on in.

In this version of multi-tenancy you rent the equipment that your applications run on.

- Typically used in IaaS.

- Isolates network and storage.

- Your VMs are isolated from other apps.

Network Functions Virtualized
Why Stop With Servers?

How Do You Virtualize a Network?

This chapter attempts to answer an important question: How do you virtualize a network? Before attempting an answer, though, it's a good time to take a step back and answer a couple of "big" questions, such as:

- What exactly is network virtualization, and how does it relate to the virtualization covered so far in this book?

- How does network virtualization fit into the grand scheme of network functions virtualization (NFV) and software-defined networking (SDN)?

Once we answer these questions, it's much easier to answer the question that the chapter title poses. More importantly, these answers provide the framework of *why* we would want to virtualize the network.

Network Virtualization

As mentioned throughout the first two sections of this book, virtualization (which typically means server virtualization when used as a standalone phrase) refers to the abstraction of the application and operating system from the hardware.

In a similar way, network virtualization is the abstraction of the network endpoints from the physical arrangement of the network. In other words, network virtualization allows you to group or arrange endpoints on a network independent from the their physical location.

It's worth noting that network virtualization is nothing new. In fact, it's been around a long time. The most common forms of network virtualization are virtual LANs (VLANs), virtual private networks (VPNs), and Multiprotocol Label Switching (MPLS). All of these technologies essentially enable the administrators to group physically separate endpoints into logical groups, which makes them behave (and appear) as if they are all on the same local (physical) segment. The ability to do this allows for much greater efficiencies in traffic control, security, and management of the network.

In many cases, this type of virtualization is performed via some form of encapsulation whereby messages or traffic between endpoints in the same logical group are "packaged" into another message that is better suited for transport over a physical segment of the network. Once the message has reached the endpoint, the original message is unpacked, and the intended endpoint receives the message in the same format as it would have if the two endpoints were on the same physical segment of the network.

Figure 10-1 illustrates one way that VLANs would be used. In this case, workers in different departments work on multiple floors of a building. A single switch can service each floor of the building, such that all workers on a given floor would be part of the same network segment. VLANs allow you to logically group endpoints so that they all look as if they are on the same segment. Further, this can be done across many buildings or even across large networks where endpoints are scattered all over the globe—although care should be taken when extending VLANs over long distances because they can create fragile networks.

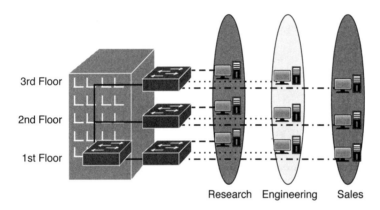

Figure 10-1 *Virtual LANs, or VLANs, were an early form of network virtualization that allowed physically separate endpoints to behave as if they were all connected to the same local switch.*

It turns out that this good old technique that has been around for many years makes server virtualization, or more accurately connecting VMs, much easier and much more efficient. It's easy to see why when you imagine the VMs being spun up here, there, and everywhere in a virtualized data center or cloud, and then being paused, moved, started again, or even being moved while still being active.

With all that spontaneous creation and movement that is done without any regard for the specific physical location in the data center (or even with regard to a specific data center), having the ability to create and manage logical groupings becomes critical.

How Does This Fit with NFV and SDN?

With a basic grasp of what server virtualization is from previous chapters and with the newly gained understanding of network virtualization, it's worth spending a few words on how they are related to network functions virtualization (NFV) and software-defined networking (SDN). To keep it in context, all four topics are summarized here.

Server Virtualization

Server virtualization is the abstraction of applications and operating systems from physical servers. This allows for the creation of VMs (app and OS pairs) that offer much greater usage efficiency on physical servers and afford enormous flexibility with regard to provisioning of applications.

Network Virtualization

Network Virtualization refers to the creation of logical groupings of endpoints on a network. In this case, the endpoints are abstracted from their physical locations so that VMs (and other assets) can look, behave, and be managed as if they are all on the same physical segment of the network. This is an older technology, but one that is critical in virtual environments where assets are created and moved around without much regard for the physical location. What is new here is the automation and management tools that have been purposely built for the scale and elasticity of virtualized data centers and clouds.

Network Functions Virtualization

NFV refers to the virtualization of Layer 4 through 7 services such as load balancing and firewalling. Basically, this is converting certain types of network appliances into VMs, which can then be quickly and easily deployed where they are needed. NFV came about because of the inefficiencies that were created by virtualization. This is a new concept; so far, only the benefits of virtualization have been covered, but virtualization causes a lot of problems, too. One of them was the routing of traffic to and from network appliances that typically were located at the edge of the data center network. With VMs springing up and being moved all over, the traffic flows became highly varied, which caused problems for fixed appliances that had to serve the traffic. NFV allows us to create a virtual instance of a function such as a firewall, which can be easily "spun up" and placed where it is needed, just as they would a VM. Much of this section focused on how this is done.

Software-Defined Networking

SDN refers to the ability to program the network. SDN is a newer technology, one that was born as a result of virtualization and the shift of where the "chokepoint" is in data communications. In short, the ability to set up or make changes to a network cannot keep up with the ability to provision applications with a click of a button. SDN makes the network programmable (which means network admins can quickly make adjustments to the network based on changing requirements). SDN is made possible by separating the control plane (the brains of the network) from the data plane (the muscle of the network). SDN is covered in depth in Part 5, "Software Defined Networks: Virtualizing the Network," and Part 6, "SDN Controllers," of this book.

All four of these technologies are designed to improve the mobility, agility, and flexibility of networks and data communication. However, virtualization, network virtualization, and network functions virtualization can all work on existing networks because they reside on servers and interact with "groomed" traffic sent to them. SDN, however, requires a new network topology and SDN-aware devices where the data and control planes are separate and programmable.

Virtualizing the Network

One of the reasons it's a good idea to make the change to network virtualization is that it allows network admins and users to fully realize many of the awesome features of server virtualization, such as vMotion, snapshot backups, and push button disaster recovery (to name just a few). Indeed, the most common reason for virtualizing the network is precisely to get VM mobility and vMotion to work.

In Chapter 9, "Multitenancy and the Problems of Communal Living," you were introduced to VXLAN, which is VLAN technology with some extensions that allow it to tunnel Layer 2 frames through the IP transport network, as well as extend the number of VLANs beyond 4096. The "tunnel" that this creates allows it to bridge virtual extensible VXLAN tunnel endpoint (VTEP) devices across a network, making data transfers easy and simple regardless of where the endpoints reside (or if they move).

As noted earlier, the VMs supporting applications or services require network connectivity via physical switching and routing to be able to connect to other VMs switching the data center or cloud and with clients of the data center over a WAN link or the Internet. In addition, in a data center environment, the network also requires security and load balancing. The first switch encountered by traffic leaving the VM is the virtual switch (hypervisor), and from there a physical switch that is either top of rack (TOR) or end of row (EOR). In other words, once traffic leaves the hypervisor, it is on the physical network, and unfortunately that network cannot easily keep up with the rapidly shifting state of the VMs that are connected to it.

The way around this issue is to create a logical network of VMs that spans the physical networks the traffic travels across. VXLAN (see Figure 10-2) does this just as most network virtualization does—through the use of encapsulation. Unlike simple VLANs, though, which are limited to 4096 of these logical networks on any given physical network, VXLAN can create about 16 million. That scale is important when it comes to large data centers and clouds.

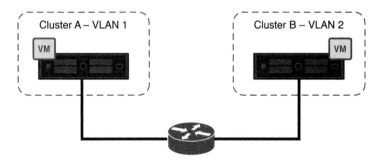

Figure 10-2 *VXLAN allows for millions of logical partitions across a physical network.*

Imagine that you have two VM clusters on a network, and imagine that a router separates those clusters because they are in different data centers. Both clusters in this case are on different VLANs. For these two VMs to talk to each other, the traffic between them must be routed. Now suppose you want these clusters to be on the same VLAN.

As shown in Figure 10-3, by using VXLAN, you can set up a VTEP that encapsulates or wraps the VM traffic on one end for transport over the routed network and then decapsulates (strips off the wrapper) on the other end. This effectively creates a logical network between the two clusters, which now appear to be on the same switched segment of a local network.

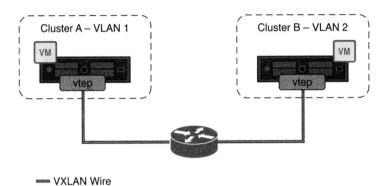

Figure 10-3 *VTEPs create a logical network between the two clusters, which then appear to be on the same switched segment of a local network.*

So, what's the big deal?

If you are new to networking, this might not seem like such a big breakthrough. If you are familiar with networking, though, you might be thinking, "This is just another way to create VLANs." There is more to it than that, though, because network virtualization in general, and VXLAN in particular, has some key benefits that become important at data center/cloud scale:

- First, this ability enables migration to a software-defined data center model. Using a vSphere administrator to provision VMs that can communicate with each other over different networks without having to involve the network team to configure the physical switches and routers eliminates one of the biggest chokepoints in the flexibility that data center virtualization affords us.

- This technology smashes through the previous limitation of 4096 VLANs

- VXLAN runs over standard switching hardware, and requires no need for software upgrades or special code versions on the switches. Therefore, you can virtualize your network using the stuff you already have.

In summary, network virtualization, although an older technology, plays a key role in the creation of virtualized data centers and clouds. It is also one of the key drivers that allows and enhances both NFV and SDN, as you will see in later chapters.

How VLANs Work

And Why They Matter in Cloud Networks

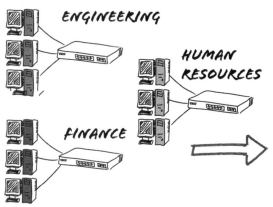

ENGINEERING

HUMAN RESOURCES

FINANCE

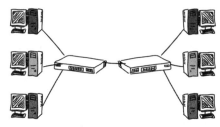

When networks were first rolled out, admins tried to keep like-users on the same switch. This local area network (LAN) model was desired, because the machines on any given LAN all received the same network instructions. It also nicely partitioned user traffic by providing physical segmentation.

As networks got bigger, it became impossible to keep like-users on a common switch. This led to the creation of the virtual LAN or VLAN. A VLAN is a means of logically grouping devices so that they appear to be connected to the same switch. VLANs provide logical partitioning and segmentation when it's not practical to physically segment.

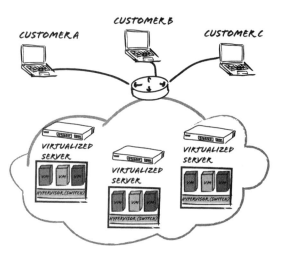

CUSTOMER A

CUSTOMER B

CUSTOMER C

VIRTUALIZED SERVER

VIRTUALIZED SERVER

VIRTUALIZED SERVER

VM VM VM

HYPERVISOR (SWITCH)

In cloud environments, VLANs are essential because a user's VMs can span multiple servers. VLANs allow easy grouping of users resources into a single logical partition. Going further, the network admins can associate a VLAN with its IP subnet. A subnet is a way to partition a layer 3 (routing) domain. This makes it easy to connect to a cloud (and all your resources) over the Internet without needing to manually configure all of your connections.

Note that VLAN segmentation is often positioned as a form of security—VLANs do segment user data, but this is a very weak form of security that does not actually protect data.

Virtualizing Appliances

To this point in the book, we have mostly focused on the virtualization of servers and the awesome provisioning speed, flexibility, and scalability it affords. This is all true, of course, but we've also been looking at this in isolation. That is to say that we've been looking at this in terms of virtual machines (VMs) being spun up and moving around within a data center without much regard for how this might impact communication with the outside world, or more precisely how this impacts the services and applications that are communicating.

Application communication is controlled at Layers 4 through 7 of the OSI model—the framework that describes how networking devices and applications communicate with each other. These layers also include information vital to many network functions, such as security, load balancing, and optimization. This framework (along with basic networking concepts) is described in the book *Cisco Networking Simplified*. Layers 4 through 7 are often referred to collectively as the *application layers* of the OSI model, and this chapter focuses on the virtualization impact on Layer 4 through 7 communication.

Layer 4 Through 7 Network Services

One of the issues with the dynamic nature of server virtualization is that all that spinning up, spinning down, and movement of VMs is really difficult to manage in terms of connecting them to network services.

The problem is that network administrators need a host of support tools and services to run the network, and most of the traffic (perhaps all) coming into or going out of the data center or cloud must be routed through these services. Some of the tools are software based, which makes things easy, but some services need to work at wire speed and are therefore typically hardware-based appliances. Examples of Layer 4 through 7 services include the following:

- Data loss prevention systems
- Firewalls and intrusion detection systems (IDS)
- Load balancers
- Security event and information managers (SEIM)
- Secure Sockets Layer (SSL) accelerators
- Virtual private network (VPN) concentrators

One of the challenges for makers and consumers of the tools is trying to keep up with the ever-increasing speed and flexibility of data center networks and clouds. More specifically, they have to keep up with the wire speed, and a constantly changing environment, but they must do this without dropping packets.

To keep up with the speed of networks, most of these appliances lived at the edge of the network. This allowed fewer (bigger and faster) appliances to be located close to the inbound WAN links where it's more manageable. Over the past few years, the line speed performance has risen from 1Gbps to 10Gbps and now even 40Gbps.

Another facet of data center traffic management is having to balance the traffic loads coming into a data center. Load balancers take advantage of the fact that redundancy has to be built in to networks. Rather than have part of an expensive infrastructure remain idle until there is an emergency, load balancers ensure maximum efficiency and traffic performance.

What follows is a brief summary of the most common (Layers 4 through 7) data center tools and services.

Firewalls

Firewalls allow traffic from authorized users but block others. Firewalls can be located at the edge of the data center, but can also be located close to the server. There has been a shift in recent years to application-aware firewalls, which give network administrators better visibility and control over security.

VPNs

Virtual private networks logically segment/isolate user traffic within the network (over the WAN). This allows many users to privately share a common infrastructure without mixing traffic. In some cases, VPNs encrypt traffic between the user and the application, which is important when traffic traverses the public Internet. If you've ever been to a coffee shop, about half of those people (the smart ones anyway) are using a secure VPN to connect back to their corporate office.

SSL Offload

Secure Sockets Layer is a web-based encryption tool. SSL has become very popular because it provides security of web-based data streams without user intervention. The SSL offload service provides a termination point for encryption.

Load Balancer

Load balancers direct and spread user traffic coming into the data center or cloud. Load balancing is a way to control the flow of traffic as applications scale up and down. There is an important distinction in the cloud, however: In the "old days," scalability meant growing over time (months and years). In the cloud, scalability means scale up or scale down right now, and the expectation is that it scales in a way that does not impact service quality. What was once an architectural consideration (you designed the network so that you could scale it later) is now an automatic function enacting real-time changes.

In many cases different tools and services work together or are chained together. For example, Figure 11-1 shows traffic coming into a firewall before being passed to the data center. Once traffic is passed by the firewall, load balancers distribute the traffic.

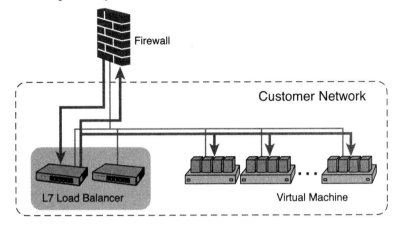

Figure 11-1   *This figure shows a service chain from a firewall to load balancers such that traffic is filtered via the firewall prior to distribution to the data center.*

These Layer 4 through 7 services have been used for many years—really ever since applications migrated from individual computers to shared servers and data centers. Therefore, they are all well understood parts of network communication. Back when they first came about, most services were relatively simple tools that did not need stateful insight—or information about what was going on inside the applications themselves. In other words, the tools really only needed to know what the rules were for connecting users to applications, without needing a great deal of information about the servers on which the application was hosted. What has changed (this should be obvious at this point) is that with virtualization, applications get spun up in an instant and tend to move around within the data center (or between them), both from session to session and within live sessions. This activity "breaks" a lot of Layer 4 through 7 services that were designed for relatively static environments.

Like almost every aspect of networking, then, Layer 4 through 7 services have to change in order to meet the needs of the users. One of the consequences of virtualization is that Layer 4 through 7 services now require stateful information about the applications and this information has to be shared across the network to ensure that services are maintained when the state and location of applications change in between or even during sessions.

This is one interesting aspect of virtualization that keeps coming up: Virtualization of applications gave the server administrators a great deal of autonomy regarding what applications people use, how they use them, and where they use them from. This level of control took hold so fast that the usage level of virtualization skyrocketed, leaving all the stuff between the users and the applications scrambling to catch up, including cabling, switching, routing, addressing, and Layer 4 through 7 services.

Fighting Virtualization with Virtualization

In response to these changing usage patterns, many providers of Layer 4 through 7 services are virtualizing their services to better match the environment they now find themselves in. This includes both generic services such as Linux (an open source operating system) and HAProxy (a free load-balancing tool for web-based applications) as well as commercial services from vendors such as Cisco, F5, Riverbed, and others.

Figure 11-2 shows the Cisco approach to appliance virtualization, which uses a Nexus switch to send traffic to virtual appliances and services. When such a switch is deployed as a top of rack (TOR) or end of row (EOR) switch, these services can be delivered very close to the traffic source, which can help maintain or even improve performance.

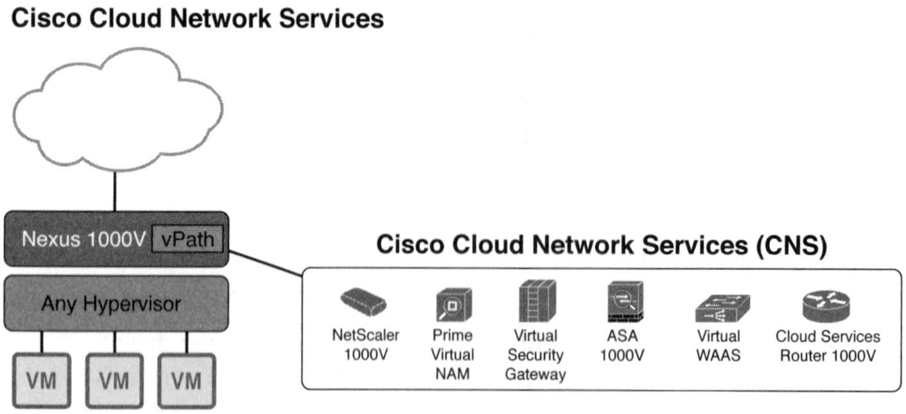

Cisco Cloud Network Services

Figure 11-2   *The Cisco approach to virtualizing Layer 4 through 7 services is to use a high-powered Nexus switch to deliver services close to the traffic source within the data center (as opposed to the data center edge).*

Virtual appliances running on VMs can use the same automation tools for deployment as VM applications do for servers. This allows the same cloud management tools that move and track all the virtual sessions to manage and track the Layer 4 through 7 services associated with the applications. In other words, by virtualizing the Layer 4 through 7 services, self-service workflows can be built that deploy servers/applications and Layer 4 through 7 services together, as a single deployment.

In this model, Layer 4 through 7 services become another set of virtual appliances, and as such they can scale up and down as needed by the application. They can also be turned up or turned off easily. For example, you need to turn on load balancers only when they are actually required, instead of running them full time, which results in efficient use of resources. This helps reduce hardware costs and simplifies operations.

What's the "So What"?

Application architectures are scaling, and application services need to match the scale and automation of VMs to ensure efficient operations and user satisfaction. The best way to achieve this is to virtualize Layer 4 through 7 services and make them part of the same fabric as the applications they support. This also means that Layer 4 through 7 services must now be statefully aware of the application traffic to ensure that they scale along with VMs as they grow, retract, and move throughout the cloud infrastructure.

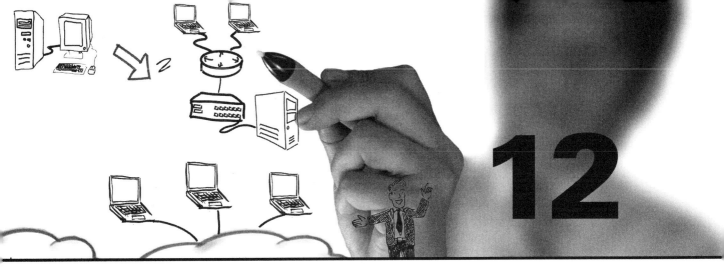

Virtualizing Core Networking Functions

The previous chapters introduced the concepts and theories with examples of network virtualization, network appliance virtualization, and even network function virtualization. These are all complex subjects, and because they are so closely related, they can blur into one confusing jumble. Therefore, before introducing network functions virtualization (NFV) in the core networks, this seems like an opportune moment to recap what you have already learned so far to keep it all straight.

Virtualization Recap

In the early 2000s, IT introduced virtualization into the organization using the VMware desktop, and later when confidence had grown, around the mid 2000s, into the data center through the implementation of server virtualization. So successful was server virtualization that IT quickly adopted this server model, and it became not only a recognized technology but also the preferred server topology for the data center. This came about due to the many benefits that virtual machines (VMs) brought IT and the business. However, early server virtualization though very successful only hinted at the true potential of VMs. If only they could be untethered from the conventional network, they would be capable of doing wonderful things.

Network virtualization (NV) in IT data centers was the next logical step in the virtualization evolution. After all, server virtualization had proven to be a highly beneficial technology, delivering cost savings, agility, flexibility, and very importantly, scalability. In fact, scalability was one of the most important aspects of server virtualization because it consolidated servers and stopped the unsustainable server spread inherent in the conventional network architecture. By embracing server virtualization, IT reduced the numbers of servers and subsequently the costs of powering and cooling them. IT created a shrinking (or at least nonexploding), sustainable data center model. More importantly, though, this made the reality of massively scalable data centers possible

The success of server virtualization led to network virtualization, because this was a prerequisite to deliver the full potential of virtual server mobility, both for applications and storage. Using the principles of a "virtualization layer," as shown in Figure 12-1, that abstracted the network functions from the hardware that housed the function, network virtualization used protocol overlays and tunnels to create logic domains that spanned the physical devices, which previously defined and confined domains. This provided a flexible network infrastructure that could discover, learn, and track in real time the virtual machines as they moved around the network. Consequently, with virtual servers now enhanced with awesome capabilities and agility, riding atop a flexible, agile virtual network, thoughts turned to the possibility of virtualization of network appliances.

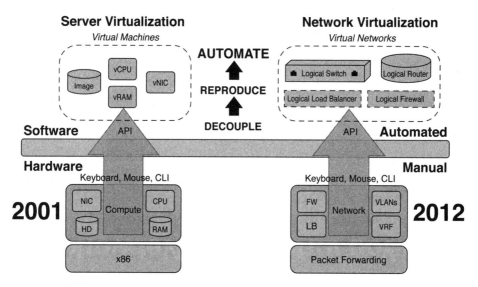

Figure 12-1 *Using a "virtualization layer" network virtualization abstracts network functions from the hardware that houses the functions.*

Virtualization of network appliances is the next logical evolution, as many questioned why it was possible to spin up a virtual server with its applications on demand rather than being bound to a hardware-based network appliance. In similar fashion to server virtualizations, all that was required was to separate the application software logic from the underlying dedicated hardware. As shown in Figure 12-2, once an application was decoupled from its hardware, and ported to run on a standard x86 server, the benefits of virtualization could be realized by firewalls, load balancers, and many other network appliances.

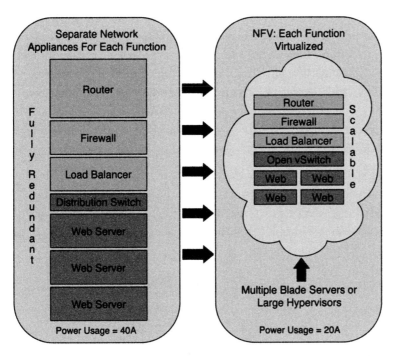

Figure 12-2 *After an application is decoupled from hardware and ported to run on a standard x86 server, the benefits of virtualization could be realized by firewalls, load balancers, and many other network appliances.*

The advent of the virtualization of servers, networks, and appliances radically changed the way administrators and engineers designed and supported the data center infrastructure. An administrator could spin up a virtual server or a network appliance on demand and deploy them anywhere in the network infrastructure within seconds. In contrast, it would have taken the administrator, supported by engineers, weeks to accomplish the same using physical servers and appliances. The lag time due to the hardware ordering process, the supply chain, disappeared. Now an administrator could spawn and deploy a server application on demand, without any technical assistance. In addition to the operational savings, capital savings were realized too, because each instance required only a license and some generic hardware, making them much cheaper than the physical entity. The real benefit, however, was in the administrative ability, and this new agility to deliver NFV.

Delivering network virtualization and subsequently network functions virtualization in the data center was a huge technological leap, which became the foundation for private and public cloud infrastructures. However, network appliance and function virtualization had caught the attention of other industries, such as mobile telephone operators who were looking for cost-effective solutions to their IP-based Long-Term Evolution (LTE) network issues.

Where Core Functions Are Being Virtualized

Enterprises and application providers are the primary drivers of server and appliance virtualization, but it is the service providers who are looking to use network virtualization to build dynamic, virtualized core networks that meet the growing demands of users. In particular, this is a key development for mobile service providers whose users have shown an unquenchable demand for bandwidth over mobile networks. This explosive growth in data consumption is forcing carries to rethink their entire approach to networking. In fact, not too long ago, carriers were all too glad to put low rate data on mobile voice networks. However, with the advent of smartphones and the explosion of video and other streaming applications, these same carriers have had to rebuild their entire networks. As a result, mobile providers now have virtualized data networks that carry digital voice traffic as they would most other applications.

As shown in Figure 12-3, using Core Network Virtualization, core network functions can run on standard IT hardware in a virtualized manner. In addition to reducing costs through the use of generic equipment (loaded with the provider-specific builds) and automation, service providers also gain the elasticity of cloud resources, ensuring the necessary network capacity is available for application usage (which can be bursty).

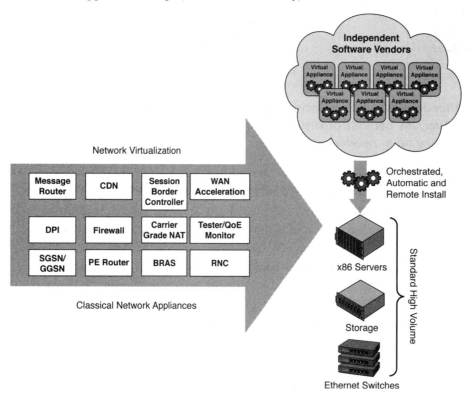

Figure 12-3 *With Core Network Virtualization, core network functions can run on standard IT hardware in a virtualized manner.*

Network and function virtualization enables telecom providers to control costs, and frees them from long-term lock-in of proprietary hardware, reducing both CapEx and OpEx. In addition, it dramatically increases both customer responsiveness and the speed to market for new services.

The benefits to the mobile operator realized by deploying network functions virtualization are as follows:

■ Lower capital expenditure

■ Lower operational expenditure

■ Increased flexibility

■ Reduced time to market

However, making the decision is the easy part, but how do you get started with network functions virtualization in a core network?

Telecoms tend to introduce virtualization into their networks in an incremental fashion, and they approach network evolution in a pragmatic manner. Because telecoms run production networks, they typically roll out changes in a controlled manner using overlay networks, which they can work on and test before switching over. When introducing virtualization, they often start by looking at the workloads best suited for virtualization. (Not all services can or should be virtualized.) Workloads suited to virtualization typically are CPU- or memory-intensive applications with low network input/output demands. The reason for this is that applications running in VMs perform well, almost on par with applications running in physical dedicated servers when performing CPU- and memory-intensive tasks. However, when the tasks are input/output oriented (for example applications with many disk reads/writes), performance can drop noticeably compared to what you would get on a physical server. For mobile operators, ideal workload candidates include services such as video optimization, content controls, URL filtering, deep packet inspection, and other value-added services (VASs).

Taking this incremental approach enables the mobile telecom provider to introduce the necessary VMs, along with their required management systems and connections to the network infrastructure. However, VAS, CPU- or memory-intensive services, and network monitoring are only a few examples of several potential areas where mobile telecom operators can introduce NFV. Another potential candidate they could target is the equipment on customer premises, because this leverages the ability to deploy virtualization anywhere within the network, not just in the data center. The point is with network virtualization it can be deployed flexibly and in the ideal location, so if that is in the customer's location or at the nearest radio mast, that would no longer be a problem. An example of when it is advantageous to deploy NFV at the customer demarcation point is when content filtering Internet access. Rather than take banned traffic all the way over the radio spectrum or a fixed line, only to drop it at the Internet gateway, it makes more sense to drop it at the customer edge device. However, planners might want NFV to be deployed at the device where data packets are managed to replace the equipment used for deep packet inspection at the Internet gateways that are responsible for policy management. What NFV gives the network planners is the flexibility to take those choices. The key is for network planners to pick candidate services, start small, and then introduce virtualized services and functions incrementally.

Network Function Virtualization

CLASSIC NETWORK APPLIANCE APPROACH

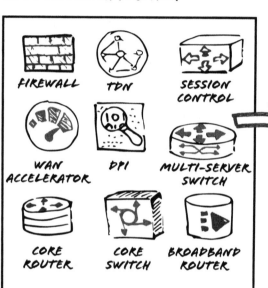

FIREWALL   TDN   SESSION CONTROL

WAN ACCELERATOR   DPI   MULTI-SERVER SWITCH

CORE ROUTER   CORE SWITCH   BROADBAND ROUTER

- Expensive equipment
- Vendor lock in
- Lack of Integration

NETWORK VIRTUALIZATION APPROACH

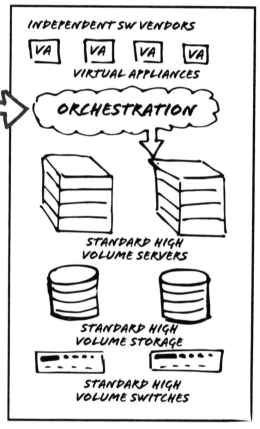

INDEPENDENT SW VENDORS

VA   VA   VA   VA

VIRTUAL APPLIANCES

ORCHESTRATION

STANDARD HIGH VOLUME SERVERS

STANDARD HIGH VOLUME STORAGE

STANDARD HIGH VOLUME SWITCHES

- Avoids vendor lock in
- Flexibility in design
- greater innovation

What About Scalability and Performance?

Scalability and performance are two key metrics when considering the effectiveness of a virtualized network, and therefore designers must understand and test for them. Very often, virtualization is deployed to reap these supposed benefits, but is done so without any real concern for these two key issues. (It's often just assumed.) Scalability should be a positive attribute in virtualization, as should performance. However, there are times when instead of complementing one another, they are in open conflict. In fact, there are times when virtualization might not be a good idea.

Scalability Versus Performance

Let's consider a scenario in which an administrator and a network planner want to shift toward a virtualized network. The administrator's ambition is to be able to easily and quickly spin up virtual servers. The planner's goal is to reduce the number of physical servers and future deployment times. Ironically, virtualization can often make the problems they are implemented to solve worse.

For example, the planner wants to consolidate the servers in the data center, because he is concerned about server proliferation and he believes that virtual machines (VMs) rather than physical servers will be the answer to his issue. Now technically this is a great idea, and so everyone agrees, and server virtualization becomes the norm, and within a year, the server count is down by 50%. The problem, though, is that the new process has removed some key constraints. For example, it no longer takes weeks of negotiating budgets, project plans, and technical meetings to install an application. Instead, the administrator has his wish; he just needs the go-ahead, and he can spin up a VM application server in a matter of moments. The planner is also happy (for now), because he has achieved his goal of reducing server count by 50%. All seems to be going according to plan.

Before too long, however, users are murmuring about performance and terrible latency and application lag. The planner investigates this anomaly and discovers that although the physical server count is down, the actual server/application count has risen by 300%. By implementing virtualization, there was a halt to server proliferation, but the speed with which an application can be spun up has resulted in unfettered VM application server spread, which is not good. To compound the problem, the network management systems have not been able to alert the business to this drop in performance because they have no visibility of the virtual switches running in the hypervisor. The net impact is that slow steady rollout with predictable performance has been replaced with ultra-fast rollout and unpredictable performance. Some users may be okay with this, but many are not.

This example highlights how implementing VM technology can be a bad thing if the technology is not controlled through technical and business policies. Furthermore, the scenario shows that although virtualization is the prime solution for scaling data centers to unprecedented capacity, network planning and monitoring is critical to success. In this case, the administrator deployed VMs without network monitoring, which resulted in too high a VM density per physical host. The administrator was probably looking at the CPU and RAM utilization and seeing they were low (circa 40%), had deployed more VMs while being blissfully unaware that the hypervisor vSwitch and network card were running at capacity.

Performance in Network Virtualization

There are inherent performance issues with network virtualization that go way beyond VM density issues and network card overutilization. A virtualized environment must allow unlimited migration of VM workloads across physical servers. Furthermore, virtualization is often utilized in multitenant environments (cloud services) that require provisioning resources across diverse geographic locations. A virtualized network must therefore be able to scale while maintaining the quality of service (QoS) customers require. Consequently, a virtualized network must accomplish the following:

- Handle vast numbers of MAC addresses and explosive growth in VMs

- Accommodate large numbers of LANs (4096—the old VLAN limit isn't going to cut it)

- Provide isolation of the physical Layer 2 network so that each tenant has the illusion of being on their own physical network without any performance overhead

Scalability and Performance in Virtual Networks

Virtualized networks use *Virtual Extensible LAN* (VXLAN) to allow servers not on the same subnet to perform VM migration, which is a key feature of server virtualization. VMs must also be able to interact with other predefined workloads and network resources regardless of their geographic location. Implementing VXLAN is the initial step to creating on-demand software-based networks that can utilize capacity wherever it is available. Technically, this is achieved by installing VXLAN in the hypervisor using VXLAN tunnel protocol and any 10 Gbps Ethernet network interface card. However, VXLAN is not without its challenges.

The main challenge when using VXLAN is that its encapsulated traffic bypasses normal stateless offload features of a conventional network card. This comes about because of the way the CPU handles packets, by either sending them individually, by calculating each packets checksum, or by using a single CPU core to handle all VXLAN tunneled traffic. The solution here is simple: You can use VXLAN-aware network cards; however, purchasing one for every device in the network might not be quite so simple (and could be very expensive).

Scalability and Performance for Virtual Appliances

It is true that virtualization has allowed servers to be spun up and down with the click of a mouse. This on-demand aspect is great for cost efficiency and agility. So, why not just do the same thing for network components? After all, applications running on these virtual servers need to be protected by firewall services, and they probably need load balances and have requirements for intrusion detection systems (IDS) and other network services such as Secure Sockets Layer (SSL) acceleration. One would think it would make perfect sense to address these requirements via virtual network appliances that an administrator could spin up on demand and deploy wherever they are required. This strategy would provide tremendous scalability opportunities because it would allow admins to avoid having to stick one huge physical device at key locations at the edge of the network. Instead, much smaller VMs could be deployed where they are needed close to the resource consuming the service or being protected.

Unfortunately, performance is an issue with network virtualization of appliances. It turns out that many of these network service applications run on dedicated proprietary hardware for a reason. Despite all the advances in software and virtualization, hardware can switch much, much faster than software; hence dedicated hardware appliances are often preferred to software-based solutions when processing and moving packets at wire speed.

Examples of this include high-speed routing, packet forwarding, and encryption. Packaging these functions in software (even when installed on high-performance x86 servers) isn't going to replicate the wire-speed performance of the dedicated silicon. Perhaps this is why most of the network functions decoupled from the devices are for firewall or load-balancing types of applications that can be handled via CPU cycles in software. The key point is that some network services are okay to run as software applications running on generic (albeit powerful) servers, but if wire-speed performance matters, there's still no substitute for dedicated hardware designed specifically for the task at hand.

Another problem with virtualizing network appliances is that they are typically performing input/output (I/O) operations, which VMs are poor at handling because the hypervisor software that is used to virtualize the server also virtualizes the network card. This means that it will use up lots of CPU cycles for every read/write function because access to the physical network means the CPU must decode what needs to be done, and then must emulate the action of a network card. For functions that do a lot of read/writes (some database applications, for example), this can be a hindrance to performance.

Another potential problem is VM overhead, which is the performance loss of going through the hypervisor. Previously, the only solution was to let the VM bypass the hypervisor and talk directly to the network card; this requires dedicated network interface cards (NICs). However, Cisco and VMware can give physical interfaces with their VM-FEX and VMDirect products, respectively.

Scalability and Performance of Virtualized Networks

Compared to conventional network and service deployments, which rely on expensive hardware from a small handful of proprietary equipment vendors, NFV offers many opportunities to reduce equipment cost and vendor lock-in. Many public cloud providers leverage generic equipment (or build their own) to increase profit margins by offering products as virtualized services. In private virtualized networks, a similar approach is taken by using generic x86 servers wherever possible to reduce costs.

Whichever approach is taken, there are still the challenges of scalability, reliability, and performance, and the approach will be similar, perhaps only differing in the scale of operation. To deploy network functions virtualization (NFV) in a data center, an enterprise-class virtualization infrastructure (private cloud) is required. Similarly, for a service provider to both consume and create functions and services and provide this service over the cloud, a carrier-class public cloud infrastructure is mandatory.

Importantly, the scale and fluidity of the virtualized compute and storage configurations need to be aligned to the ability to dynamically change network behavior. This is why robust and reliable network virtualization, performance, and stability are critical. SDN is also an important technology in meeting these needs.

One other consideration for maximizing scalability and performance is ensuring that the correct network management tools are installed and that there is end-to-end vision, monitoring, management, and provisioning of the entire network infrastructure. Similarly, for service providers, there is a requirement for tools for automating onboarding, deployment, and scaling of virtualized functions.

Summary

This chapter covered a lot of downsides and cautions. This is not to detract from the power or goodness of virtualization in its many formats. Rather, it's a reminder that virtualization is not always the right solution, and even when it is the right solution, not taking user behavior into account can often have disastrous results. It should be obvious that if you build a system that allows users to spin up an application with the click of a button, there will be an awful lot of button clicking, but designers miss this all the time. Systems that are fast and easy to deploy won't just make it easy to deploy, they will also make it more enticing—which means that demand will usually skyrocket. If there is one big takeaway to virtualization, it's this: It is best to plan for a massive uptake rather than the current rate of consumption.

Virtual Appliances

FIREWALL APPLIANCE

Traditional appliances we put
in front of a data center or cloud.

ALL
INCOMING
TRAFFIC

-BIG
-FAST
-$$$$
-POLICY FOR
ALL TRAFFIC

PROS:

Really fast (purpose built HW)
Lots of features.

CONS:

Very expensive
All traffic through a few devices
has to cover many policies
(a big problem for multitenant).

VIRTUAL FIREWALLS

Virtual appliances can be put on the
same servers where the VMs are.

PROS:

Really cheap and easy to scale
Individual policies for clients

CONS:

Limited performance
Limited features

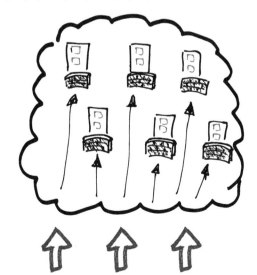

TRAFFIC   TRAFFIC   TRAFFIC

Modern Networking
Approaches to Virtualization

From Consumers to Creators

Server, storage, and network virtualization served as the foundational technologies that enabled cloud computing back in the mid 2000s. Back then, it was a very different world from a technology perspective. High-speed broadband Internet access was readily available, but from fixed-line sources, and mobile telephones were still using GPRS and WAP, rendering them useful for email (with no attachments) and SMS text but little more. Not only were the technologies different, but looking back we see that the way businesses ran IT departments and how applications were delivered and how data was stored differed from today.

Back then, small and medium-size businesses (SMB) actually ran their own services, hosting them in mini to medium-sized server rooms on dedicated high-powered servers. IT departments would maintain and provide hosted email, customer relationship management (CRM), financial packages, enterprise resource planning (ERP), and an array of homemade web-based applications to the company's users. Security was a major concern even then, so typically those web-based services were available only on the private LAN or over secure remote-access virtual private networks (VPNs). Other applications may have required thin clients on the user's desktop PC, with the main application residing on a dedicated computer in the server room. This was an "on-premises self-hosting" solution, and there were few alternatives. IT management may have decided to host the company e-commerce website on service provider networks, but the level of service and lack of control made that a less-than-ideal solution.

This on-premises model was actually good for IT because is gave them tremendous levels of control over their environment. Not only did they have control over performance, networking, and capacity, but they were their own masters when it came to change rollout upgrades, new deployments, reconfigurations, and backups. Subsequently, they had more flexibility when developing their web applications because they could manipulate their environments at will. Similarly, they could reconfigure the web servers and load or drop modules without going through layers of bureaucracy at their service provider's help desk

Consequently, it was IT's responsibility to maintain these servers and the applications that were running. This was great for IT (in the sense that IT departments had a lot of power, a lot of control, and really big budgets), but very bad for the business, because this autonomy came at great expense.

The Emergence of SaaS

Over the past 15 years, however, network technology evolved to allow a different way of delivering software applications. Increases in bandwidth, reliability, performance, and the improved security of Internet access have allowed web applications to scale beyond the control of IT and be accessible from sources outside the company network boundaries. This, of course, made the provisioning of a third-party vendor's web-based application over the Internet not just feasible but attractive (and ultimately a best practice). Early adopters such as SalesForce.com found an instant market for this method of application delivery. By hosting their application on the Internet and making it available by subscription through the client's browser, they could reduce costs to their customers who no longer needed to host and maintain an application server on-premises. This model was to go on to be very successful and was categorized as software as a service (SaaS).

Initially, service providers used a conventional model of deploying an individual server in their data center for each customer. This was still inefficient (it simply shifted the server inefficiencies from one provider to another), but at least the cost of those inefficiencies was consolidated on the vendor side. Virtualization, however, radically changed the cost structure. By virtualizing the data center, including the compute, storage, and network functions, service providers were able to consolidate the server count and become a multitenant provider for their application on shared servers. Virtualization and the capability to support multiple tenants on shared hardware using virtual machines (VMs) and database identifiers was the boost that SaaS required to go mainstream as a software-delivery model. Figure 14-1 shows various multitenant models.

Multitenancy Models

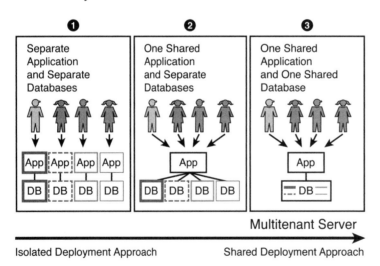

Figure 14-1 *There are many ways to create multitenant environments based on the nature of the users, the environments, and the applications.*

At the time, this was quite revolutionary, and it brought about many changes to how other services were delivered to business clients. Soon, it was not just software but also other hosted services that were being offered over the Internet. For example, the same technologies allow Voice over IP (VoIP) virtual telephone IP/PBX, which enables businesses to obtain hosted cloud-based IP/PBX telephone features and functions for a fraction of the total cost of ownership for an on-premises platform.

Soon, this application service provider model became widespread, with large service providers creating software, development platforms, infrastructure, security, and micro-services over the Internet as services. This was only feasible due to virtualization and cloud adaptations in the data centers of the providers. However, the providers were not necessarily the creators of the service.

Cloud Business Consumer-Creators

The cloud business model has three distinct roles: cloud service consumers, cloud service providers, and cloud service creators. As you will see, the functions of these roles are clearly defined, but the lines between the roles are greatly blurred:

- **Cloud service consumers:** A consumer is an organization, individual, or IT system that consumes the cloud service instances that are delivered to them via the cloud service provider. An organization may still maintain a conventional IT team that will require cloud manage-ment platform tools to integrate in-house IT with the consumer provider's cloud services.

- **Cloud service provider:** A provider has the responsibility of delivering services to the service consumer. Those services are delivered via a cloud management platform over a corporate performance management (CPM) infrastructure or by consuming one as a ser-vice from another provider. Consequently, a provider may also be a consumer of services. The cloud service providers deliver services that can be any type of IT capability that the service consumer requires. Typical capabilities are software as a service (SaaS), infrastructure as a service (IaaS), platform as a service (PaaS), and business process as a service (BPaaS).

- **Cloud service creators:** A cloud service creator is someone who creates a cloud service that can be provided by a cloud service provider and consumed by a crowd service con-sumer. A cloud service creator designs, implements, maintains, and supports runtime and management objects, such as software, infrastructure, a development platform, or a business processes suite.

What you can see here from the definitions is that the roles are not fixed; a provider of services can also be a consumer of other services. In large-scale operations, a cloud service provider will most likely be a vast data center with cloud infrastructure and generally be self-sufficient. However, smaller-scale cloud service providers may well provide many IT services, but will likely have to consume other services from larger cloud service providers to fulfill all of the tasks required to deliver service to their end customers. More interesting, though (and more common now), are the cloud service consumers who are also cloud service creators.

What is interesting here is how fluid the roles can be between creator and consumer. For example, if a large software house produces a CRM package delivered via a SaaS model, they will create all the required artifacts that will make it a service, such as billing, multitenancy, management tools, and so on. By definition, they are a cloud service creator. However, that software house might not want to go and spend a billion dollars building their own cloud service provider infrastructure. Instead, they may decide to go to an existing cloud service provider who will host their SaaS CRM application on spare capacity infrastructure. The end user, the client that uses the SaaS CRM application, is therefore the cloud service consumer.

Many of the massive software houses, such as SalesForce.com, Oracle, IBM, and Microsoft, started out as cloud service providers. They would then use Amazon or build their own cloud infrastructure to deliver the services to the small business and enterprise cloud service consumers.

However, these consumer organizations do not just exist to consume the cloud services of the software giants. Many of them also have their own products and services to offer the world, albeit on a much smaller scale. Consequently, the small consumers also have the opportunity to become cloud service creators. This is the driving force behind the software revolution we are now witnessing. Small business and enterprises of all sizes have discovered for themselves the vast potential of the cloud for delivering services. Whether they are software applications for smartphones, less-complex business software, or security products, these businesses have grasped the opportunities to become cloud product creators, and their participation is feeding the cloud ecosystem from the bottom up.

Large established enterprises have their own on-premises custom applications, and they are taking the initiative to become cloud service providers through their own private clouds. Simultaneously, they are also cloud service creators who make their in-house developed applications available to other subscribing organizations.

This ongoing democratization of the cloud infrastructure has been growing steadily for some time and is becoming ubiquitous. The differentiation between consumers and creators is shrinking as more and more small businesses are utilizing the cloud infrastructure to deliver their products to market. Indeed, in the small business marketplace, some organizations are building their own hybrid cloud infrastructures using a mixture of private and public clouds to bolster new business initiatives.

Anyone Can be a Creator in the Cloud

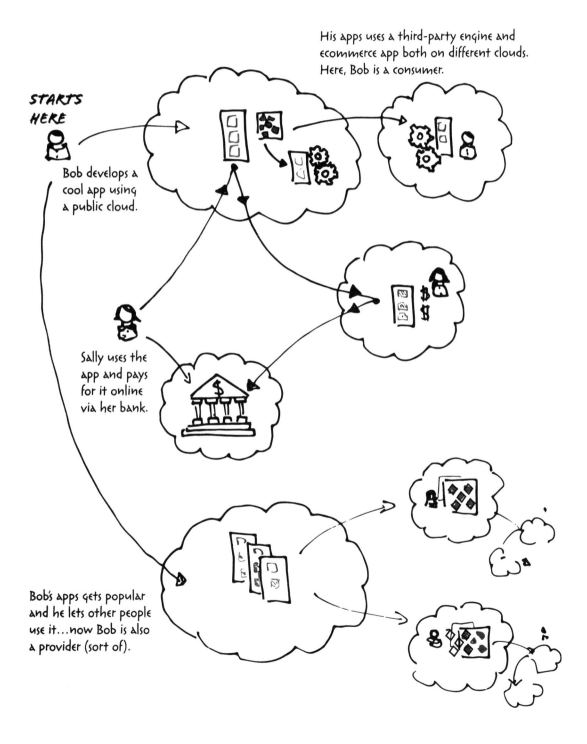

His apps uses a third-party engine and ecommerce app both on different clouds. Here, Bob is a consumer.

STARTS HERE

Bob develops a cool app using a public cloud.

Sally uses the app and pays for it online via her bank.

Bob's apps gets popular and he lets other people use it...now Bob is also a provider (sort of).

OpenFlow

One big problem that network engineers have with virtualization of network infrastructure devices such as routers and switches is that these devices are closed proprietary systems. This means that vendors do not reveal the inner workings of their hardware or software products to public scrutiny, and this is a major problem when it comes to programming because each switch or router is a closed system containing both the control functions (the logic that determines how traffic is handled) and the data functions (the actual moving of packets). With these two functions contained in the same appliances, network engineers are forced to configure each device in isolation. You can imagine what a daunting task this is in a large network, and it is worsened by the fact that most networks are in a constant state of flux, meaning that programming updates take a long time. It also means that the network is slow to respond to state changes in the network because updates have to be passed from device to device, such that by the time all devices in the network are "aware" of a new state, the state has probably already changed again. It turns out that the key to fixing this problem has already been used before on networks, and it has nothing to do with virtualization.

The key to solving this problem is to separate control and data planes such that devices can be controlled and programed from a centralized controller. To accomplish this without swapping out all network hardware (which would be prohibitively expensive), an application programming interface (API) is needed to allow centralized control. It turns out that this is exactly how manufacturers approached the problem with enterprise Wi-Fi. A few years back, when Wi-Fi was rapidly replacing wired ports as the standard connectivity, administrators in a large network infrastructure were having to manually configure hundreds of access points to configure or update their firmware. In some cases, these access points had to be updated daily, which was nearly impossible. Manufacturers subsequently designed access points that the administrator could manage through the use of a centralized controller. As a result, access points became "thin:" they were stripped of their logic, functions, and services, such that they were only capable of packet forwarding. All the brains and the value-added services were migrated to the central controller. By utilizing this controller and dumb AP terminals, administrators could manage hundreds of access point from a single terminal. This same transformation is taking place in networks as they migrate from traditional hardware networks to software-defined networks (SDNs), and OpenFlow is the protocol that allows centralized management to take place.

The key to OpenFlow is that it is able to take advantage of the fact that routers and switches have common hardware architectures whereby the upper logic and code for value-added services reside in a portion of the hardware described as the control plane. The packet forwarding (the actual routing and fast switching of packets) resides on a lower-level data plane. Much in the same way that virtualization abstracts the application and OS from the server, OpenFlow allows us to abstract the control plane from the data plane, thus virtualizing the network.

It's worth noting that equipment manufacturers have made this possible recently by agreeing to separate the logic functionality from the packet forwarding by segmenting the control and data planes within their equipment. This might seem odd that manufacturers would do this, but the reality of living in the virtualization era means that companies either play along or get left out.

As a result of this segmentation, all devices in the network can be centrally controlled, thus creating a programmable network. Consequently, administrators can manage, configure, and define policies centrally from their management console just as they did with Wi-Fi over a decade ago.

OpenFlow History

The history of OpenFlow is interesting and provides insight into how it developed such a critical role in the foundation of SDN and the virtualization of network functions. OpenFlow began as a project at Stanford University when a group of researchers were exploring how they could effectively test and experiment with protocols (including the replacement of the ever-present Internet Protocol) on a realistic network without disrupting production traffic. This was important research; after all, organizations are naturally cautious of experimentation on production networks because the effects of making changes are often unpredictable. This not only creates a high barrier to entry for new ideas, but it also means that many new ideas go untested or untried (at least that's the case with companies). Universities, in general, and Stanford, in particular, not only do not have this concern, but in fact they have large networks built specifically for experimentation.

It was in this environment that the researchers at Stanford tried to find a way to address this problem by attempting to segregate research traffic from production traffic, thereby creating a reserved slice of the network for research traffic. In researching how they could do this, they discovered that although hardware manufacturers were designing their products very differently, all of them used flow tables to implement network services such as Network Address Translation (NAT), quality of service (QoS), and firewalls. Furthermore, although the implementation of network equipment manufacturer's flow tables differed, the researchers found that they could exploit some common function sets.

The result of the Stanford University team's research was OpenFlow, which provides an open protocol that enables admins to program the flow tables in different switches and routers. A network administrator can program switches and routers using OpenFlow to partition traffic into production and research, for example, each with its own set of features and flow characteristics.

As shown in Figure 15-1, OpenFlow works by interfacing with the device's flow table and assigning flows with an action. The action tells the router or switch how to handle the data flow. By specifying through OpenFlow which data flows are handled and how, there is no need to physically connect to and configure each individual router and switch in the network. This not only improves efficiency, but it also greatly reduces complexity and configuration errors.

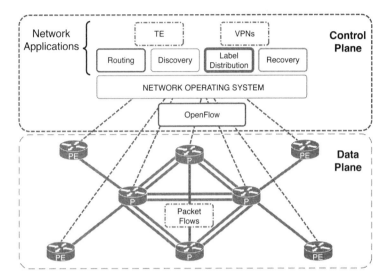

Figure 15-1 *OpenFlow provides an open protocol that enables admins to program the flow tables in different switches and routers.*

How OpenFlow Works

In OpenFlow, a flow table has three fields: (1) A packet header that defines the flow, (2) the action that is to be taken on packets for each flow, and (3) statistics that keep track of the packets and bytes for each flow. Each flow in the table has a simple action associated with it. The four basic actions that all OpenFlow ready switches must support are as follows:

1. Forward <defined> packet flows to a given port. This allows packets to be routed through the network.

2. Encapsulate and forward <defined> flow to a controller. This is typically an action for the first packet in a new flow so that the controller can decide whether it needs to be added to the flow table.

3. Drop <defined> packet flow. This is used for security. For example, it can be used to curb denial-of-service attacks.

4. Forward <defined> packet as normal.

Some implementations of OpenFlow use VLANs to separate experimental and production traffic. The OpenFlow controller adds and removes flow entries into the flow table using OpenFlow protocol over a Secure Sockets Layer (SSL) channel.

There are some legitimate concerns and questions as to the performance, reliability, and scalability of controllers that dynamically add and remove flows. However, in their testing, the researchers were able to process over 10,000 new flows per second running on a low-end PC. At that scale, you could support a large college network. Additional scalability can be achieved by making the controller and the transactions stateless, hence allowing simple load balancing across multiple controllers (which are typically much more powerful than the low-end PC used in the example).

The goal of the Stanford research for OpenFlow was to demonstrate the viability of the protocol such that vendors would integrate OpenFlow into their devices. Switch vendors were surprisingly enthusiastic about supporting OpenFlow, and many have since installed OpenFlow as an integrated feature. One of the main drivers of this support is that OpenFlow gives users unprecedented ease of control when managing networks, something that all manufacturers want, and even the few who were not initially keen about supporting were forced to in order to maintain parity.

Another big advantage of OpenFlow is that it enables users to define their own flows and determine the "best" paths through the network. An obvious question at this point is, "Isn't that what routing protocols are for?" It is true that routing protocols are designed for that, but many routing protocols do not take into consideration congestion or available bandwidth when calculating their best route. By using the OpenFlow protocol, users can engineer the traffic based on available bandwidth, or use paths with less latency or less congestion, and find alternative routes that are preferable to the shortest congested route. This is also one of the features of Multiprotocol Label Switching (MPLS) traffic engineering (so it is not a new concept), but MPLS is a Layer 3 protocol and is limited by the vendor's capabilities. In contrast, OpenFlow is a Layer 2 technology and has particular applicability to data center scenarios (where MPLS does not play).

In contrast to MPLS, OpenFlow works on three layers, enabling a controller to manage the forwarding process of data flows through the network by manipulating the flow tables of both physical and virtual switches and routers. These layers are as follows:

- **The application layer:** This layer handles the business applications and helps accelerate new features and service introduction by decoupling applications from vendor platforms.

- **The control layer:** The centralization of intelligence simplifies provisioning, optimizes performance, and enables greater control, granularity, and simplification of policy management across all network devices.

- **The infrastructure layer:** It is at this layer that hardware is decoupled from software and the control plane is decoupled from the data (forwarding) plane. Decoupling these planes facilitates logical configuration through software on a central controller rather than physical configuration of each device.

Today, OpenFlow is widely accepted due to its promotion by the Open Networking Foundation. OpenFlow-based technologies are at the heart of SDN and enable IT administrators to address the high bandwidth and dynamic nature of modern applications. Furthermore, administrators and applications can dynamically adapt network devices to suit ever-changing situations and requirements. For example, an application can reconfigure the network devices to forward packets (because of congestion), and it will be able to dynamically reconfigure every device along the path. This defines how the network routes traffic and is the foundation of SDNs. Although it doesn't let you do anything that you couldn't do on a network before, it does provide a programmable interface to the network, greatly improving manageability. It also is better suited to data centers than MPLS is because it is a Layer 2 protocol. Consequently, it is often compared with VLANs, but OpenFlow is much more than a VLAN because it allows for genuine dynamically programmable virtual networks.

OpenFlow

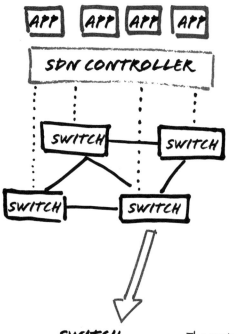

SDN IS A GOOD THING

SDN makes the network programmable by abstracting the control plane (the intelligence about how packets flow) from the data plane (the "muscle" that moves the packets really quickly). SDN makes the network adaptable and agile and is widely viewed as a good thing.

BUT THERE'S A PROBLEM

Within each proprietary switch is a data plane and a control plane...there's not a huge difference between the data planes of switches from different providers but there's a huge difference in the control planes.

The control plane is where the network companies put most of their development efforts, and there's a lot of money invested in these control planes. Because of this, the network providers are not going to support anything that exposes their proprietary code. The result is that these switches are not easily programmable—especially on a network with many different vendor products.

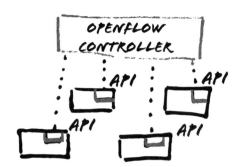

OPENFLOW IS THE ANSWER

OpenFlow is an open source control protocol that all the vendors can equally support. An API can be placed on the vendor switches, enabling them to be programmed without exposing their code.

VMware Nicira

In 2012, VMware acquired Nicira, a five-year-old software-defined networking (SDN) start-up company for a whopping $1.2 billion. Nicira was founded by a team of engineers from Stanford who had built pioneering research in how to change the way networking had worked for decades. The price tag seemed rather staggering for a company that is rumored to have had only about $50 million in revenue at the time of acquisition, but it turns out that VMware not only saw this as a strategic acquisition but also was in a bit of a bidding war with Cisco Systems. Not only did they pay a ton of money for Nicira, but the acquisition ultimately led to some disruption of a lucrative partnership that VMware had with Cisco along with VMware's parent company EMC in the form of a company called VCE (which sells a "data center cloud in a box" solution).

So why would VMware (or Cisco for that matter) want to buy a start up for a 25x multiple and also frustrate a good partnership over it? The answer was that Nicira was the leading SDN controller company, and the companies who wanted it were willing to pay a king's ransom to take the lead in this new market.

The Nicira product allows you to create SDN environments that can be dynamically programmed to make adjustments in the network. Nicira works by treating the network as a flat network by removing traditional hierarchies, which tend to create bottlenecks in performance. Through devices that connect directly to switches, Nicira is able to distribute traffic effectively across its infrastructure.

VMware believes that this technology will allow it to compete with Amazon Web Services and OpenStack, as a viable alternative for building out cloud environments. Ironically, though, Nicira is a significant player in OpenStack, providing an application programming interface (API) for the OpenStack Neutron network interface. This means VMware has also become a significant part of the OpenStack community.

Today Nicira technology is the basis for the VMware NSX virtual network platform.

VMware NSX

The NSX platform enables network virtualization for the software-defined data center (SDDC). What this means is that VMware has brought the same virtual machine (VM) capabilities to the data center that it provides for compute and storage. Now administrators can reduce network provisioning times from weeks to minutes using VM capabilities such as create, save, delete, and restore to virtual networks on demand without having to reconfigure the underlying physical network.

NSX provides network agility in that it reduces provisioning time in multitier networks by abstracting virtual networks from the underlying physical infrastructure. This provides for faster deployment and greater agility, while providing the flexibility to run on top of any vendor's hardware. In addition, NSX can improve and fine-tune security policies by tying them to VMs.

Network Virtualization with NSX

To date, the biggest problem with bringing virtualization into the data center has been in realizing the full potential that VMs bring to compute and storage to nonvirtualized network infrastructures. The problem is that networking and network services have not evolved at the same pace as compute and storage. By comparison, they are slow to provision and require manual provisioning and are anchored to vendor-specific hardware. This is not good because applications require compute, storage, and networking to provide all the benefits of virtualization. Moreover, network provisioning is error-prone due to complexity that increases risk. This is compounded by the fact that the network changes necessary for one application may inadvertently adversely impact another application. As a consequence, changes within a data center where there is that rapid provisioning of compute and storage assets still takes weeks for IT to repurpose the network for changes.

The solution to these problems is to virtualize the network, and this is what the NSX platform is designed to manage. With server virtualization, a software abstraction layer reproduces the familiar attributes of an x86 server (namely the CPU, RAM, disk, and network interface card [NIC]). This allows them to be programmatically assembled in any combination as a unique VM in a matter of seconds. This speed of provisioning for network infrastructure puts it on par with server provisioning.

With network virtualization, the functional equivalent of a network hypervisor reproduces the complete set of Layer 2 to Layer 7 networking services. For example, routing, switching, access control, load balancing, firewalls, quality of service (QoS), Dynamic Host Configuration Protocol (DHCP), and Domain Name System (DNS) software are decoupled from the underlying hardware. As a result of this decoupling, network services can be re-created in software and then programmatically assembled in any combination to provide a unique VM just like with server virtualization. The benefits virtualization brings are also similar to those obtained through server virtualization. When network services are independent of the underlying x86 hardware platform, IT can treat physical hosts as pools of transport capacity that can be consumed and repurposed on demand. It also allows IT organizations to leverage the pricing differentiation and speed of innovation that happens in hardware versus software.

The NSX platform enables IT to introduce software-defined data center (SDDC) as opposed to hardware-defined data center (HDDC). The reason that SDDC is preferred in today's data centers is that software-defined networks have been proven to bring the elasticity and agility that is required in the largest data centers. Both Amazon and Google introduced software-based intelligence into their applications and platforms that enabled them to build the largest and most agile data centers we have today. Furthermore, software innovation is delivered faster because its only constraint is the release of the upgrade. Hardware, in contrast, requires application-specific integrated circuit (ASIC) redesign and hardware upgrades that may be on a two-to three-year refresh cycle. What's more, software-defined data centers can work with the hardware already in place and IT can introduce SDCC through VMware NSX nondisruptively.

How VMware Leverages Nicira (NSX)

Since the VMware acquisition of Nicira, NSX has become a market leader in implementation of network virtualization in the data center. Importantly, NSX is a nondisruptive solution, because it deploys on hypervisors connected to the existing physical network infrastructure, as shown in Figure 16-1. NSX also does not require any changes to be made to the existing hardware's configuration, applications, or workloads. In addition, it allows IT to make incremental changes and implement VMs at whatever pace they choose, without it having any impact on existing applications and workload. NSX extends visibility to existing network monitoring and management by introducing visibility into the virtualized networks. However, it requires network teams to manage and monitor separate physical and virtual networks.

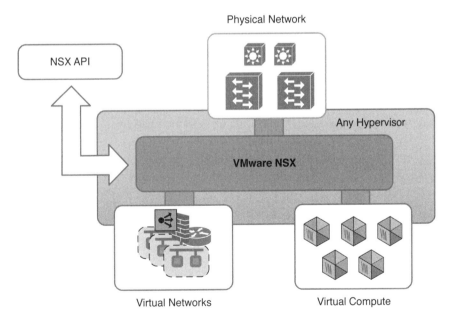

Figure 16-1 *NSX deploys on hypervisors connected to the existing physical network infrastructure.*

NSX works as a multihypervisor solution that leverages the vSwitches currently part of the server hypervisor. NSX handles network VMs similarly to server VMs. Insomuch as a server VM is a software container that provides compute services to an application, a network VM is a container that provides logical network services—vRouting, vSwitching, vFirewall, vLoad-Balancing, and so on—to connected workloads. These networking and security services are delivered in software and require the physical device to handle the packet forwarding in hardware. This is again a separation of the control and data layers, which is a feature of network virtualization.

The way NSX manages the network VMs is through a cloud management platform, which uses the RESTful application programming interface (API) exposed by the NSX controller to request that network services be initiated for a corresponding workload. The controller then distributes the required logical network or security functions, the vRouting, vSwitching, and so on, to the corresponding vSwitches on the VMs that require these combinations of network functions. An advantage to using this approach is that different virtual networks can be associated with different workloads on the same hypervisor. Consequently, this allows very basic networks to be virtualized. For example a virtual network that involves only two nodes is capable of becoming a virtual network comprising multisegment network topologies delivering multitier applications.

The real beauty of virtual networks is that they look and operate like a traditional network. As shown in Figure 16-2, workloads "see" the same network services that they would in a traditional physical network; it is just that these network services are logical instances of distributed software running in the hypervisor and applied to the vSwitch virtual interface.

Another advantage to virtualizing networks is the removal of hair-pinning, which is the undesirable feature of conventional networks whereby traffic that is east-west in nature (that is, server to server) is forced to traverse the north-south network (the access and aggregation switches) to reach essential network services such as routing or firewalling. An example of this is two server VMs on the same hypervisor but in different networks will have to traverse an inefficient path looking for a routing service. With NSX, this efficient east-west communication is eliminated.

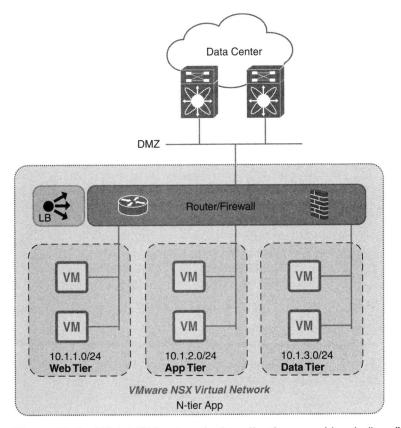

Figure 16-2 *With NSX network virtualization, workloads "see" the same network services that they would in a traditional physical network.*

NSX has many compelling features and services, but the most attractive aspect of NSX is its promiscuity, in that it works with

- **Any application:** Workloads need no modification.

- **Any hypervisor:** NSX supports XEN, Microsoft, KVM VMware ESXi, and any other that can support standard vSwitch capabilities.

- **Any network infrastructure:** NSX is independent of hardware because it requires only connectivity and packet forwarding from the underlying hardware. All control plane features have been decoupled from the data plane.

- **Any cloud management platform:** NSX works with CloudStack, OpenStack, VMware vCloud and can be integrated with other through the NSX API.

NSX simplifies networking by abstracting virtual networks from the underlying physical network that enables increased automation. Administrators no longer need to concern themselves with VLANs, ACLs, spanning tree, or firewall rules because these are no longer a concern when the network is virtualized. In addition, NSX has proven performance and scalability; the processing requirements of distributed network services is only incremental to what the vSwitch is doing at the time, which is typically on a percentage of one CPU core on each host. Furthermore, virtual network capacity scales linearly alongside VM capacity, with the introduction of each hypervisor host adding 40 Gbps of switching and routing capacity. In a real-world production environment, NSX can potentially support more than 10,000 virtual networks and 100,000 VMs, but this varies based on design, server CPU, controller CPU, and other factors.

Cisco Insieme

The advent of industry support for communication protocols that decouple the applications and the data-forwarding functions of physical network devices such as OpenFlow must have unnerved the network hardware vendors. This concern was also compounded by the subsequent introduction into the data center of network virtualization platforms such as VMware NSX. Recall, too, that Cisco Systems lost a high-stakes bidding war with VMware for Nicira, the software-defined networking (SDN) company whose technology was the foundation of what would be become NSX. It was little wonder then that there was great interest as to how the giants of networking, particularly Cisco Systems, would react. What would be their response to the first significant technology threat to their dominance (SDN)?

Cisco's Hybrid SDN Solution

Cisco System's interest in SDN was compounded by the fact that they had previously played down the significance of SDN by stating a position that while customers did want programmability, they did not care about decoupling the control and the data plane (a point central to SDN technology). To that end, Cisco released a program called OnePK, which opened up a host of application programming interfaces (APIs) to developers to access and attach programs. As welcome as the release of the APIs was through OnePK, it was only marginally related to SDN. By maintaining that the intelligence and value-added applications and features remain in the control plane of the switches and routers, they initially distanced themselves and their customer base from SDN in an attempt to defend their strong market position. This, of course, was perfectly natural because SDN is a major threat to Cisco and other network hardware companies, because if SDN is broadly adopted, routing and switching hardware could potentially become commodity devices used to simply handle packet forwarding. Therefore, they would be priced accordingly, something no Cisco shareholder would want to hear.

Interestingly, while Cisco was stating that position on SDN, they were reacting positively to OpenFlow, albeit without supporting the idea of using centralized intelligent software controller and dumb switches, for obvious reasons. Cisco's main objection to OpenFlow was that it required a central controller deployed on a server. The controller uses the OpenFlow protocol to communicate over the network with agents on switches and routers. Applications then use APIs on the OpenFlow controller to create and deploy a distributed network policy. Cisco believed that the model should not be restricted to only the OpenFlow centralized controller/switch approach. They believed that the centralized control planes offered the advantages of easy operations and management. However, they also introduced scalability concerns and pointed out that the model limits developer options for application deployment. Cisco's model, through OnePK, would decentralize and expose device APIs, yielding a broader range of application possibilities.

What Cisco was proposing was a hybrid solution that used decentralized control planes with direct-access APIs, and a centralized controller to provide a more flexible SDN model. Crucial to Cisco was that this approach would mean retaining the intelligence in the switches and routers. Effectively, Cisco had agreed that it was a good thing to be able to instantiate a service anywhere in the network based on dynamic demands. However, they insisted that decentralized control planes were the right option for application deployment. Consequently, Cisco came up with their own OpenFlow killer protocol called OpFlex, which maintained intelligence in the network devices rather than using a centralized controller and dumb switches. OpFlex keeps network infrastructure hardware as the foundational controlling element of the programmable network. In effect, Cisco tried to reinvent the OpenFlow wheel, providing a protocol that will be to its ACI SDN architecture as OpenFlow is to the SDN.

Cisco SDN and Insieme

It was against this backdrop that the industry received the news that Cisco had acquired the SDN company Insieme. The stated purpose of this acquisition was to get hold of Insieme's SDN products, which indicated a major shift in Cisco's SDN strategy. The ultimate outcome of the Insieme acquisition was the SDN technology, which has since been introduced into the Cisco product line as Cisco application-centric infrastructure (Cisco ACI), which is aimed at automating IT tasks and accelerating data center application deployments as an SDN architecture.

Cisco's SDN architecture is a policy-based automation solution based on the integration of physical and virtual environments under one policy model for networks, servers, and storage. The aim of Cisco ACI is to reduce the deployment time of services and applications from days to seconds and to better align with modern business requirements.

Cisco ACI is built on the Application Centric Policy, which itself is based on the Cisco Application Policy Infrastructure Controller (APIC). In addition, there is the Cisco ACI Fabric, which is based on the Nexus 9000 series switches and the Cisco Application Virtual Switch (AVS).

The basis of the Cisco SDN network is to decouple the connectivity requirements of applications from the complications of network configuration. Application-based policies result in automated processes that significantly remove most of the complexity in a device's network configuration. ACI can provide the transparent support necessary to support heterogeneous physical and virtual interfaces with Layer 2 to Layer 7 network and security services. In addition, the application of a consistent policy and greater visibility into the virtual networks provides for easier troubleshooting across the entire infrastructure.

There are problems with cloud and the deployment of new network applications (routing protocols, firewalls, and so on). It seems that programmable infrastructures have made provisioning applications using virtual machines (VMs) a trivial task. However, onboarding the applications remains problematic with DevOps teams struggling to comprehend how numerous applications can operate within a common network and furthermore how changes to the network configuration of VLANs, firewalls, security appliances, and other such network functions can affect individual applications. The problem is that changes must work within the shared domain with no effect on existing tenants and applications, and that is never easy.

The Cisco approach through ACI and the APIC controller allows for granular security policy down to the individual application, tenant, or workload, as shown in Figure 17-1. Cisco's ACI solution is designed as an open architecture by providing a technology ecosystem to partners and customers to leverage the SDN and automate IT tasks.

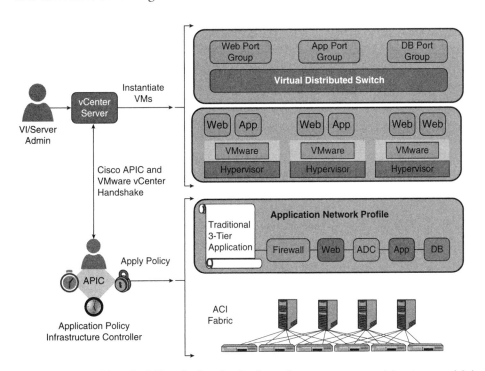

Figure 17-1 *Cisco's ACI solution is designed as an open architecture, which allows for granular security policy down to the individual application, tenant, or workload.*

With the release of ACI, it appears Cisco has finally developed an SDN strategy, and is making up for lost time by going way beyond a low-level controller and virtual network management model. Instead, Cisco is including enterprise-wide regulation and automation of application policies for security, performance, and use. Not content with that, they are also incorporating the orchestration of virtual network services and management of both physical and virtual networks into the mix. To achieve all of these goals, Cisco uses an APIC controller that includes a plethora of supported APIs and protocols that surprisingly include OpenFlow, its own onePK, NETCONF, OVSDB (Open vSwitch), and its own application virtual switch. Tellingly, though, there is still no embracing of the dumb switch centralized control plane philosophy. In fact, it is quite the reverse, with Cisco launching a new line of the Nexus 9000 that will be tightly integrated with the ACI and APIC controller via a new generation of firmware. Therefore, it looks like although Cisco is willing to embrace SDN, it is unwilling to sacrifice hardware intelligence to centralized software controllers. By allowing the Nexus 9000 switches to operate in ACI or non-ACI mode, they allow customers to leverage the hardware in the manner they are most comfortable with today, and allow them to upgrade to an SDN model if desired.

Whether Cisco's vision of SDN strikes a chord with data center customers will depend on their willingness to accommodate a new hardware and software architecture. Other competitive SDN solutions such as VMware NSX do not require a hardware upgrade. Cisco's does, and it's both expensive and disruptive. It remains to be seen whether customers will do a "rip-and-replace" upgrade to accommodate SDN when clear upgrade paths exist that do not entail such costs and disruptions. This is a problem that all SDN vendors have, and it's not unique to Cisco. Some customers may prefer overlay solutions to physical layer hardware and software protocols such as OpenFlow, but not all. As of this writing, there are no clear winners or losers.

Cisco claims that ACI and OpFlex use a declarative model of forwarding control that differs distinctly from OpenFlow's imperative model. A declarative model is abstracted from the network and not the network configuration, as is the case with an imperative SDN model. The difference in layman's terms is that with a declarative model the network acting on an applied policy from the APIC decides how to reconfigure itself rather than have the controller dictate a configuration. However, in the imperative model applications, operations, and infrastructure requirements must be configured, which does nothing to remove the complexities of device and network configuration.

Cisco is lining up support and partners for OpFlex to write the APIs and it is proposing it as a standard in the IETF and to the OpenDayLight open source SDN project. However, even if OpFlex does become a de facto standard, and even with Cisco's huge influence in the market, ACI and OpFlex are such a deviation from the conventional SDN model that even mighty Cisco Systems may find it difficult convincing customers of the need for a hardware and software upgrade.

OpenStack

Up until now, we have looked at transforming conventional data centers—with their inefficient, expensive architectures and server sprawl—into more streamlined models that consolidate many small servers onto a few larger ones through the use of virtualization. This transformation from a conventional model to a virtualized model could be accomplished using any of the server virtualization technologies to create a private cloud. By now, you should be well aware of the benefits of turning a data center into a private cloud, but this still falls short of cloud computing, which suggests that cloud computing is more than "just" server virtualization. This, of course, leads us to this question: What is the difference between virtualization and cloud computing (or cloud networking), and why is it important?

Consolidating enterprise applications onto fewer larger servers is a well-understood and proven solution for large enterprise applications such as Microsoft's Exchange and Oracle's PeopleSoft. Traditionally, these large applications ran on conventional monolithic architectures, and the shift to a virtual server model with each instance migrating from a single large physical server to a single large virtual server was pretty straightforward. Once the conversion takes place, the application can grow by scaling up the single physical server running a bare-metal hypervisor. To provide redundancy and high-availability, these enterprise applications can be run as VMs in vSphere clusters, which leverage the proven vSphere high-availability and vMotion technologies.

Applications on Modern Networks

In essence, what you have after such a conversion is a traditional application running on VMs. These VMs are managed by some coordination technology such as VMware vSphere, and all these servers are sitting on a traditional network infrastructure and accessing traditional resources such as storage-area network (SAN) storage. The network and storage pieces are designed for high availability (and they are highly available), and by now you should be well versed in the benefits of server virtualization.

All of this works fine when we consider legacy applications, but cloud computing is different, or more specifically, cloud-based applications are different, and for them to work the way there were intended, a different approach is needed. It turns out that cloud platform architecture and philosophy are quite different from the legacy way of managing traditional data center applications and servers. Typical enterprise applications are built for efficiency, but cloud-based applications such as MySQL and Hadoop are architected to scale horizontally by adding more application instances and rebalancing the workloads across those instances. They are also "designed for failure," meaning that 99.999 percent network and resource availability is not assumed, and so they are built to be more robust in the face of outages. Consequently, these new breeds of applications are not well suited to run on the same monolithic architectures as traditional applications. Instead, these distributed applications must manage their own resiliency, independent of the underlying infrastructure.

To meet the needs of these new applications, cloud platforms have different design principles to virtualization of legacy applications via VMware or other similar products. Cloud platforms remove the requirement for "shared-everything" by moving application resiliency up the software stack. Horizontal scaling (the ability to increase capacity by connecting multiple pieces of hardware that can act as one unit) is provided through commodity servers and other hardware to build the cloud platform. This creates an architecture that can scale out rapidly. Consequently, resiliency and high availability is not required in the infrastructure. Failure is anticipated and can be dealt with at multiple layers of the software architecture. In fact, in cloud-based applications, failure handling is designed into the application to reduce the associated hardware costs of redundancy and high availability.

With this new design and new philosophy comes new tools to manage and maintain the resulting architecture. OpenStack is one cloud management vehicle through which these tools and technologies are provided. Built as an open source project (where a community of developers maintains, upgrades, and debugs the software), OpenStack "sits on top" of the compute, network, and storage technologies, providing the relevant application programming interfaces (APIs) and tools to interface with the resources in an agile and programmatic way. Figure 18-1 shows the OpenStack model relevant to modern applications and the commodity hardware the clouds run on.

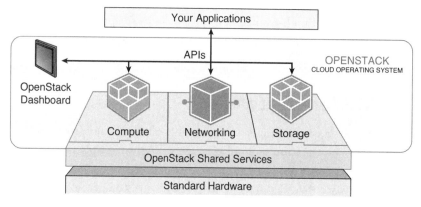

Figure 18-1 *OpenStack is an open source cloud management vehicle that sits on top of the compute, network, and storage technologies, providing the relevant APIs and tools to interface with the resources in an agile and programmatic way.*

The best way to think of OpenStack is to view it as an operating system for public and private clouds. This is where we take the first steps away from virtualization and software-defined networking (SDN) and actually enter the domain of true cloud computing. OpenStack provides the means that allow both large and small organizations to build cloud infrastructures without the risk of vendor lock-in. Despite being open source, OpenStack has the support of many heavyweights in the industry, such as Rackspace, Cisco, VMware, EMC, Dell, HP, Red Hat, and IBM, to name just a few; so, it's no small-scale open source project likely to disappear overnight or be snapped up by a brand name and lose its open source status.

Beyond the high-level description, OpenStack is a suite of applications and tools that provides for identity management, orchestration, and metered access. However, it's important to note that OpenStack is not a hypervisor, although it does support several other hypervisors, such as VMware ESXi, KVM, Xen, and Hyper-V. Therefore, OpenStack is not a replacement for these hypervisors; it doesn't do virtualization as such, but is a cloud management platform.

OpenStack has many individual modular components, each of which is driven by an open source technical committee that determines features and roadmaps. A community-driven board of directors determines which new components get added to the OpenStack roadmap. At the time of this writing, the following modules are available:

- **Compute (Nova):** This is the main controller that is the main component in any IaaS (infrastructure as a service) system. It is designed to manage and automate pools of computer resources. Nova can work with a wide range of virtualization technologies.

- **Object storage (Swift):** This is a scalable redundant storage system. Objects and files are written to multiple disk drives spread throughout servers in the data center. Storage clusters scale horizontally simply by adding new servers. Should a server fail, OpenStack will replicate its data to new locations in the cluster.

- **Block storage (Cinder):** This is the block storage system that manages the creation, attachment, and detachment of block devices to a server. Snapshots provide the functionality for backups of block storage volumes.

- **Networking (Neutron):** This is a system for managing the cloud network IP addresses to ensure that the network is not a bottleneck in a cloud deployment. Dynamic Host Configuration Protocol (DHCP) floating addresses allows for traffic to be dynamically rerouted to any resource in the infrastructure. In addition, users can control their own networks, connect servers and devices, and use SDN technologies such as OpenFlow to support multiple tenants.

- **Dashboard (Horizon):** This is the administration and graphical user interface (GUI) used to access, provision, and automate resources. It also incorporates features for billing and network monitoring and has other third-party management tools.

- **Identity service (Keystone):** This provides a central repository and directory of users who are mapped to the services they can legitimately access. Keystone acts as an authentication service for users supporting standard user credentials, token-based systems, and Amazon Web Services (AWS)-style logins.

- **Image service (Glance):** This is an image service that provides discovery, registration, and delivery services for disk and server images. An image is an OS that has been installed on a server. Images can be used as templates or backups. Glance can add many features to existing legacy networks. For example, if working with vSphere, it can facilitate vMotion, high availability, and dynamic resource scheduling.

- **Telemetry (Ceilometer):** This provides a single point of contact for billing systems by providing all the necessary counters needed to establish customer usage and billing. The counters are traceable and auditable and are easily extendible to support new projects.

- **Orchestration (Heat):** This is an orchestration service and the main project within OpenStack. The Heat engine allows you to launch multiple composite cloud applications based on templates.

- **Database (Trove):** This is a database as a service provisioning component for relational and nonrelational databases, although relational databases, such as MySQL, are the most used databases in operational deployments.

- **Bare-metal provisioning (Ironic):** This is not a hypervisor but an API and set of plugins that allows OpenStack to communicate with a bare-metal hypervisor such as VMware ISXi.

- **Multitenant cloud messaging (Zaqar):** This is based on Amazon's Simple Queue Service (SQS) messaging product and provides event broadcasting and the ability to send messages between components of their SaaS and mobile applications.

- **Elastic map reduce (Sahara):** This provides the methods to provision and deploy Hadoop clusters. Sahara can also scale an already-provisioned cluster by adding or removing cluster nodes on demand.

Note that OpenStack continues to grow and evolve. The OpenStack organization and community regularly releases new code and versions. To see the latest updates, visit OpenStack.Org

Figure 18-2 shows how some of these modules work in concert to form a cloud-based operating system.

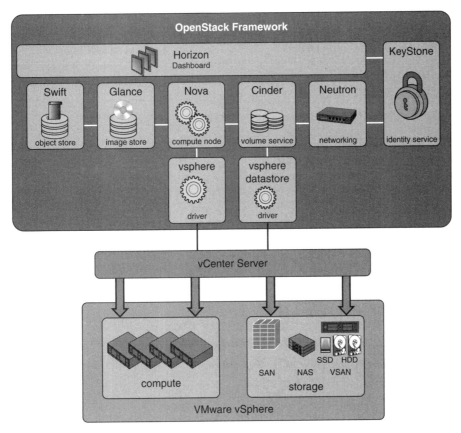

Figure 18-2 *OpenStack modules work in concert to form a cloud-based operating system.*

Despite the fact that OpenStack is a free open source distribution, many corporate users such as Yahoo!, Deutche Telecom, AT&T, eBay, NASA, PayPal, and Rackspace (to name just a few well-known brands) have adopted it. This is a big shift from the early days of enterprise applications, where going with a big name software vendor was preferred and safe. (The "nobody ever got fired for buying Cisco or IBM or Oracle" phenomenon.) Today, however, there is a shift toward mature open source options that reduce overall costs and avoid vendor lock-in. As the OpenStack brand has matured, additional development has resulted in broader deployment options, thus increasing adoption, development, and quality in a virtuous cycle. As a result, OpenStack can be deployed as an on-premises distribution within a private network, as a hosted OpenStack private cloud, or as OpenStack as a service.

OpenStack

Core Services

- Open source cloud-computing platform

- Modular architecture

- Designed to easily scale out

- Made of a growing set of core services

Software Defined Networks
Virtualizing the Network

The Evolution of the Data Center Network

To this point in the book, the focus has been on virtualization of servers and transformation data centers, which began in the early 1990s. During the time period when these second-generation data centers came on line, and then began to "max out," the industry was also making enormous strides in increasing networking capability. With fixed network connectivity providing almost every employee with access to application servers (and to each other), the demand on these data centers began to rise, creating more and more stress on networks as many more users began to rely on them. Newly formed data center networking teams, which split off from IT and core networking teams, implemented hierarchical designs and high-availability architectures to ensure that users had access to programs and data with little or no service interruptions.

Advances in modern networking also made wide-area networks (WANs) very fast and reliable, which meant that companies could consolidate their data centers, first among buildings in a campus and then among regions and even worldwide sites, but only large companies could afford dedicated long-haul network connections. During this time, the term *data center* came into popularity, and several innovations quickly positioned data centers as critical business assets. In addition to disaster recovery sites, which were created so that even natural disasters would not disrupt service, a whole new business model for outsourced data centers called *co-location* came into popularity. Soon, just serving and hosting data and applications became a multi-billion-dollar industry. For many companies, the data center became one of the most important assets—IT or otherwise.

This seems all well and good, but there was a problem. Despite all of the capacity built in to the system, it never seemed to be enough. It's crazy to think that at one point in the not too distant past if it only took 30 minutes to download one song, you thought you had a fast connection. Now your kids expect to watch streaming videos on their phone while you drive down a highway at 65 MPH, and they complain if it buffers here and there. Further still, many people (and companies) are no longer satisfied with buying large software packages from companies; they want to create and use their own, and they want them right now.

And here is the heart of the problem. With all the advances made and all the added capacity, it still failed to satisfy the needs of the users (both individuals and companies). It merely got to the point where we realized the network we had, despite all the advances (or perhaps because of them), was not the network we needed anymore. In fact, it works just well enough to make us realize we had to scrap the whole thing and start over.

Now, of course, that's not to be taken literally. Instead, the point is that the industry had to rethink how networks were built and operated, and it would eventually mean a whole new approach to networks.

This chapter, and the ones that follow, explain where it all breaks, and what the industry is doing about it.

Networks Worked Great, Until They Didn't

At first blush, it's easy to miss the real reason why traditional data center network designs don't work that well when you virtualize applications. After all, we just package the same old applications with an operating system, and then decouple it from the hardware. How hard can it be? The whole point is that we can get more efficient use of the servers, which saves on space and lowers our power bills, right?

The truth is, it's not that simple. Yes, virtualization does package app-OS combinations and decouples them from the servers. Yes, this does allow more efficient use of servers, and yes, it does result in lower power bills, all other things being equal. But here's the reality of virtualization: Virtual machines (VMs) are different things than the servers they replaced, with different properties, and as a result, they are used differently and in ways that traditional data centers were not built to handle.

Fortunately, the advantages VMs yield make it worthwhile to scrap legacy data center architecture and start over. In fact, it's worth scrapping (over time) the entire network and starting over, which is what software-defined networking (SDN) is really all about. It might not happen overnight, but it will happen over the course of years. It's hard to believe that it's taken this long. After all, the industry has already re-architected storage, and we've re-architected servers to make them virtualized. In fact, both of those transformations took place quite some time ago. So, why did we wait this long for the network?

It's not that the network designs were bad. (In fact, they were great for the task at hand.) It's that the nature of the resources that they were providing access to changed, which precipitated changes in how the users consumed those resources. Those changes are so profound that it's worth it to have a "do over" now on the network.

As a side note, there is a similar argument that the ease of video creation and the corresponding wide availability of videos has resulted in behavioral changes. Pundits claim sites like YouTube have turned us into a "video society." Others make the claim (and the author agrees with them) that we've been a video society for a long time; after all, the generations that grew up with TVs as babysitters and the primary source of entertainment have always been "tuned" to consuming video. Thus, YouTube did not create a new need for video but rather satisfied a latent desire for video that had been there all along.

The situation with virtualization and cloud (and the networks that support them) is similar. Virtualization is not creating the desire to use application and computing resources differently as much as it is satisfying a long latent need or preferred usage model for servers that had been there the whole time. Virtualization was the crack in the dam. Now cloud networking is allowing the whole river to flow.

Traditional Data Center Design Goals

As a part of understanding traditional data center design, let's review what the design criteria were. You'll see some common attributes between the old design criteria and the new, but even within those common attributes, there are some major differences.

High Availability

It should be a surprise to no one that one of the prime directives of the data center (virtualized or not) is availability. If you're going to lump all your data or applications in a single room or building (or several of them) and then have those rooms or buildings be remote from the users, you better make sure those users can get to the data and applications when they need them (which is all the time).

Low Latency

One of the impacts of consolidated and offsite data centers was that it took longer to send and receive information—not so much because of the distance (the speed of light is pretty fast), but more because of the complexity of the network designs, different types of traffic, differences in link speeds between here and there, and a whole bunch of network-specific instructional traffic. This created a need to design low-latency networks, and this was (and is) especially important in the data center.

Scalability

The cloud has altered our view of what "scalable" is, and we'll discus this a bit more later, but data center networks needed to be scalable relative to the growth of data consumption at the time. Back then, scalability meant that you architected for future growth at a measured pace. In today's "rocket car" world of data-consumption acceleration, it's kind of quaint to talk in terms of having a "faster horse" back in the old days, but in the context of the time, having a faster horse was a big deal. (It sure as heck beat having a slow one.) Today, scalability means the ability to not only scale up almost instantaneously, but to also scale back down just as fast. As a result, the fundamental tenets of data center design, such as power density per square foot, have changed radically as network speeds increased and as demand for cloud services grew.

Security

Security has always been a concern in the data center, but we're talking about a whole different view of security for the traditional data centers. In the "old days," security still meant letting authorized users get to their stuff without too much hassle and keeping the "bad guys" out. It's relatively simple to have an enterprise network perimeter when servers stay put. Putting a perimeter around constantly changing, reconfiguring, and moving servers, and the network that is tied to the servers, becomes a daunting and ultimately futile task.

As a result of all these changes, it did not take long for this system (both data centers and long-haul networks) to strain against demand as both businesses and individuals began to consume more and more data. Then, just to make things harder on everyone, we went mobile. As if keeping up with demand (and ensuring authorized access and adequate security) was not hard enough with ever-increasing demand, users started moving around (and not once, but constantly). And they started expecting video, which places demands on data centers and networks that their creators never envisioned. As illustrated in Figure 19-1, when data centers ballooned in sized, going from rooms, to buildings, to campuses, to what now look like small towns, complexity outstripped performance.

Figure 19-1   *Data centers became monuments of complexity.*

The Cost Model Explodes

While all of this was going on, the demand for data grew relentlessly (and continues to do so). Out of necessity, this growth (and the strain it caused) drove a great deal of innovation. What's interesting about the latest era of innovation—virtualization and cloud networking—is that economics has as much to do with it as operational efficiency and keeping up with data demand. Data centers are now built in far-off places where land is cheap. Ideally, they are near a hydro dam or other power source, because moving power over long distances is less efficient (and more expensive) than moving data. Figure 19-2 shows a layout of a modern data center. We've come a long way from when the data center was a few servers in the basement.

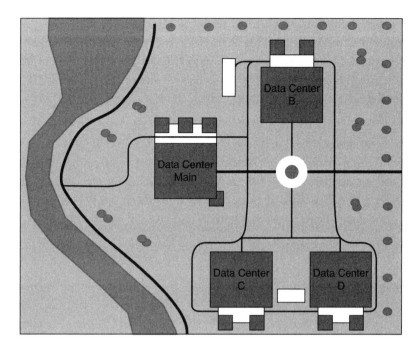

Figure 19-2   *A mock up of a data center site plans. Note that data center site designs account for multiple buildings on dozens or even hundreds of acres.*

This is a bit different from what had come before. Once companies learned to harness the power of computing and universal data access, we basically threw money at the demand problem because the economics were so good. It was all businesses could do to keep up with it. For nearly 30 years, every dollar we threw into connecting people with data yielded a dollar plus return on the investment. In recent years, however, the balance started to shift due to server sprawl and the unsustainable growth in the number of servers and the energy required to power and cool them. This is important, too. It's not that data centers and data center networks were not good enough. They were actually great. But after about 20 years (we're only counting modern data centers here), data center investments reached their point of diminishing returns. This really underscores how much value we derived from data centers.

How We Got Here

Trying to cover 30 years of data center evolution in one chapter is a bit tricky, so a summary is in order.

Original data centers were usually a collection of servers in a building or a room in close proximity to the users. As demand for the applications grew and as the speed and reliability of networking grew, data centers became quite large. Security and availability demands dictated the need for large remote data centers with backup sites that were geographically diverse (so that a natural disaster would not hit both the primary and backup data center). This model worked well for many years.

The advent of virtualization, however, changed both the scale and the demands of the data center. (Think about the number of videos loaded on to YouTube every day and the number of videos watched.) In the virtualization era, data centers are now built on a scale that is orders of magnitude larger than the previous generations. They also behave differently (internally) and have more and different demands put on them, and virtualization also changed the cost model of how they were operated.

So, while the original data center designs were great for about 10 to 15 years, all good things must end. Here's the really interesting part, though: At some point, even a massive change in how data centers are built and operated started to have a diminishing value on the overall quality of experience for users. To really maximize the upgrades to data centers, we had to evolve the networks that connect data centers and users. SDN and cloud networking are the results of this evolution.

What's Wrong With the Network We Have?

One of the most important shifts in networking technology has been the trend toward user-developed applications. Whether it's a phone application, corporate financial tool, or web widget, we have arrived at a place where the user community is now a legitimate creative force and a significant driver of application development rather than being just passive consumers.

Users are now so accustomed to this that they are no longer willing to wait for, or completely rely on, the company or large suppliers and vendors to create the tools and applications they want to use, and have shown not only a willingness but also an expectation that they will go find (or even create) the tools they need. In some cases, this means downloading an application on their smart device or subscribing to a software as a service (SaaS) application (as an individual). In some cases, it means using open source software, and in rare cases where the users are very technical, users can actually be open source creators or contributors.

Often enterprise IT staffs have to scramble to keep up with all these tools and figure out a way to support them. In some places, very harsh restrictions are placed on employees, who can be fired if they fail to comply, but such restrictions are rare because they are hard to enforce and often create morale problems. On the other end of the spectrum is a new willingness with enterprises to allow the use of open source tools even on business-critical systems. One example of this is MySQL, an open source relational database, which has broad adoption even within large enterprises.

This drive toward user innovation has extended to the network as well. Users (who may be departments within a company or companies in a multitenant service) want (and to some degree expect) the ability to customize their environment in terms of services and applications. In this case, the word *applications* refers to networking applications such as routing, optimization, and security. To accommodate this, the industry needed to change how networks work.

In essence, the desired outcome is to make networking programmable. In doing so, it becomes much, much easier to accommodate changes, implement customized environments for certain types of users, and make it easier to truly leverage the full power of data center virtualization. The result of these changes is embodied in what is known as software-defined networks

(SDN). This chapter takes a look at the way networks work now, why a change was needed, and how SDN solves the problem.

A Brief Review of Networking

A brief review of networking will help to explain the problem that SDN attempts to fix. As you recall, a network is a collection of specialized computers called *routers* and *switches* that send and receive packets to each other. Packets consist of blocks of data that are sent over physical links. The packets are a series of 1s and 0s that contain a small amount of data (typically the data is broken up into small chunks on the sending side and reassembled on the receiving side) and instructions for the routers and switches about where to move a packet along to its intended destination. This information is put at the front of the packet and is referred to as the *header*.

As shown in Figure 20-1, the information passed between computers is referred to as the *payload*. Multiple layers of data are assembled, each with its own specific set of instructions that the corresponding computer on the other end of the communication line will use to put the data into usable form. These different instructions/information layers are collectively referred to as the *OSI stack*.

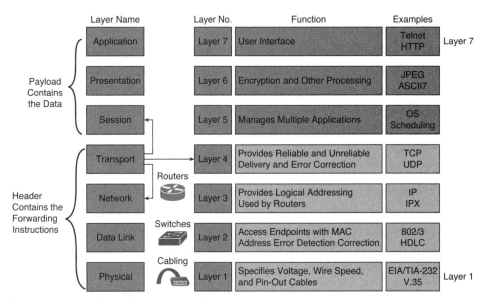

Figure 20-1   *The OSI model defines the communication functions of network components independent of vendors and specific technologies.*

For a network to be useful, information must be passed from one part of the network to another. This could be between servers or computers or dedicated communication devices such as IP-based phones (Voice over IP [VoIP]). When a network session is initiated, the first packet is sent to the next network device in line. That device has to figure out what to do with the packet, and the process of how this decision is made (and the software behind it) is at the heart of why something had to change for users to be able to create their own applications and programs.

The first issue is that each networking device is really an island unto itself. So, although each device is part of a large architecture of mass connectivity, these specialized computers are self-contained portals through which traffic flows. This is an artifact of how the Internet was built; it's designed to work even if large parts of it are missing. The result is that every node on the network is self-sufficient.

Control Planes and Forwarding Planes

These specialized computers called switches or routers have two logic planes (or functions) called the *control plane* and the *forwarding plane* (sometimes called the *data plane*). The control plane is where the intelligence of the device lies. It is here where all the instructions (in the form of applications and large tables of rules) are stored. The other part is the forwarding plane, where packets are moved from one network interface on the machine to one of the many other network interfaces on the machine. You can think of the control plane as the brain and the forwarding plane as the muscle.

This seems like a perfectly reasonable way to architect a networking device, and it has worked well for a long time, but the problem is that over time it has created an enormous amount of complexity in the network, because every function, application, and rule set has to be programmed into every single device because each device relies on its own little brain to run applications and make forwarding decisions. Given that it's not out of the ordinary for a network to contain tens of thousands of these devices, this complexity can achieve nightmarish status. It also means that if a user does something unpredictable to one node on a network, it can break other ones. That's bad news.

As a result, every new thing that comes along has to be added to and learned by every device in the network, and generally all these new rules and programs get stacked on top of every other thing already running on these devices, which creates "towers of complexity" throughout the entire network, and often many of these rules and tables are tied together. So, the complexity (and by extension errors) cascades throughout the device and the rest of the network.

The Cost of Complexity

This complexity is then significantly compounded by the fact that the new usage models such as cloud and mobility result in an almost constantly shifting array of machines that not only move but often move during active communication sessions. It's become untenable, and network configuration errors are a significant cause of downtime.

This also impedes the pace of technology innovation, when the software (control plane) and hardware (forwarding plane) are deeply integrated. Decoupling these (much in the same way that the application and OS were decoupled from the server for virtualization) offers the ability to innovate at different speeds, potentially offering new value to IT organizations.

Figure 20-2 attempts to illustrate how complex systems that add variables at an even rate can become exponentially complex after only a handful of iterations. In this case simply doubling the options creates a $2 \wedge x$ exponential response. After just 10 iterations, the 2 original options increase to 1024.

Now apply this to a network. Imagine a network device running just a few applications, each of which with some overlap of resources, rules, or tables. If a new application is added that affects more than one of the existing rule sets, the complexity impact is disproportionate to the linear addition of the application. In just a very short time, adding a single application or rule can have significant and far-reaching consequences. This added complexity also greatly increases the chances for configuration errors, which then creates even more complexity.

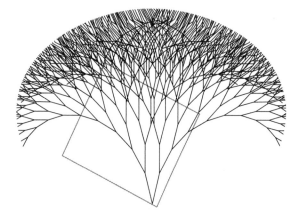

Figure 20-2 *In complex systems, adding variables can drive complexity. Simply doubling options creates exponential complexity.*

Systems such as this are especially inefficient when it comes to collecting and disseminating information about how devices on the network are doing. Device information sharing is the source of a great deal of network traffic, because in addition to enabling communication between end devices, information must be shared between devices to monitor and ensure the health and reliability of the network. In fact, this is a case where centralized network intelligence can significantly reduce complexity and add efficiency.

By way of example, let's take a look at one of the most common networking activities: discovering the most efficient path through the network. Because each device in the network has to make and then carry out packet-forwarding decisions, each must know where (which port and, by extension, which of the many other devices it's connected to) to send data to ensure that packets are taking the "best" path through the network. In most networks, this is accomplished with a routing protocol called *Open Shortest Path First* (OSPF).

As its name suggests, OSPF creates a set of rules that tells a device what the next best path is to get traffic to its final destination and each point throughout the network. *Best* in this case is a relative term (it could be based on speed or number of devices, and so on), and it is based on "link state," which means that the map it creates is constantly changing based on any number of factors that could impact the millions of combinations of connections between any two points on the network. OSPF basically creates a "snapshot" of the network at any given time, and it requires constant updating.

To make OSPF work in a network where all of the decision making is distributed through every device, the networking community has created a 245-page specification to describe the process (and associated codes) required for each device to "look, report, and learn" repeatedly until all the information has been passed through the network.

To put the complexity into context, imagine if on your commute home you had to know at all times the state of every intersection you might choose to drive through so that you could get home quickly. It would be a daunting task because the state of those intersections changes constantly. Networks have this problem, too, and the cloud has made it worse because it has increased the rate of change in networks. However, this problem exists only because each network has to figure this information out for itself.

By way of contrast, if there was centralized intelligence to the network, this "link-state map" could be done in a very simple and straightforward manner. The single shortest path throughout the network can quickly and efficiently be found with a simple process and just a few lines of code using something called *Dijkstra's algorithm*. This algorithm is an efficient graph search method devised by Dutch-born mathematician Edsger Dijkstra (which he did way back in 1956). This algorithm accomplishes the same thing as OSPF, but it can be described in half of one page (500 times smaller than the OSPF description). The only caveat is that you need centralized network intelligence to do it.

Decoupling Networking Applications from Networking Gear

In addition to the problems caused by network-wide distribution of intelligence, there is also a problem with the way we develop network applications and code on these systems. Again, keep in mind in this context that we are talking about networking applications such as routing and optimization as opposed to the applications that run on your computer or smartphone. Current practices also inhibit user innovation. The problem here is that in addition to each network device having its own control plane, each device also has its own complicated operating system, which also has to be set up, secured, maintained, and reconfigured every time a change is made.

If you look at a block diagram of the code stacks (see Figure 20-3) on one of these systems (from the manufacturer's point of view), it would appear that there are distinct functional blocks. At the bottom would be the specialized hardware running on the device. Sitting on the custom hardware is the vendor's proprietary software, and on top of that are the various network applications such as routing functions, management software, access lists, and a host of others. You'll note an obvious similarity to the relationship of applications, operating systems, and server hardware from the chapters on virtualization.

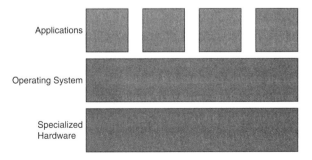

Figure 20-3   *Most device manufactures claim to have code stacks (functional sections of code) that are distinct from one another.*

This would be all well and good if it actually worked like that, but as shown in Figure 20-4, in reality the code bases of these sections are irrevocably intertwined and interdependent such that a problem with one of the applications can impact the operating system, which can in turn impact the specialized hardware instructions and vice versa. This is why application or configuration problems can often cascade through the network, creating performance issues or, worse, causing outages and reboots.

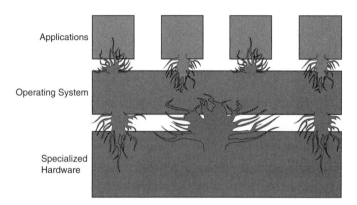

Figure 20-4   *Despite the claims of manufacturers, their code stacks are irrevocably intertwined.*

These systems also increase the level of complexity even beyond that which is caused by the distribution of control. Recall that each one of these devices literally has millions of lines of code that sit on various versions of hardware and memory, and all of this complexity, well… it's complex.

This is part of the reason that innovation is slower than most users want and customization is difficult (for multiple users on a common network), because each of the major networking companies is faced with the same complexity issues, and any new application that comes along must be compatible among all the different vendors' gear. The compatibility issue is addressed through standards bodies, but even so, getting a new application designed, and then reviewed and then produced, can take years.

It's worth noting here that this is not the result of some nefarious plot by the big networking companies. When these systems were first created, there was a great deal of innovation and collaboration that rapidly changed the business and communication landscapes over the course of two decades. In fact, it's still going on, and it's actually quite remarkable. The issue is that what is really needed today are programmable networks, rather than networks where a collection of devices are individually programmed.

The hard part of this is that using a centralized controller to program the network potentially requires network vendors to open their code up to the public, not something they are willing to do. Fortunately, there are some workarounds to this, as we discuss in the part on controllers. In fact, you'll see most of the big networking vendors are supportive of the SDN initiative even though it means a change in their business and a loss of some market control.

How SDN Works

The preceding chapter discussed the lack of programmability with traditional networks and noted that the key to transforming networks is to decouple the control plane (software) from the data plane (hardware). In doing so, we can provide centralized control and enjoy the benefits of a programmable network. Accommodating this new model involves two key steps.

First, we want the control of the network to be centralized rather than having each device as its own island. This greatly simplifies network discovery, connectivity, and control, all of which are complex and problematic in large traditional networks. Having overarching control actually makes the whole network programmable instead of having to individually configure each device every time an application is added or something moves. It's the difference between a general telling a whole army to march north versus a general telling one soldier to whisper "march north" to the soldier next to him. The first method results in orderly movement; the second creates chaos that may eventually lead to the army moving in a north-ish direction.

Second, we want to have a clear delineation between the network operating system and the applications that run on it, through a well-defined application programming interface (API). This makes it possible for third parties to develop applications quickly and easily, which as mentioned in the preceding chapter allows for a pace of innovation beyond what large vendors are able to achieve. This is also a big change in networking. Applications need to talk to network control systems way more than they did a decade ago. Allowing this to happen without have to wait for large vendors to work through their very long development cycles is a big plus.

As simple as it sounds, this is exactly what software-defined networking (SDN) does.

Understanding SDN

If we take a simplified view of SDN, we can think of it as really just an extensible networking control system that allows separate applications to control the forwarding plane of network hardware through a defined API. It effectively pulls network intelligence out of the many network devices and places it in the hands of a central authority. In the military example earlier, SDN is the mechanism that lets the general give an order to all the troops at once instead of letting an order trickle through the ranks slowly and randomly.

Figure 21-1 shows a simple network diagram for a traditional network. In this case, each switch/router has applications loaded on to it, and each one must be programed individually. In this case, applications could include intrusion detection, monitoring, Voice over IP (VoIP), and load balancing. As traffic flows through the network, each switch/router makes decisions on where to route packets based on the local logic. In this network, any changes to applications or flows must be systematically programed into each switch/router.

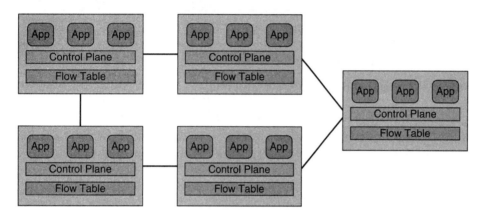

Figure 21-1   *In a traditional network, each device includes both control plane and a forwarding plane. Each also has applications loaded on to it, and each device must be separately configured.*

Figure 21-2 illustrates an SDN. In this case, the applications and the intelligence are removed from the switch/router. A centralized controller becomes the control plane for all devices, which makes the network programmable. Applications interface with the controller, and their functions are applied across the network.

Traffic flows are now under the supervision of a centralized controller that distributes and manages a flow table to each switch/router. Flow tables can be based on a number of factors, and there's a lot of flexibility in how they can be defined.

The flow table also collects statistics, which are fed up to the controller. This improves both visibility and control of the network because issues are immediately reported to the controller, which, in turn, can make immediate adjustments across the entire network.

Figure 21-3 shows a logical view of SDN. One of the cool things about SDN is that because most applications are not residing on the actual devices, and most only interface with them through the controller, the network appears to be one big switch/router. (Note that some applications are just nodes on the network.) There could be 3 devices on the network or 30,000. To centralized applications, it's all the same. This makes upgrades, changes, adds, and configurations much, much simpler than they used to be.

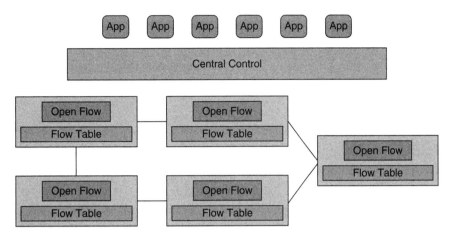

Figure 21-2 *With SDN, a centralized controller is used to program flows for the entire network. Applications interface with the controller, and services are applied where they are desired.*

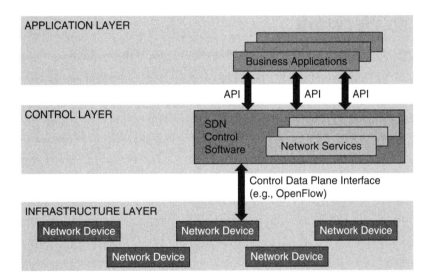

Figure 21-3 *Centralized applications and a programmable network make the network much more adaptive and responsive because changes have to be accounted for only in a single controller.*

The Application Layer

As the name suggests, this layer includes the network applications. These can include communication applications such as VoIP prioritization, security applications such as firewalls, and many others. This layer also includes network services and utilities.

In traditional networks, these applications were handled by the switches and routers. SDN allows us to offload them, making them easier to manage. It also means that the hardware can be stripped down, saving companies a lot of money on networking gear

The Control Layer

What used to be the control plane of the switches and routers is now centralized. This allows for a programmable network. OpenFlow is an open source network protocol that the industry seems to have settled on, although the big network vendors (such as Cisco) have their own variants.

The Infrastructure Layer

This layer includes the physical switches and routers and the data. Traffic is moved based on flow tables. This layer is largely unchanged in SDN because the routers and the switches are still moving packets around. The big difference is that the traffic flow rules are managed centrally. This is not to say that the actual intelligence is stripped out of vendor devices. In fact, many of the big network providers accommodate SDN centralized control via an application programming interface (API) to protect their intellectual property. That said, it is possible to use generic packet forwarding devices built specifically for SDN at a much lower cost than traditional networking gear.

A Programmable Network

Taking this one step further, developers have added a virtualization layer between the hardware layer and the control system so that network administrators can easily create "slices" that allow generic networking hardware to support multiple separate configurations in the same way that a hypervisor allows for multiple virtual machines (VMs) on a single server. In other words, with SDN an admin can create one set of (forwarding) rules and applications for one group of users, and an entirely different set of (forwarding) rules and applications for another set of users.

See Figure 21-4. This allows network administrators to pick and choose which applications they want to allow (and where), based on the needs of user types (or groups) rather than treating all users the same or having to individually program every device individually (every time there is a change). SND, in effect, allows you to create multiple virtual networks on a common infrastructure.

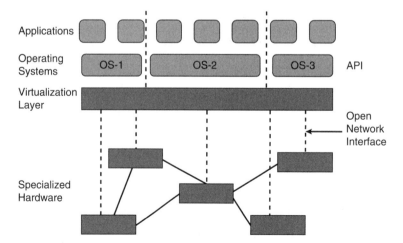

Figure 21-4 *With SDN, you can create multiple virtual networks on a common infrastructure.*

Recall from the chapter on virtual machines that a VM is a self-contained app-OS combination that is abstracted from the server. SDN can be thought of as the virtualization of the network. It frees network administrators from having to reconfigure hundreds of network devices in a cloud or backbone network every time a new application, networking device, or VM is added. What's more is that SDN allows us to take full advantage of server virtualization and cloud computing; it eliminates the chokepoint that inhibited the full power of virtualization from being harnessed.

So What's the "So What?"

The big takeaway here is that SDN makes it really easy (well, much easier than it used to be) for network operators to provide customized, isolated services for individuals that use the network. With SDN, the *network owners* have all (or at least most) of the power and control by gaining the ability to customize their networks. For example, they can get rid of features they don't use; quickly and easily isolate parts of their networks (or users or types of traffic) from other parts or users or types for efficiency, performance, and security; or create customized applications. Again, the key here is centralized control and programmability.

It's also a good bet that SDN will result in an increased rate of innovation. (It's well known that if you let users create applications, they will…in fact they will create lots of them.) Chances are this will result in some real breakthroughs, too; it should be an exciting time for networking. It's worth noting that this will not diminish the value of the large vendors creating applications. It will actually add to it, and it will help the vendors be more innovative as well. This is a case where more is more and it's also better. From a cloud networking perspective, network virtualization in the form of SDN will accelerate cloud providers almost as much as server virtualization has.

As shown in Figure 21-5, with SDN the entire network can be virtualized. The use of centralized controller software (such as OpenFlow) allows programmable control of how VMs connected with each other or with users. It also allows logical (and location independent) groupings to be created quickly and easily. This is something that was complex, slow, and error prone in traditional networks where device-by-device configuration was required.

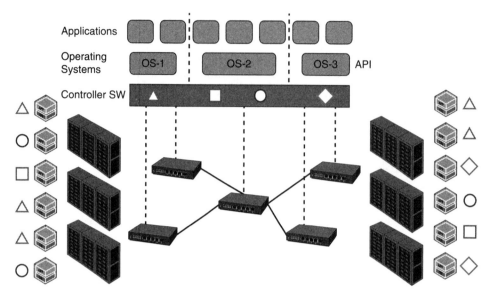

Figure 21-5 *SDN allows programmable control of how VMs connect with each other or with users. It also allows logical (and location independent) groupings to be created quickly and easily.*

The really big takeaway, though, is that SDN will make networking a lot less complex, which will also make networks faster, more reliable, more agile, and more secure. No one intended for current models of networking to become massively complex and generally at odds with the way that the customers want to use and move data around. The reality is that networking based on distributed control, intertwined hardware-software systems, and stacked code bases is approaching the end of its useful life. SDN, with its centralized control, virtualized applications, and programmable networks, has emerged to take us into the next golden era of networking.

SDN and NFV Benefits

SDN AND NFV ARE
RELATED BUT NOT
THE SAME

DRIVERS FOR SDN/NFV

CARRIER CHALLENGES

- Decreasing revenue to cost ratios
- Slow service velocity
- Vendor lock-in
- Exploring traffic demand

DATA CENTER TRENDS

- Virtualization is the norm
- Rapid tech advances
- General purpose servers preferred

BENEFITS

Increased Service Velocity	Opex Savings	Capex Predictability	Elastic Scaling	Vendor Independence

SDN

- Separates control plane from data plane
- API driven forwarding rules
- Stateful L4-L7 is critical
- Came from data center world
- Standardization efforts in open networking forum (ONF)

NFV

- Decouples HW from SW
- Flexible network function deployment
- Focused on L3-L7 OSI
- Initiated and driven by carriers
- Standardization efforts in ERSI-NFV ISG

The Economic Impact of SDN, NFV, and the Cloud

There is endless marketing chatter about software-defined networking (SDN), network functions virtualization (NFV), and the cloud, and the gist of most of it is that "this is a good thing, and lots of people/companies are going to make or save a bunch of money." Although this might be true, it's not exactly useful information. Mostly it sounds like combinations of buzzwords and generalizations. In this chapter, we sort out the marketing blurbs from the economic realities by focusing on three subtopics:

■ **Winners:** These are the folks who directly benefit from SDN and the cloud. Who are they, and what benefits do they gain?

■ **Losers:** As with any disruptive technology, not everyone will be better off because of it. It's worth trying to understand who these folks are and why/how they lose out.

■ **The overall economic impact:** When you strip away specific individuals and look at the larger economic picture, you get a better understanding of the true economics of SDN, NFV, and the cloud.

Winners in SDN, NFV, and the Cloud

It turns out that almost everybody wins when it comes to these new technologies, and this should be a surprise to no one. In fact, there are so many winners that it is best to break this section into a few pieces.

How the "Little Guy" Wins

For all the talk about how large enterprises and government agencies will save "gazillions" of dollars on SDN, NFV, and the cloud, it's also the little guy who wins. *Little guy* here refers to the pair of college kids who have a great idea for a new application, or the start-up that wants to ramp up development, or the small but growing company that wants to invest in a customer relationship management (CRM) system or other business application. What SDN, NFV, and cloud networking allows them all to do is get the benefits of owning the resources it would take to accomplish their goals without actually making the large capital investment that those resources once required. This, in turn, allows them to invest that capital elsewhere (or allows them to avoid raising expensive outside capital). Let's run through an example or two to illustrate this.

Two college students developing an application:

> Jeff and Carol have this great idea for an application that helps couples settle arguments. They have the skills to do the programming themselves. They do some preliminary research and estimate that the server and the operating system they need is on the order of $5,000—not an amount they have readily available. They also need to connect the server to the Internet, so they'll need a contract with an Internet service provider (ISP) for a business-grade connection, which will cost several hundred dollars a month. They probably cannot get their parents to help out either, because it's all they can do to keep up with the tuition.

> With SDN, NFV, and cloud networking, however, they can rent the computing resources they need on a "pay as you go" model that is easily affordable on their budget; it starts out at about $30 per month. Additional bandwidth is built in and available at any time, and they only pay for it if their app gets a lot of traffic (and thus hopefully makes money). This is within their budget, and they can be up and running (and coding) literally within minutes.

The start-up considering a data center:

> Spackler Industries is a software development company that has been steadily growing. They now find themselves with multiple sites, each with multiple servers. It's clear that the inefficiencies of distributed servers, as well as the risks of inconsistent backups, is bad and will get worse as the company grows. They need to invest in their own data center, one that will meet not only today's needs but also accommodate the two- to three-year growth that the company expects. The problem is that rent on the 1000 square foot building will be around $25,000 per month, plus the upfront cost of retrofitting the building to accommodate the required power and cooling (not to mention the racks, servers, build out, licenses, and power). The network will require fiber-optic connectivity to the nearest fiber line, which will cost tens of thousands of dollars and require tractors and lots of conduit. By the time the company adds it all up, they are looking at a minimum of a million dollars of upfront and ongoing costs, which will require additional funding. Based on this, they rethink their plans.

> With SDN, NFV, and cloud networking, however, this same company can enter into an upgradable contract for the computing resources they need. Not only does this eliminate the upfront costs, but it also allows them to very quickly and easily scale their compute and storage resources up or down. The networking problem goes away; not only do they avoid paying for Internet bandwidth, they also avoid paying for the cost of redundant switches to interconnect their multiple servers with each other in a data center. They can also customize which applications they use on the network based on what they actually need rather than on what the vendors give them. In fact, this type of service allows them

to gain access to the maximum amount of resources laid out in their business plan for growth rather than the minimum. This plan could allow them to hire more development engineers as opposed to buying servers, networking gear, and long-haul bandwidth, and then paying to maintain them.

There are a couple of implications here worth pointing out (one pretty obvious, another not so much). The obvious one is the preservation of capital. Money is expensive, it's hard to make money over costs, and it's sometimes even harder to raise it from an external source. For years, though, companies, start-ups, and entrepreneurs had to find a way to fund development, and these efforts took a lot of time and effort and often resulted in great dilution of ownership or loss of control. In many ways, SDN, NFV, and cloud networking has eliminated the capital barriers to computing resources, or at least it has drastically decreased the threshold to obtain the benefits of having them. It's not a stretch to say today's start-up can spend $10,000 to get what would have cost the founders of Hotmail or Google $10,000,000.

In fact, networking is so fundamental to cloud and data centers that it was a networking problem that drove the creation of the first modern cloud computing company, Exodus Communications. In the mid-1990s, the founders of Hotmail (now owned by Microsoft) built a tiny data center by putting some servers under a desk in their start-up offices and paying a lot of money to the phone company for a T1 (a 1.5-Mbps broadband network) connection. The problem was that their e-mail service was so popular that they needed a lot more T1 lines. So, they called the phone company to get more T1 lines, but the phone company said it would take six to eight weeks to install another network connection.

The Hotmail founders quickly realized that they could add servers to their popular service much more quickly than the phone company could string copper or fiber to their start-up headquarters. To keep from going out of business (because they could not meet the high demand), they approached a local ISP and asked to put Hotmail servers next to the Internet backbone network, instead of taking the time to bring the network to the servers. Thus, the colocation model was born. It was so economically addictive that it grew that service provider (Exodus) into the top-performing stock on the NASDAQ only three years later, with more than a billion dollars in revenue and 42 data centers globally.

So you see, it was the network limitations that caused colocation to form, and it was colocation that created the infrastructure for modern cloud services, both software as a service (SaaS) and infrastructure as a service (IaaS), to evolve. SDN, NFV, and cloud networking are the result of users taking control back.

Another implication of the rapid growth of networks and data centers is that because these compute resources are so inexpensive to obtain, demand grows, which increases the overall amount of innovation (this is the not so obvious benefit). Because the cost of the resources is so low (and by extension, there is a much lower risk associated with "misusing" them), users tend to be more risky, which actually improves the overall quality of innovation as more users "push the envelope." Real breakthroughs happen when smart people make connections no one has made before and very few can see in advance. But these types of innovations tend to come after long strings of "failures." Inexpensive and flexible resources make failures much easier (and less expensive) to deal with, which improves innovation.

How Large Enterprises Win with SDN, NFV, and the Cloud

If you've read anything at all about the economic impact of these technologies, what you read was likely from the enterprise perspective. In Part 1, "Virtualization 101: The Basics of Virtualization," you read about issues with the static server model; companies had to build out data centers to the expected maximum usage, which, of course, is terribly inefficient. This point might be better explained with the following diagrams.

As you can see by the shaded area of Figure 22-1, there is a great deal of inefficiently used resources, but this is only part of the problem.

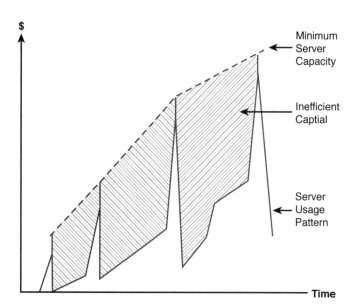

Figure 22-1   *Traditional server utilization is economically inefficient.*

The other issue with companies that have this usage pattern (and there are a lot of them) is that they have to house the equipment, power it all, cool it all, maintain full-time personnel to run and maintain it, and several other costs that trend up and to the right. This is shown in Figure 22-2. Just the cabling alone is hundreds of thousands of dollars for a modest-sized data center. From an economist's and CFO's perspective, this is obviously a lousy model, but it's the one pretty much everyone adopted. The question is why.

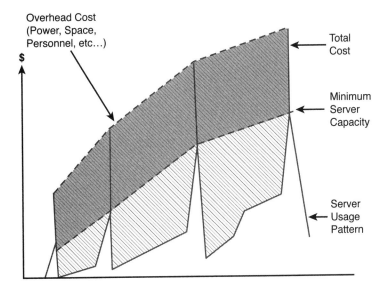

Figure 22-2   *Total data center cost*

This looks like a pretty lousy model, but the reason everyone put up with this inefficiency is that companies were making a lot of money through the use of all these servers despite the inefficiencies and overhead. As shown in Figure 22-3, all the numbers were going "up and to the right;" so while organizations were spending more money, they were also making more money in proportion and buying more servers and network equipment and hiring more people, and it was more, more, more, which is great while it lasts, but it usually does not last that long.

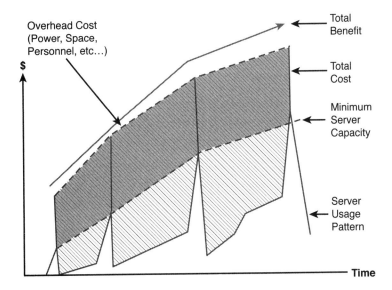

Figure 22-3   *Data center costs versus benefits*

Typically what happens is that the benefit of a new technology reaches the point of diminishing returns, which means that the relative amount of benefit received becomes less than the cost of achieving that benefit. At that point, it stops making sense to keep investing in that benefit, as illustrated in Figure 22-4. The problem, however, is that it's not that easy to stop if you are a large company seeing customer growth or you have a committed development schedule. In many cases, there is a very high barrier to exit. In other words, they are stuck.

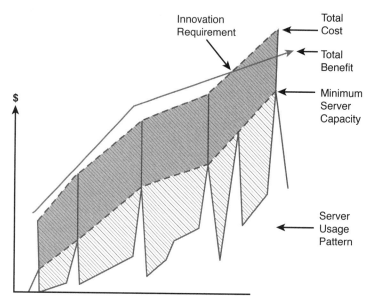

Figure 22-4   *Data center diminishing returns.*

The good news is that this particular system was massively inefficient due to the combination of very high overhead costs and the bursty usage patterns, which required companies to maintain assets that supported an infrequent and disproportionate peak-usage pattern. This model was ripe for innovation because there was still a great deal of money to be made; we just needed to get rid of all the very expensive overhead.

This is exactly what SDN, NFV, and cloud networking technologies do for large companies or organizations that traditionally maintained large data centers. With SDN and cloud networking, you can basically rent the capacity and decrease the cost without decreasing the revenue derived from using less-expensive resources, as shown in Figure 22-5.

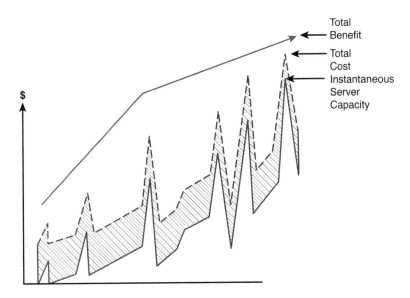

Figure 22-5   *The cloud cost versus benefit.*

From the user's perspective, cloud networking technologies enable them to maintain the same bursty (but increasing) usage pattern by renting the resources on an as-needed basis, without all the other costs. Virtualization allows the hosting companies to remove a lot of the inefficiencies of dedicated servers. The cloud networking model allows them to offer these computing resources to clients in a way that saves the users a lot of money while at the same time making a good amount of money for the providers. The SDN model eliminates the networking inefficiencies and the expensive vendor-driven solutions.

Losers in the Cloud

With all the hype around the cloud, it's easy to forget that there are some individuals and companies who will lose out. It's worth spending a few paragraphs on them.

First and foremost, there are some individuals whose lives are disrupted in this shift. If you are part of an IT staff that gets drastically reduced because the company you work for decides to outsource their one huge data center to a cloud provider, you might not be all that excited about the shift. In some cases, it's not that disruptive because IT skills have remained in high demand, but macrostatistics don't matter for much if you're the one who gets a pink slip.

At the company level, some lose out, too. Local power companies can lose revenue when big data centers (and big-paying customers) wind down their operations. Server companies and companies that make server operating system software can lose out, too, because big cloud providers often prefer to use commodity servers that run their own software. These companies need to find alternative lines of revenue or risk having to go out of business.

Other potential losers are companies that adopt cloud technologies when they don't really need to, which wastes time and money—both of which could be spent elsewhere. It should not come as a surprise that in some cases it is perfectly okay to keep using a dedicated server. The old adage applies here: If it isn't broken, don't fix it. Still, some will get caught up in the hype and waste precious resources converting to cloud and SDN when what they have works perfectly fine.

On the whole, there are far fewer losers than there are winners, and in a macro sense, the economy as a whole is better off in the shift to cloud and SDN. Economic theory holds that big picture gains trump individual losses, but as mentioned earlier, if you're the person who loses his or her job, or if it's your company that goes under in one of these technology shifts, it's hard to see the greater good in that moment.

The Economic Value of Increased Innovation

Classical economics theory holds that the accumulation of capital is the primary driver of economic growth and that additional inputs into a process will drive higher rates of productivity, which in turn allow the creation of more capital. This "virtuous cycle" basically says that if you have more money, you can buy more parts, to make more widgets, which you can sell to make more money, which you can use to buy more parts (and on and on). It's not quite that simple, of course, and there are limits (the diminished point of returns and such), but that's pretty much the gist of it.

According to this way of thinking, the primary economic benefit of the cloud would be derived from the additional capital that organizations enjoy from the savings of using cloud and SDN technologies. In other words, we could quantify the total economic value of the cloud by adding up all the "areas under the curve" (the solid shaded section in Figure 22-6) for all the companies taking advantage of the technology. This is the simplified version of the recovered capital that the cloud model gives us, and it's a really big number.

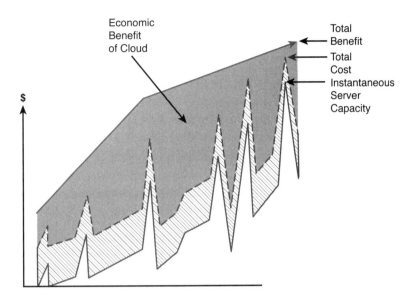

Figure 22-6   *Capital benefits of the cloud*

What's interesting, though, is that as big as that number is, it might not even be the main driver of the real economic value of the cloud. The theory that explains this view is the relatively new school of thought called *innovation economics*. This theory states that it's not the accumulation of capital that drives economic growth but rather the innovative capacity of a market that is the primary growth driver. And the cloud and SDN enable boatloads of innovative capacity (in addition to all the newly freed-up capital discussed earlier).

As mentioned previously, the cloud/SDN model will allow large companies to consume more computing resources, which provides an increase (likely a linear one) in innovation. In addition, the low cost of cloud resources de-risks the consumption of those resources, which goes a long way in fostering innovation within large companies, which tend to be risk averse. At the other end of the spectrum, the cloud and SDN allow access to very powerful innovation tools (formerly expensive computing and networking resources) to those who tend to be big risk takers, such as start-ups and entrepreneurs. These players are often the drivers of disruptive innovation, but they typically lack the capital required to put their ideas into action. Inexpensive computing and networking resources can be viewed as driving an increase in the overall pool of active innovators, which according to the theory will drive more growth than what the freed-up capital from less-expensive computing costs would enable on its own.

In others words, it is a good bet that all this innovation will drive a lot more innovation.

Cloud Networking Economics

The Real Impact on the Economy

The benefits of data centers and advanced computing are well known, which is why everyone is so interested in it.

The problem is, it's really expensive.

On-going costs of people and power…

…which is incurred even when they're idle.

This limited who could use the data center, and there was an awful lot of waste.

All of this limited innovation is because the expense and the risk of loss was high. It also kept the "little guys" out who tend to be the best innovators.

Cloud networking greatly lowers the cost barriers to big computing power, which means less risk, and less costs, leading to more innovation from more people—and more innovation means greater economic growth.

SDN Controllers

SDN Controllers

Much of what has been discussed previously has focused on SDN, but has only skirted around the devices that make SDN possible: SDN controllers. We know from the SDN architecture that the controller is the keystone, the top of the architecture hierarchy, which serves as the brain of the system. However, what is not so clear is how that controller functions or even fits into our network topology.

This section looks at how controllers function and how they play an integral part in regulating the data flow between the application layer (the applications we use) and the physical layer (the routers and switches our data has to cross). For instance, if you are going to replace the control layer of every device—router or switch—you must have another means of centralized control. That is where the central controller comes into play.

Centralized Control

The controller is a centralized "brain" in the network; it will have a global view of all the network devices, their interconnections, and the best paths between hosts. Having this single global map of the network enables the controller to make swift, intelligent, and agile decisions with regard to flow direction, control, and speedy network reconciliation when a link fails. As shown in Figure 23-1, the network no longer has to converge, through multiple devices in the network swapping routing tables, running an algorithm, before they update their routing tables and then recalculate the preferred routes. After all, the time to converge in a network is as follows

The time to detect a failure + the time to announce a failure to all parties + the time to run the algorithm + the time to update the databases in each device

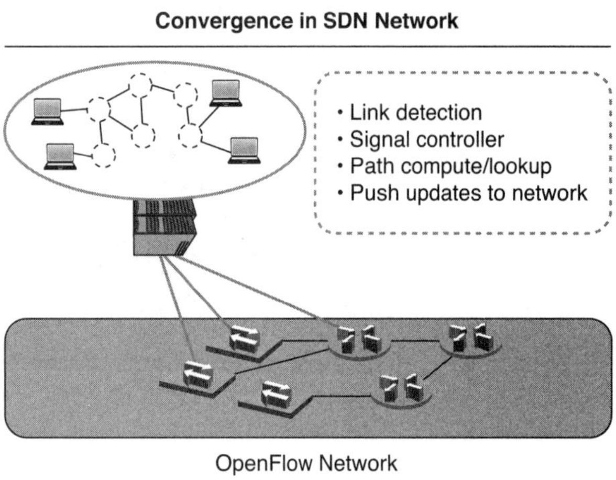

Convergence in SDN Network

- Link detection
- Signal controller
- Path compute/lookup
- Push updates to network

OpenFlow Network

Figure 23-1 *Network convergence is much more efficient in SDN.*

However, in a software-defined network (SDN), the controller already has a global view of the entire network and a selection of predefined alternative routes (flows) for every link so that it can fail over to an alternative route quicker and more gracefully than a traditional routing protocol such as Open Shortest Path First (OSPF) or Enhanced Interior Gateway Routing Protocol (EIGRP). After all, it doesn't have to recompute the shortest path for every link; it already knows them, and therefore there is no time required to run a routing protocol algorithm or update the routing tables—which is not an inconsiderable time during network convergence.

Commercial Versus Open Source Controllers

If the controller is going to be the brains of the network, we have to consider how we get from where we are today with a traditional network topology to an SDN centralized network. This is where controllers come into play, and they are hugely important. So, let's look at some of the open source and commercial versions available:

Commercial controllers

- Cisco Application Policy Infrastructure Controller (APIC)

  The Cisco APIC acts as a central point of control, data, and policy and provides a central API.

- HP Virtual Application Networks (VAN) SDN Controller

  This uses OpenFlow to control forwarding decisions and policy in an SDN topology.

- NEC ProgrammableFlow PF6800 Controller

  The NEC controller is programmable and standardized in that it integrates with both OpenFlow and Microsoft System Virtual Machine Manager.

- VMware NSX Controller

  This product is a distributed control system that can control virtual networks and overlay transport tunnels over the existing infrastructure. The controller communicates with the applications to ascertain their requirements before configuring all the vSwitches.

Open source controllers

- OpenDaylight open source SDN controller

  OpenDaylight can provide centralized control over any vendor equipment. This is the subject of the next chapter.

- OpenContrail SDN controller

  This controller is actually a stem from Juniper's commercial offering and can be used as a platform for network virtualization under open source licensing.

- Floodlight

  This is a Java-based controller for SDN that supports a range of OpenFlow virtual or real switches. It is part of the Big Switch open source project and has been successfully used in a number of SDN projects (for example, the OpenStack Quantum plug-in and the Floodlight virtual switch).

- Ryu OpenFlow Controller

  Ryu is an open source SDN controller framework that supports several protocols, including OpenFlow, Netconf, and OF-config.

- Flowvisor

  This is a specialist OpenFlow controller that acts as a go-between for OpenFlow switches and multiple OpenFlow Controllers.

Although there is a choice between a commercial and an open source controller, most operational SDN deployments use a mixture of vendor-sponsored projects—and not surprisingly, there are some common requirements that all SDN controllers should meet. For example, all controllers should support features such as the OpenFlow protocol, which vendors have adopted for southbound application programming interfaces (APIs) to their switches. To support OpenFlow, it is a requirement for the switch to be able to understand the contents of the OpenFlow header. This is because when a packet enters an OpenFlow switch, it is first compared to existing entries in the flow control table. If the switch cannot find a match, the packet is sent to the SDN controller. The controller then has to make a decision on whether to drop or forward the packet by creating a new flow defined by a programmable policy.

Network Virtualization

Another essential feature of a controller is the ability to support network virtualization, because this is one of the most important aspects of SDN. Network virtualization is nothing new; there have been VLANs (virtual local-access networks) and VRF (virtual routing and forwarding) for many years, but both are limited in scope. For true network virtualization, there is a requirement to abstract and pool network resources in a similar manner to server virtualization. This is illustrated in Figure 23-2. The capability enables tenant-specific virtual networks to be designed and constructed over the physical infrastructure, ensuring complete isolation of traffic flows.

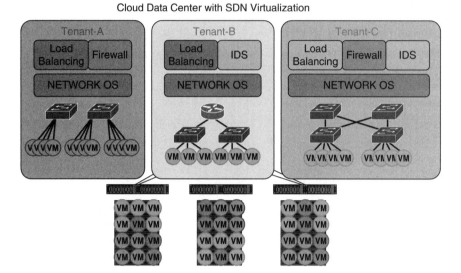

Figure 23-2 *For network virtualization, there is a requirement to abstract and pool network resources in a similar manner to server virtualization.*

Isolation of tenant traffic is not just the concern of cloud service providers, it is also relevant to enterprise and data center solutions. Security is an issue with all sizes of business. Furthermore, government regulatory compliance that demands the separation of financially sensitive information, such as Sarbanes-Oxley (SOX), is just one example. However, there are other reasons why network traffic should be isolated. For example, traffic isolation provides the opportunity to apply different levels of quality of service (QoS) on a flow basis.

Subsequently, having the ability to isolate and apply policy on a flow-per-flow basis allows a controller to determine per-flow best routing. The controller can establish the best routes from a source to a destination. In fact, a controller can even determine multiple routes and load balance across them if appropriate. Having multiple routes from a source to a destination also provides for network redundancy as the controller can redirect traffic flows instantly. This functionality can do away with the need for higher protocols such as TRILL (transparent interconnection of lots of links) and SPB (shortest path bridging), which address both the functions and restrictions of the Spanning Tree Protocol (STP). You'll recall that STP is required in Layer 2 networks to detect and prevent loops, but is a major inhibitor to Layer 2 network scalability.

Consequently, a controller should be able to handle network scalability by managing the network as if it was one device. A controller, by having a global view of the network, can mitigate looping issues and provide efficient east-west traffic flows not feasible with the traditional multitiered (north-south) architecture. However, large-scale Layer 2 flat networks also have issues, one such issue being the proliferation of MAC addresses in the content-addressable memory (CAM) and Address Resolution Protocol (ARP) tables. An SDN controller should be able to mitigate this problem by minimizing the number of flows in the flow table entries. This is typically achieved by using techniques such as header rewrite in the core of the network, which is similar to provider backbone bridging (PBB). This technique replaces the source MAC address in the header with that of the core ingress device, greatly reducing the number of entries stored in the tables.

Moreover, a controller should have the ability to set up the required number of flows and maintain them. Therefore, two of the key performance indicators for an SDN controller are flow set up time and the number of flows it can handle per second. These are very important key performance Indicators (KPIs) with regard to performance. However, it is not quite as simple as beefing up the controllers' processing power, because the processing power of the individual switches, which they control, play a part. Similarly, the OS on which the controller runs can be an issue. For example, a controller running on C tends to run faster than one running on Java, but Java is often preferred by developers.

Programmability is another major consideration for controllers. As you have seen, some operating systems run faster than others do, but that is only part of the equation. The whole purpose of SDN is to programmatically control the network, and to do this there must be a programmable interface that is familiar to the company's programmers. There must also be APIs supported that control the switches (southbound) and those that control the upper-layer applications (northbound). The more APIs that the controller supports makes it far more flexible, and in the case of northbound APIs allows the applications to dynamically configure the network to their specific requirements.

These are just some of the main features that a controller should support; another obvious one is centralized administration and monitoring. However, to look into the workings of the controller in more detail, we need to consider one of the most industry accepted SDN controllers in closer detail. Consequently, in the next chapter, we look at OpenDaylight's version of an SDN controller.

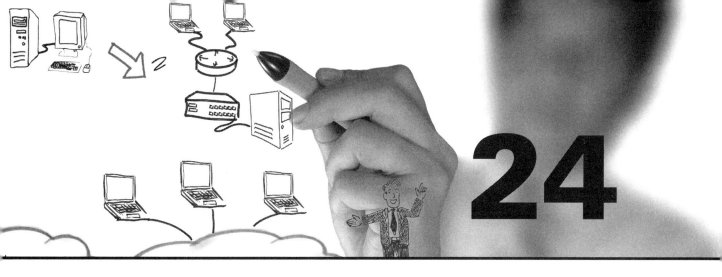

The OpenDaylight Project

The OpenDaylight (ODL) project was initiated in 2013 when The Linux Foundation (TLF) announced the funding of a community-led SDN open source framework. One of the more interesting aspects of this project kickoff was that the founding members consisted of some of the heavyweight vendors such as IBM, Cisco, HP, Big Switch Networks, Arista Networks, Microsoft, Brocade, and Juniper, among others. Furthermore, these giants were prepared to not only throw their considerable technical resources behind the project but also to finance and support the aspirations of this SDN open source project. This, of course, raised some skepticism, because it was not clear as to what end these vendors were working; some had clearly different visions of their approach to SDN. Among the open source crowd (who tend to be outspoken), this caused some consternation at the time. It was felt that major sponsors could actually hinder rather than promote innovation—especially in this case where there were some obvious conflicts of interest.

Another point of concern was the lack of what is now the Open Network Foundation (ONF), which is a nonprofit organization that forms around open source technologies. Consisting of consumers and developers, the ONF is attempting to be a standards body for SDN. In addition, several of the major router/switch manufacturers had strategic technological and business goals that seemed incompatible with many of the ODL partners. Many vendors also had conflicting interests and alternative development projects in the pipeline, which used different protocols. As a result, many industry analysts predicted that these players would be reluctant to fully engage in the project.

These doubts proved to be unfounded, and since the ODL initiation in 2013, ODL has had three major releases. These releases included the first version of code (called Hydrogen) in 2013, Helium in 2014, and Lithium in 2015. As a result, despite the initial skepticism, ODL has respect and acceptance from vendors, users, and analysts alike.

So, what are the ODL project and the current Lithium version in particular, and how does it get us from being a traditional hierarchal network to being an SDN?

The ideals of the ODL project are to further the adoption and innovation of the SDN through a common framework, as shown in Figure 24-1. As noted in the diagram, the framework defines the key APIs for both the applications that run on the network and for the traffic flows (the instructions for the switches on how to forward packets). This framework makes it possible for many vendors to work together, and ideally to be interchangeable.

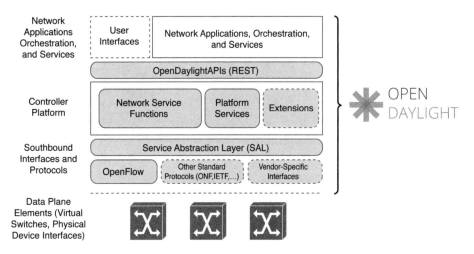

Figure 24-1   *ODL common framework for SDN*

That goal of adoption and innovation of the SDN through a common framework can be interpreted as a purpose to create code that is open source and available for all to use. Another important goal was acceptance, through vendors supporting and using ODL as a product. By signing up to the ODL project, vendors committed to that goal, which future-proofed ODL for users. It also proved to be a great incentive to get many vendors as well. After all, with all their competitors onboard, no one wanted to walk away and relinquish their seat at the table. Consequently, having all the major vendors onboard prevented any single vendor or alliance from influencing the direction of the project roadmap. Of course, at the time, the SDN market was very fragmented, and still is. Not surprisingly, most vendors agreed on the position of the goal line, but not how to get there. As is the norm in this case, each vendor has their own projects under way and will fight for implementations that closely resemble what they are already doing. In addition, there is also the case of the product's investment potential and the coding community's interest and, of course, their subsequent support; no open source project can thrive without the support of the community. However, open source has a poor reputation within some enterprises; the support of powerful sponsors went a long way to alleviating this problem. It is worth noting that acceptance among enterprises to use open source software, even for critical systems, is growing and becoming the norm.

To understand why this unlikely alliance of powerful competitors came to support an open source project in such numbers, we need to look at the ODL manifesto. After all, ODL as a project was designed to fulfill the following:

■ Design a framework for delivering a network architecture that can deliver diverse applications and customer experience

■ Provide the means for a programmable network

■ Abstract the control plane logic from network devices into a centralized entity

The final aspiration would cause some problems, because it is not in the interest of major manufacturers of switches to dumb down their products. Subsequently, the ODL initiative designed the ODL controller to support both a centralized and distributed model. The latter topology might seem to be out of step with SDN, but there are rational reasons why there might be several, if not many, SDN controllers in a network. Hardware redundancy and the avoidance of a single point of failure are two such reasons. To mitigate these potential issues, controllers are often deployed in a cluster configuration. Of course, this only applies to a data center deployment; when considering a regional or global network, a distributed architecture becomes a necessity.

So, let's look at how the ODL architecture works.

How the ODL Architecture Works

The ODL controller, as you have seen, sits between the application layers and the data (packet forwarding) layers. This is important because it provides the mechanisms to control both upstream and downstream traffic flows.

Upstream traffic flows are delivered via northbound APIs (application programmable interfaces), and they interface with the high-layer applications. Southbound APIs are used to interface with and control the individual switches to influence their traffic flows (see Figure 24-2).

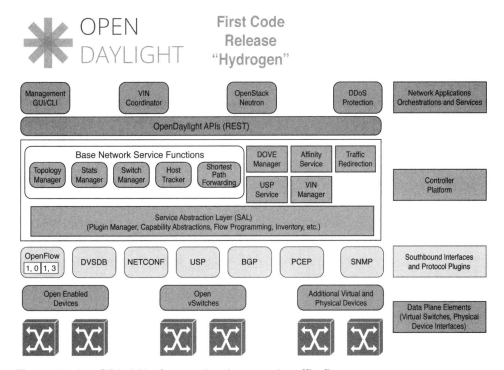

Figure 24-2 *ODL APIs for applications and traffic flows*

To understand how ODL operates, it is first useful to take a black-box approach and consider only the ODL interfaces. The ODL controller acts as a service abstraction layer that mediates between southbound and northbound communications. ODL sits between the applications (northbound) and the lower-layer switches (southbound). ODL accomplishes this using APIs, which are programmable interfaces. APIs can be considered to be snippets of code that act like templates that the application developers use to connect to the advertised (exposed) services provided by applications. Examples of these are the REST web services, but there are several others.

Northbound APIs allow applications to collect and analyze traffic data, and therefore adjust traffic flows by sending corrective signals to the network devices via the ODL controller. These northbound APIs carry the data that allows applications to dynamically adjust to their environment. Applications will analyze and collect data from the network via the northbound APIs (upstream); and, for example, if more bandwidth is required, the application can instruct the controller through the bidirectional API channel to provide that service by distributing the load. Northbound APIs provide the mechanisms that enable the programmer/application to perform dynamic rerouting, establish quality of service (QoS) levels per flow, and provide for network survivability.

Furthermore, the ODL controllers, to manage specific traffic flows, establish policy and update the switch's flow table using southbound APIs. The southbound APIs provide the interface to control the physical or virtual switches. The most commonly used, standardized, and integrated protocol in ODL is OpenFlow.

OpenFlow is a southbound API that has become synonymous with SDN. Though it is strictly a protocol, it is a vital piece of SDN architecture. That said, it doesn't really define SDN. OpenFlow will interface with the switches in the infrastructure, whether they are real or virtual, to tell the switch how to forward the individual traffic flow. It is, therefore, necessary for vendor switches to support southbound APIs such as the OpenFlow protocol.

However, to understand how the ODL controller interfaces with the network switches, we have to understand that the controller just sends updates, via southbound APIs, to that switch's forwarding table. The updates, contained within OpenFlow frames, will instruct the switch how to forward a particular traffic flow. The switch does not need to know any more; therefore, there is no requirement for a switch to have a control plane. This separation of a switch's control plane from its forwarding plane is what centralized SDN is all about. However, in the case of a distributed system proposed by the major hardware manufacturers, ODL will still send the control messages via the southbound API, but they will use a vendor proprietary API channel, and the switch's own control plane will manage the request. This ensures the intelligence remains on the switch.

The ODL Controller Platform

With an understanding of what ODL is and how it operates, let's look at the ODL controller platform. After all, the controller is the "brain" that controls both northbound interfaces and southbound interfaces, but there is much more than that to a controller's function:

- **Topology manager:** Stores and manages information about all the network devices.

- **Statistic manager:** Collects and analyzes data for each network segment. The northbound APIs also supply information (data) on switch port, flow meter, table, and group statistics.

- **Forwarding rules manager:** Manages basic forwarding rules such as through OpenFlow.

- **Host tracker:** Stores information of all entities on the network, their OS, device type, and version.

A controller, therefore, crosses the boundaries of application, development, and most importantly, networking. So, whereas ODL provides the abstraction layer between high-layer applications and lower-layer switches, and it has become successful due to its multivendor support through The Linux Foundation open source project, it has blurred the lines within DevOps. The multivendor collaboration and mutual support provided by the major manufacturers has been successfully achieved—which is no simple feat—despite initial skepticism. However, other political storms need to be weathered. One is within the organization itself: Where are the demarcation points of responsibility within networks, applications, development, and operations?

It's hard to say at this point exactly how it will all shake out, but it's a good bet that because it's a community-driven effort, the outcome will be positive and (of equal importance) continue to improve over time.

The Fight to Control Your Network

The advent of software-defined networking (SDN) has created a shift in the networking landscape, and as a result there are two main fights going on for control of the network. The first is the external "fight" in the marketplace—which company or companies will become the dominant player in the multi-billion-dollar market for networking? Will it be a traditional network player such as Cisco, a company from the server virtualization world such as VMware, or will some new company come along and become the next big thing? The previous chapters discussing controllers were about that external fight.

Interestingly enough, there is also an internal fight inside of companies as various factions try to parse out who controls what on corporate networks. This is not only a "turf war" between departments that may be looking to expand control (and budgets) but is also a legitimate concern for companies. By making the entire network programmable—from spinning up servers (virtualization), provisioning resources (network functions virtualization [NFV]), and programming paths and flows (SDN), companies have lost the ability to know and control who and what is on the network at any given time.

This is a bit of a paradox. As odd as it might seem, there was a huge benefit of having autonomous systems that required several weeks of cross-departmental collaboration to provisions apps and servers, set up security rules, and program switches and routers. Namely, there was a long lead time, during which people in authority could put a stop to activities that were deemed too risky for the company. This is the big catch with all of this technology: Although all this autonomy and speed and flexibility may be great for the users, it might not be so great for the company that owns all the repercussions of the things that are on those same networks.

Separation of Internal Controls

The fact is that networks of any size need to be controlled. Even in the smaller organization, having a single talented person (who may be able to design, build, administer, and maintain the servers, firewalls and routers) is not sustainable or even acceptable in larger networks. Businesses have responsibilities to ensure separation of duties (SoD), and it is for that reason that large companies have change control and best practices to prevent inadvertent configuration changes. The problem is that with virtualization and SDN, once-well-established boundaries blur, and what once was a server is now a router, switch, or firewall. As these technical boundaries blur, so too do the areas of responsibility, authority, and accountability that are such a critical aspect of corporate and government networks.

To establish and maintain SoD, organizations with large networks typically use silo structures with the following functions/departments:

■ Application Development

■ IT & Server Operations and Support

■ Networks

■ Security

These departmental business units operate autonomously but have to interact to provide service to the business. This model worked well before the days of fast technological development, and importantly, changes within the software development lifecycle (SDLC) could be managed at a pace that was most often faster than the pace of a technology rollout, which made change control manageable, if not cumbersome.

Typically, project teams using the SDLC waterfall methodology—which undertook major application development projects—would spend months defining the specifications and requirements. This methodology provided a detailed blueprint or SRS (software requirement specification) that the project team would adhere to (and it was the authority). However, as the technology climate changed and predefining requirements and specifications was no longer feasible due to the fast-changing nature of the marketplace, application development moved to a more agile methodology.

The agile methodology required that you started small and invested time in development of the software rather than in documentation and predesign. What this meant was that projects could be easily adaptable, always have some earned value, and be flexible to change as the market evolved. This was a wonderful change of strategy for web application development; they could change their requirements and specifications at will, but it did increase the tension between the application development and IT operational and support staff, which would, after all, have to deploy the application. Even with this faster deployment method, though, deploying a new app still took quite a while and required approval and coordination between departments.

This was, of course, not a new phenomenon. For a long time, there had been friction between application development and operations, and there were already initiatives to merge them under DevOps. Such mergers brought together development and operations only at the higher managerial level. After all, there were few MS administrators wanting to try their hand at Java programming, and vice versa. Subsequently, the DevOps initiative was successful in merging the two departments.

When SDN came into play, it also helped to aid the merger of development and operations. For example, it further reduced the time to spin up an application in a virtual environment.

That deployment lag—the time required to order, physically build, and rack servers—was significantly reduced, as was the operational burden. Now, all operations were required to do was spin up virtual machines (VMs) for applications whenever required. DevOps and virtualization was a winning combo, except they were not the only players in the game.

The network department's responsibility is to construct, monitor, and maintain the physical or wireless communication network. They accomplish this task using network management software (NMS) that interrogates switches, routers, and other network entities by querying agents about their interface status. By using Simple Network Management Protocol (SNMP), the NMS can build a map of the network's links status and, if necessary, relay alarms to the network control center agents in the network control center (NOC, pronounced "knock"). It is the NOC's responsibility to monitor and manage the network 24/7.

However, herein lies the problem: In the earlier editions, the virtual switches and hypervisors were supplied by vendors. There was no way to communicate with the NMSs: these were just dumb virtual switches. This meant that the NOC had no vision of these applications (VMs). They only had vision to monitor and support up until the last physical switch port.

To monitor and control the network, the NOC required real-time visibility of the entire network. Indeed, they required not just link status but operational status and metrics, such as bandwidth congestion levels. In short, the NOC required visibility and control of the following:

- Each endpoint where traffic can be routed

- The transport and control layer (Ethernet, IP, Layer 4, and so on)

- Every service running through those layers, and quality of service (QoS) metrics for each

However, with SDN, the controller dynamically decides the traffic flow, so it is more difficult for NMSs to track individual traffic flows from the data plane. Obviously, this was far from ideal, but vendors in response produced virtual switches, which addressed these problems, and virtual switches could then support many of the features present in a physical switch.

These intelligent vSwitches worked together with the hypervisors and gave insight into the gray area between the physical and virtual switch interfaces. These new vSwitches went a long way to resolving many of the management issues with products, such as the following:

- **Cisco Nexus 1000V Switch for VMware vSphere:** This software virtual switch worked alongside the VMware vSphere hypervisor to extend the network edge from the physical switch into the hypervisor. This provided the feature and management tools for integration of the virtual network into the physical infrastructure.

- **VSphere:** This provides the controller that works with Cisco Nexus and the VMware vSphere hypervisor and was developed jointly with Cisco.

- **Citrix Netscaler:** This again worked with the Cisco Nexus range and acts as a central controller for many distributed vSwitches in the network.

You Can See It, But Who Controls It?

These products helped to solve the visibility problem, but they did not cure all the problems; there was a deeper cause for friction, and that was the perception that each department team held. For example, application development wants their software to run fast and efficiently, whereas networks want their networks to run fast and efficiently but also to have the NOC monitor and control the status. The problem here arose from DevOps taking a pragmatic approach to application deployment.

Consider a traditional application, which included the following:

- A web server

- An application server

- A database server

Networks would traditionally build this in three layers; it was a sensible and secure architecture with a security element between them. However, the design did introduce latency. With the advent of virtualization, DevOps could and often did spin these functions up on the same physical server. What's more, they installed them so that they worked with an east-west communication path via a virtual switch. The result was that all communications ran through the host server's memory rather than having to traverse the wire, which meant the NOC had a blind spot.

In addition, although there was a performance boost, it came at the cost of security and network management. To DevOps, this newfound flexibility was wonderful, but to networks it was invisible, and to security it was a worse-case scenario.

The takeaway here is that there were unintended consequences. Although there was greater speed and agility that greatly sped application deployment, this new ability circumvented many checks and balances. Whereas once it would have taken weeks and strict change control to introduce a new application (on a dedicated server) into the data center, now a VM running an app can be spun up in minutes. As a result, there was a proliferation of unaudited VMs and unmanaged network traffic. Making the situation worse, many of these VMs were zombies, which are undocumented, unmonitored, and unmanaged application VMs.

Obviously, this was not an acceptable situation, so more control had to be applied to network management and administration, especially with respect to security. However, security cannot be merged into DevOps, for an obvious reason: IT should never control security, as it is a major conflict of interest. Security, however, cannot just have DevOps deploying applications wherever they like, regardless of the performance improvements. Again, the solution was the need for greater real-time visualization into the entire network, which was beyond traditional NMSs.

Lately, with advancements in virtualization and virtual switches in particular, many of these issues were resolved as NMSs could again see into the virtual gray area within the hypervisor and track and monitor VM installed on the physical host servers. In addition, control of the network was eventually regained by using a coming together of SDN and NFV concepts to provide the real-time tracking of dynamic service delivery traffic flows through virtual instrumentation. This technique and set of NVF tools provided the methods for the controller to tap into information on the data plane of each network device, and they effectively provided feedback to the SDN controller on the performance-monitoring data. This allows SDN to have a ubiquitous, real-time vision of the data planes, and it effectively monitors itself.

The early implementations of virtualization and SDN were fraught with problems about network control and management. These ranged from the political to the administrative to the technical. Political/administrative issues were resolved through reorganization and the merger of departments and the enforcement of policy. Technical issues, which are discussed in depth in a later chapter, such as upgrading and resolving issues with the traditional connection-oriented NMS, have also been worked out. As a result, in current deployments, the problem of controlling the network is no longer the issue it once was, but there will likely always be tension between DevOps, network teams, and security, but that's actually a good thing.

The Fight for Control of the Network

"BACK IN THE OLD DAYS"

The lines of demarcation between groups were quite clear. The IT, networking, and security teams all had clear roles, and the users were dependent on all of them.

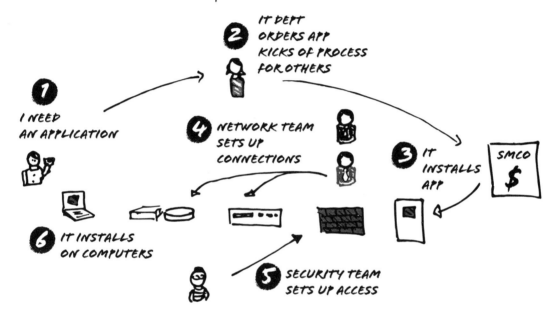

1 I NEED AN APPLICATION

2 IT DEPT ORDERS APP KICKS OF PROCESS FOR OTHERS

3 IT INSTALLS APP

4 NETWORK TEAM SETS UP CONNECTIONS

5 SECURITY TEAM SETS UP ACCESS

6 IT INSTALLS ON COMPUTERS

SMCO $

SDN AND MODERN TIMES

Today, the users can do so much themselves, and the lines have been blurred between the functional groups. It's great for the users, but the core teams are often left confused.

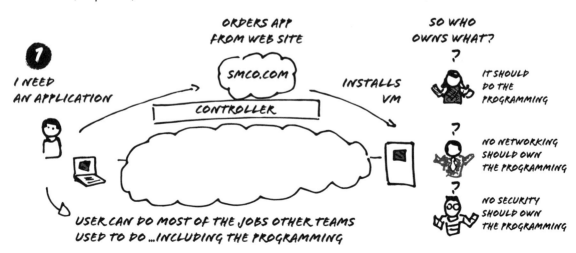

1 I NEED AN APPLICATION

ORDERS APP FROM WEB SITE

SMCO.COM

CONTROLLER

INSTALLS VM

SO WHO OWNS WHAT?

? IT SHOULD DO THE PROGRAMMING

? NO NETWORKING SHOULD OWN THE PROGRAMMING

? NO SECURITY SHOULD OWN THE PROGRAMMING

USER CAN DO MOST OF THE JOBS OTHER TEAMS USED TO DO ...INCLUDING THE PROGRAMMING

What's the Business Case for SDN?

The previous chapters covered some of the "teething" problems that deploying software-defined networking (SDN) and network functions virtualization (NFV) can introduce into the business. At this point in the technology lifecycle, there's enough information available such that a CIO can identify and define these problems during the planning stage, and there are several technologies and techniques to mitigate them. In addition, because the potential benefits of SDN and NFV clearly make this a worthwhile exercise, these problems are not going to be insurmountable. Moreover, identifying the benefits of SDN is also well understood and documented. What isn't so well defined is what the business case is for SDN.

To quickly reprise the benefits of SDN, let's consider that it will make network environments leaner and cheaper to operate and bring major improvements in application delivery, time to market, and network provisioning. Just some of the technical benefits include the following:

- Simplifying configuration and link provisioning

- Bringing network agility and increased speed of application and service deployment

- Allowing traffic engineering on a per traffic flow and service basis

- Increased application performance and user experience

- Support for the dynamic movement, replication and allocation of virtual resources

- Establishing virtual bridged Ethernet networks without complex and limited VLANs

- Enabling applications to dynamically request services from the network

- Enabling central orchestration for application delivery and provisioning

- Reducing capital expenditure (CapEx) by using white-box switches

- Deploying network applications and functionality more rapidly based on a software development lifecycle

- Easier implementation of quality of service (QoS)

- Implementing more effective security functionality on a per traffic flow basis per service

As can be seen from this incomplete list of the benefits SDN can bring to the network, building a business case would or should be a trivial matter. Unfortunately, it is not, and in this chapter, we discuss why there is trouble defining the business case for SDN.

When discussing business cases, you typically refer to a specific use case, which is a scenario for deploying SDN to address a specific business problem or pain point. Use cases typically highlight the potential solution, the deployment method, and the soft benefits derived from the deployment. There is also the financial business case; this addresses specific financial benefits derived and how they will influence the business capital and operational budgets.

The financial case will be prepared predeployment at the planning stage by project managers or CIOs by comparing the deployment of SDN against the present operational conditions and making financial comparisons using a multiyear financial analysis and plan. Calculating the theoretical economic benefit of SDN starts with adding up the cost of the networking hardware it will make redundant, this takes care of the CapEx element and then adds the reduction in labor support costs for network management, application provisioning, to find the savings in OpEx. The next stage is then to subtract the total from the cost of the proposed SDN implementation, including the operation, and management burdens. The project manager can then use these results as a comparison against present operational conditions or other proposed solutions.

One of the problems, though, is that the financial business case is unlikely to do SDN justice, because the hard financial benefits are certainly present, but much of the value of SDN comes from soft benefits, such as agility and improved customer experience, and these are notoriously hard to quantify.

Moreover, the financial business case varies between industries and use case. For example, savings on network equipment in the telecom industry, where the network equipment burden accounts for less than 20 percent of the CapEx, is not going to make much of an impact. In contrast, SDN savings in software-defined data centers, where a large proportion of the CapEx is in network hardware, may have a major financial impact. The problem is that it is difficult to define without a specific use case. This is because SDN is not like other network architectures such as Multiprotocol Label Switching (MPLS) (to use one example), where you scale up or down to fit the business requirements for a 3- to 5-year period. Instead, SDN is extremely flexible and can address a multitude of areas using different techniques and architectures. Therefore, SDN is more commonly referred to in articles in the form SDx, as it could apply to service-defined WAN, or service-defined virtual customer premises equipment (vCPE), or many other variants. Consequently, defining the business case requires that it matches the purpose it is being deployed for, and must match to a specific use case. It is only then that we can define key areas of financial benefits.

SDN Use Case Examples

Up until now, this book has focused on the two most common use cases for SDN: data center networking and Ethernet bridging for mobile virtual machines (VMs). There are, however, many other applications for this technology, including the ones discussed in the following subsections.

Data Center Optimization

This is the model discussed in the preceding chapters using SDN and NFV to optimize networks using Ethernet extensions and overlays to improve application performance by providing a method for VM mobility and by detecting and taking into account traffic flows and individual services. SDN allows for orchestrating workloads with networking configuration and per application dynamic adjustments.

Network Access Control

This type of use case is often deployed in campus networks and enterprises running "bring your own device" (BYOD) because it can be used to set appropriate privileges for users or devices accessing the networks. Network access control (NAC) also manages access control limits, service chains, and controls QoS.

Network Virtualization

This is a cloud and service provider (software as a service [SaaS]) model that creates an abstracted virtual network on top of a physical network. This model is appropriate when the goal is supporting a large number of multitenant networks to run over a physical network. Network virtualization is capable of spanning multiple racks or even data centers in different locations.

Virtual Customer Edge

This is the preferred model for telco, Internet service providers (ISPs), and over-the-top service delivery providers because it virtualizes the customer edge device. This model is covered in detail later, but for now suffice to know that vCPE either uses a virtualized platform on customer premises (large customers) or uses a virtualized multitenant server in the provider core network.

Dynamic Interconnects

This is a software-defined WAN (SDW), and it creates dynamic links between locations, typically between data centers (DCs) and other enterprise locations. It is also responsible for dynamically applying appropriate QoS and bandwidth allocation to those links.

Virtual Core and Aggregation

This is another service provider and telco model for virtualizing core systems and support infrastructure such as virtual Information Management System (vIMS), evolved packet core (vEPC), as well as dynamic mobile backhaul, virtual Premise Equipment (vPE), and NFV Gigabit LAN infrastructure

SDN's benefits aren't limited to actual networking. SDN provides a whole host of possibilities for solving business problems, from product development to sales and marketing and, importantly, customer fulfillment. Consequently, this is where the focus for the business case must land, not just on the network but the applications and the beneficiaries.

This is where early adopters saw the immediate potential of SDN (not in the reduction in equipment expenditure to improve CapEx spending, but in reducing OpEx, through automated customer provisioning and customer support). One industry that saw the potential of deploying SDN very early and rapidly adopted the technology was telecoms and service providers. What they saw was an end to the truck rolls and vastly reduced operational spending on manual provisioning and supporting CPE.

These were both hugely expensive operational burdens that could be virtualized relatively simply, and they mapped ideally to the concepts of SDN. Moreover, the solution, the investment, and the deployment were relatively straightforward, and the return on investment (ROI) was delivered almost immediately and could potentially be vast.

By applying a use case to a specific business pain point, as in the case of the software-defined vCPE and SDWs, there were obvious business cases that highlighted SDN as the technology of choice. Financial benefits could then be quantified with confidence and soft benefits highlighted as value adds to convince even the most skeptical of CFOs.

Summary

The next section does a deep dive into the deployment of SDN in the telecom and service provider networks. The chapters examine how the companies derived huge operational cost savings while increasing customer experience through improved service delivery, a larger service portfolio, and faster problem resolution. By applying the correct business case, they were able to achieve these financial and soft benefits by identifying SDN as the technology using a use case model that mapped to their specific requirements.

SDN Business Cases (for Service Providers)

Although it's easy to see the benefits of SDN, the business case is not always so obvious- but for service providers, there's a clear business case.

TRUCK ROLLS

With SDN, the cost of truck rolls is greatly reduced. This is a big deal given the pace of service expansion and BW growth.

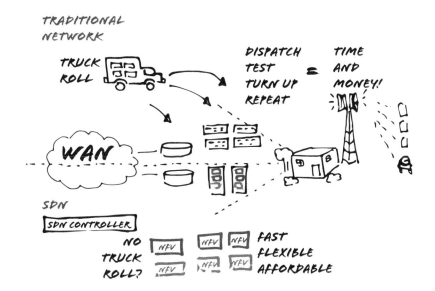

VIRTUAL CUSTOMER EDGE (VCE)

Creating VCEs is a big deal. With SDN, providers can use generic servicers at the customer edge and port all the intelligence to centralized controllers, saving a great deal of time and money.

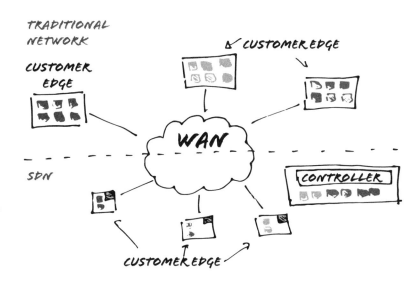

Virtualized Networks
Connecting It All Together

PART 7

Goodbye Truck Rolls

One consequence of server virtualization and the build out of massive data centers and clouds is a shift in how companies deploy new servers and how they upgrade existing servers when they need replacing. Referred to as a *truck roll* (because building a new data center meant you had a bunch of delivery trucks that were heading your way), the build out of cloud data centers and networks changed in some profound ways—both in scale and design philosophy. These changes have also driven new ideas about repairing or replacing servers and networking devices. This chapter provides an overview of both.

Software-defined networking (SDN) and network functions virtualization (NFV) also change things, because network upgrades and truck rolls specifically for network equipment are different because of the way cloud deployment cycles work.

Data Center Scale

The first thing to understand about truck rolls and maintenance of modern data centers is the massive scale to which they are built. In the early 1990s, a large data center might comprise the floor of a single building, or for a really big company, maybe a building or two. The use of the word *building* here means a regular, perhaps even large, office building. This would have been considered a large data center for many companies back then, and as shown in Figure 27-1, they are full of equipment.

Figure 27-1 *Data centers are often packed floor to ceiling with servers.*
Photo Credit: Mark Oleksiy

Today's data centers are massive, with the largest ones topping 2,000,000 square feet. To give you a better idea of the scale, that's about 26 soccer fields—filled with row after row after row of racks filled with high-density servers. The scale of it boggles the mind. Add to that all the routers, switches, connectors, cables, lights, and the myriad other items required to network a data center together and you get an idea of the massive undertaking of a modern data center truck roll. In fact, just the number of screws needed to secure the servers to the racks (a trivial line item in the grand scheme of things) would fill an entire tractor-trailer. Think about that for a minute. Twenty years ago, everything you needed to build out a data center, including the network, would have probably fit in a large tractor-trailer. The entire data center in one big delivery truck. Now that same tractor-trailer is filled with screws that will hold the servers to the rack, and there's a fleet of trucks behind that one for all the other stuff.

To manage this new scale, cloud providers have done what companies have always done to manage changes in the scale, scope, or speed of business: They innovate. One of the coolest innovations in data center truck rolls and designs comes from Google. As shown in Figure 27-2, Google has developed (and patented) a design that stuffs more than a thousand servers and several high-speed, high-density switches into shipping containers (the big steel boxes used on cargo ships).

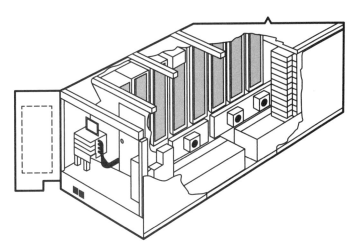

Figure 27-2 *In very large data centers, servers come in pods that can be connected and combined at large scale.*

As shown in Figure 27-3, this design idea was quickly adopted by Sun, HP, and others, and is now becoming a common deployment method. These shipping containers are designed in such a way as to cram as much computing power and switching capacity into modular units as possible, taking into account power, cooling, and connectivity.

Figure 27-3 *Server pod shipping containers are designed in such a way as to cram as much computing power and switching capacity into modular units as possible.*
Photo Credit: chesky

The result is what amounts to LEGO blocks filled with servers that can be plugged into the data center. The efficiency gains are incredible. First, the sheer amount of computing power stuffed into the containers easily gives these containers the greatest CPU density of any other space (such as a server room of comparable square footage). Second, this makes truck rolls much easier because each of the shipping containers can be configured and tested offsite, and once it's ready, it just gets plugged into the data center. The IT staff of the data center now "plugs in" thousands of servers and switches into the data center in much the same way that they used to plug in a server blade or switch into a rack. That innovation in truck roll scalability gives Google (and other large data center owners) the ability to roll out massive data centers in terms of months instead of years.

Why is that important? Well, beyond the obvious reason that sooner is better, the ability to deploy data center blocks at once also helps them keep up with exploding demand while at the same time avoiding near-instantaneous obsolescence. You can imagine the horror of ordering hundreds of thousands of servers, then taking two to three years to network them all together, only to find that the day your data center comes on line, the servers and network are a generation or two behind on performance.

A New Maintenance Philosophy

Back when each server in a data center held a specific application for a group of users, maintaining each server was one of the key aspects of the IT team's day-to-day responsibility. In fact, the IT team's yearly evaluation was often based in some part on the user satisfaction of the various departments that they served.

To keep the servers running at max performance, there was regular maintenance and upgrades. This usually required periods of scheduled downtime called *maintenance windows*, during which server firmware or operating system software could be updated. In some cases, it also meant hardware swap outs or server replacements. The maintenance windows were most often scheduled at off-peak hours or periods, usually over the weekend or during a tradition-ally slow time of the month or year. If a secondary data center was available, traffic would be routed to it after ensuring that those servers were fully operational.

All this careful scheduling was done to ensure that the business was impacted as little as possible, to avoid situations where a department was not able to access a server. The reality, however, is that even back then, the various departments did not really care at all about the server. What they really wanted was access to their applications and their data, which just happened be residing on a specific server (or storage unit in the case of data).

Today, of course, it's not all that different, in that the various departments or users are only really concerned with having access to their applications and data. What's very different (and much better), though, is that the importance of any single server has essentially been eliminated because of virtualization and cloud networking. The ability to freeze and move and thaw an application from any server in the data center to any other server, even while that application is being used, means that maintenance windows are becoming a thing of the past.

As long as the data center has excess capacity (which is one of the criteria of clouds, given their need for elasticity), and the network is fast and flexible enough, IT personnel can avoid maintenance windows altogether. There are, of course, some exceptions, but for the most part, any application, operating system, or server can be upgraded without disrupting services (thanks to the properties of virtualization).

This is good news for the users of the applications, but it still leaves a great deal of work to do for the IT staff because they still have to deal with hardware and software issues, and now there are literally hundreds of thousands of servers to deal with. Software issues are not a big deal because most issues can be dealt with via remote management tools. Hardware issues are a different matter, though.

Let's say that you are a data center manager and you get an indication that a server has an issue that cannot be fixed with one of your remote software management tools. Let's also assume that the server is located in a shipping container, or pod, and of the one thousand plus servers within that pod, it's the only one not working. Now consider the following. If the pod is running at a high temperature that is within the server heat specs but outside "human heat specs," you have to cool it down. Once they get a person in there, they have to physically handle the server and either test it there (bringing tools and diagnostic machines with them) or pull it out and test it on a bench somewhere. It could be a quick fix, but maybe not.

If the problem is not an easy one to fix, there is a growing school of thought that says ignore it. This seems a little nonintuitive at first, but think about the time, energy, and potential collateral damage to other servers and networking gear that are tightly packed together in pods, where the environment is tightly controlled and generally safe from clumsy, error-prone humans.

This actually makes more sense if we look at the cost and effort of server repair relative to the scale of a modern data center. It's not too far fetched to view individual servers in a data center the same way we view sectors of a hard drive on a computer. Many of you reading this might be familiar with the idea that the hard drive on your computer is made up of many small sectors. Hard drives are created this way because information is stored as it arrives on the computer. There may be some partitions set aside for applications, but generally speaking, new information is stored as it comes in.

At times, certain sectors on the hard drive become damaged and unusable. As long as the number of damaged sectors remains small, your computer will not even bother letting you know about it via a user alert. Instead, it will just "de-list" that sector so that the operating system does not attempt to store data on that bad sector.

In modern, massive data centers, the importance of any single server has been diminished to the point that it might not be worth the effort or risks to go in and "mess with it." As long as these errors are few in number and fragmented from rack to rack or container to container, the data center staff is better off leaving them alone. If the problem spreads within a container, the whole container can be replaced, and the old one can be sent to a repair depot.

Summary

This chapter focused on truck rolls and maintenance, but the point was to give you an idea of the massive scale of modern data centers and some of the necessary changes that this scale shift has forced.

The big takeaway here really is that relevance of individual servers to the overall data center has been greatly diminished because we now think of data centers in terms of thousands of servers operating within a pod or sector. This scale shift has driven a great deal of innovation, both in the technology itself and in how we deploy and manage it.

Swap Outs

How Clouds and Cloud Networks Have Scaled Truck Rolls and Components

 It was not too long ago that IT staffs would open a chassis and replace parts. They would not crack open a hard drive if a few sectors went bad, but they would swap out hard drives or upgrade/replace memory boards.

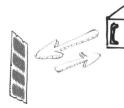

2 Once we started dealing with racks of server blades and switches, it did not make sense to replace internal components. At this scale, we actually started thinking of servers or switches as components that could be swapped out or upgraded.

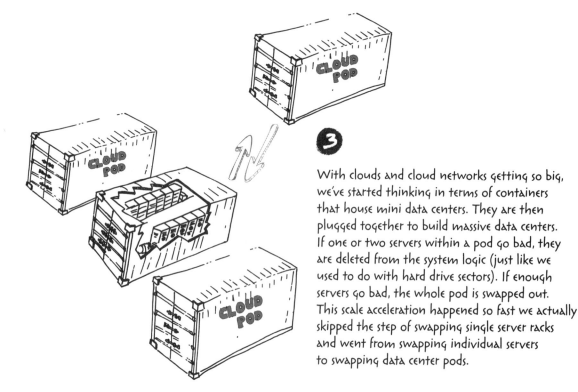

3 With clouds and cloud networks getting so big, we've started thinking in terms of containers that house mini data centers. They are then plugged together to build massive data centers. If one or two servers within a pod go bad, they are deleted from the system logic (just like we used to do with hard drive sectors). If enough servers go bad, the whole pod is swapped out. This scale acceleration happened so fast we actually skipped the step of swapping single server racks and went from swapping individual servers to swapping data center pods.

What If the Shoe Doesn't Fit?

Throughout this book, you've now seen case after case of how virtualization, software-defined networking (SDN), and network functions virtualization (NFV) have transformed businesses and lives, and it's all been rainbows and unicorns so far. The problem is that although these technologies do work for most organizations, they're not a great fit (a least for the time being) for all companies. Such is the problem when a new technology comes along, especially one that works; there's a lot of hype. As a result, some companies jump in when in fact they should not—and the result is usually not good. This chapter focuses on why these technologies are not right for everyone, at least right now.

But first, let's look at where it does fit. A good example of a great fit for SDx (the collective term for Software Defined technologies) is in the telecommunications industry, and their search for a solution to the problems of high capital and operational expense, particularly at the customer edge. Indeed, such are the costs of supporting the customer premises equipment that it severely affects service provisioning and maintenance, as truck rolls are often required to keep up with customer demand. The solution that the communication operators discovered lay with NFV. As discussed earlier, NFV is a highly compatible technology that works well with SDN in providing the sort of programmable, dynamic network that the communication providers envisioned. The use case they adopted and vigorously pushed forward utilized NFV to create virtual customer premises equipment (vCPE). The concept was simply to replace the expensive branded physical CPE with COTS (commercial off-the-shelf) switches for residential and a COTS server or switch for business and enterprise.

The initial capital savings were obvious because the COTS equipment was much cheaper to buy. However, there were also operational savings as operators found that their provisioning and support costs plummeted due to many fewer truck rolls. This was because with NFV only the basic functions required by the customer were retained on the vCPE; all the other functions were pulled back into the operator's network. This made support much easier as the customer support agents could access and configure the vCPE without any truck rolls because all the equipment was located within their own network. Furthermore, there was a vast improvement in service delivery and provisioning times, and new services could be developed and delivered as managed services or packages in hours rather than months. As a bonus, the operators also experienced gains in marketing and sales as the vCPE model using NVP and SDN delivered data mining and service personalization opportunities that were not possible using a conventional CPE.

Where SDN Does Not Fit

While the vCPE use case is a major success for communication service providers, and one that is often pointed to as the "proof that it works," it is a highly specialized example—one that would hold little interest in the enterprise data center. Similarly, a data center use case may be better suited to a more conventional SDN model by flattening the conventional hierarchal network and separating the control intelligence from the forwarding data planes. The advantage to the data center manager is that it simplifies the network and provides the flexibility and agility that the server network has enjoyed for years. Moreover, she can convert the data center network a piece at a time, starting with only a row or two and then escalating the migration when she sees the results. Of course, this too is quite a specialist use case because SDN brings increased simplicity to the infrastructure design, making it very scalable, both horizontally and vertically, and adding the concept of service elasticity. It also introduces better traffic management and quality of service provisioning through programmable traffic engineering and orchestration. Although these are hugely valuable tools to the likes of Google's and Amazon's data centers, not all enterprises need that kind of scalability. In fact, most don't.

The point here is that many use cases for SDN are very specialized and not suited to every organization. There is no one-size-fits-all design, and success depends on matching an SDN use case to your network to ensure SDN or NFV best suits the network's core purpose. Indeed, in many cases, deploying SDN may be the wrong decision altogether because it might not be right for the network. Telecommunication services providers solved their specific problems in vCPEs and WAN links; these were major problems where a solution was required that no one had ever solved before. Similarly, the massive cloud service and storage network providers such as Google had to commit to innovation and be adventurous. Google was an early adopter of SDN because they had a real problem with massive scalability that required solving and there was no roadmap at the time.

Admittedly, these are cool stories, but they are not reflective of typical enterprise data center problems. In most cases, managers are rarely wandering off a vendor-supported strategic roadmap, and in most cases, it would be highly inadvisable to do so. Therefore, it should not be necessary for most enterprises to take radical action such as redesigning their entire infrastructure unless there is a real identified and quantifiable requirement.

When Should You Adopt SDN?

So, how do you know whether your network should be migrated to SDN or whether it just doesn't fit the SDN model?

The case where you don't need SDN is the easiest to identify and resolve. In this scenario, you simply determine that your enterprise network or data center traffic is predictable and the application response times meet or exceed expectations. It would also be the case that the network is easily managed, as it is stable due to few new upgrades and deployment of new applications is a rarity. In addition, it would probably indicate that the applications themselves relied on network hierarchy such as a client/server model, where having predominantly north/south traffic is the norm or at least not an impediment to application performance. Furthermore, WAN links would be provided to remote sites as managed services through a service provider and would meet capacity requirements and use WAN optimization software such as Citrix to minimize the traffic traversing the WAN links.

In this case, there would be no reason to even contemplate undertaking an SDN transformation. In fact, doing so would bring little or no immediate benefit, at the price of tremendous levels of anxiety, effort, and cost.

In contrast, when a business network is a prime case for SDN deployment, the business case can be just as clear-cut. If the business is supporting fast-moving development of web and mobile apps that generate vast unpredictable traffic flows that require real-time response, the conventional network hierarchal network may no longer be able to meet those performance demands. Similarly, if those apps require mobility and elasticity, insomuch as new instances may require that VMs be spinning up, spinning down, or moving to servers with lower or greater capacity depending on application usage, SDN is likely going to be for you. In addition, if traffic patterns are unpredictable and you are continually battling with overprovisioning of bandwidth and congestion on best paths through the network, SDN will be a highly attractive proposition.

Stuck in the Middle

The real problem, however, is when you are somewhere in between (for example, if you have a mainly traditional stable network that performs just fine for all your legacy applications but you have just launched a few web and mobile apps and you are struggling to meet their demands on resources). In this scenario, you could theoretically just deploy SDN in the racks that house the new apps and keep the rest of the network in its conventional architecture. That way you are not compromising the existing applications, but instead are introducing a new technology only for the new and future apps. This is the way most data center managers approach the problem of having mixed apps in their architectures. One of the benefits of this approach is that it is a good, controllable way to introduce SDN into the network without too much risk. The drawback is that there are rarely people with both skills, conventional and SDN, onsite. This means the team is managing two totally different networks. Another issue is the question of where one stops. These can end up being very complicated matters—both technically and politically.

There are, of course, ways to solve the problem of the lack of SDN skills to deploy SDN. One of the better ones is via preconfigured appliances that contain all the components you require in one rack-mounted box. This technique is called *hyper-convergence*, and vendors have started to push these appliances out to the market. This is certainly an attractive way for mid-level enterprises to enter the SDN technology field with full vendor support and requiring few onsite skills. The appliances contain virtual compute, storage, network, and orchestration elements that are all configured to work together; all the customers have to do is load their applications and they then have a fully virtualized SDN environment in a box.

Hyper-convergence is already becoming a popular method for those wanting to test the SDN network technology without fully committing to expensive proof of concepts or full-blown trials. However, hyper-convergence is still only an emerging technology and will not be—in its present form—the solution for large-scale deployments; however, it will be well suited to low- and mid-level entrants into the market.

The reality is that SDN and NVF are eventually going to take over all networks, if no yet to be developed-disruptive technology emerges before the conversion is complete. The key, though, is that this will be a slow-rising tide. Some companies will be ready earlier than others and will do fine, others will wait too long and get left behind. Some, however, will wade in before their time; which, given the expense and distraction it can cause, is perhaps more dangerous than waiting too long.

Service Chaining

When reading about software-defined network (SDN), the phrase *service chaining* comes up a lot, and it is not initially clear what relevance the term has to SDN. Service chaining, after all, is nothing new; it's been around in networks for some time, and it relates to the way hardware, typically security appliances, were attached to one another to form a physical chain of devices that provided the combined functions, which you required. For example, you may have wanted Network Address Translation (NAT), followed by intrusion detection (IDS) and then antivirus (AVS), followed by URL and content filtering and a firewall (FW). If that were the case, the network administrators would build these appliances and see to it that they were physically connected in series with the traffic stream passing through the chain of devices. It would then be up to the access lists and rule bases on each appliance to determine which traffic streams were to be processed.

This works well for a whole network, but it's not an optimal way to configure services on a per-customer basis (for example, in a multitenant environment).

As shown in Figure 29-1, Client A may only require FW and AV, yet his traffic will travel along the same path as Client B, who requires NAT, IDS, and FW, even though he has no requirement for IDS or NAT. Similarly, Client C will travel the same path to receive IDS, AVS, and CF.

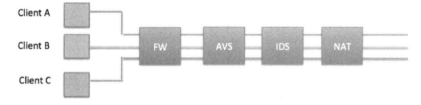

Figure 29-1 *Service chaining with no client customization: Every client gets every service.*

In addition to the increased risk of configuration errors, this method also introduces latency into the process. The lookups are applied to all the traffic whether the appliance was due to process it or not. In fact, the traffic that does not apply is the last traffic to get processed due to the nature of access lists. It's easy to see why this is a process ripe for change.

The new idea was to use a more logical approach, especially in IP/MPLS networks. The reason for this was that in IP/MPLS you have better control over what path the traffic passes over by creating label switch paths (LSPs). By predetermining a path for a particular traffic stream, you can ensure that the packets go through only the appliances they need to go through and bypass the others. This was an improvement in some ways though a lot depended on what induced the greater delay; the unnecessary flow through an appliance or taking a longer path through the network.

Whichever technique was used to provision the service chain, whether it was hardware chaining, then appliance configuration to apply the service per client data stream or using MPLS LSP, it required lots of manual configuration to provision and deploy the service chain to the client.

Service Chaining in SDN

So how has service chaining improved now that we are dealing with SDN networks? Well, the most important thing is that we now have virtual network functions (VNF) working in conjunction with SDN to provide the important virtualization required to separate the functions (in the form of virtual network functions) from the expensive physical appliances. These virtualized network functions are similar to virtual machines (VMs) in server virtualization, but there is a big difference. VNFs are not bound by a hypervisor or on a virtualized server of any kind because they can run purely as an application on a standard server. This makes them extremely flexible when deploying them in the network.

The other point of interest is the VNFs can be deployed on COTS (commercial off the shelf) servers or switches running a basic form of Linux. What this means is that they can be deployed wherever and however they are best suited, based on the cost-effectiveness of either approach. This was, of course, not possible with the expensive appliances, which had to be located at traffic aggregation points and be overprovisioned as a result of that. If they were to be chained, it would mean going back to the old hardware serial chaining of before. However, there are other options; NV (network virtualization) is used by SDN to create tunnels based on customer data flows through the NV overlay that sits on top of the conventional data center network. It is possible to place a COTS server directly into the customer's tunnel, thereby ensuring you capture the data flow, because the traffic flow would have to pass through it. However, adding a hardware device per customer is not very scalable or cost-effective, and even if the deployment of NFV servers were rationalized, it still is not an ideal way to go because it is adding more hardware and additional complexity into the network.

Now here we seem to be going back to an old way of doing things. Adding hardware is not the best way forward, so how can we move service chaining forward to meet the goals of rapid automated deployment? It isn't initially clear until you consider SDN's role in service chaining and function deployment. SDN can play the part of MPLS—and do it more effectively. What this means is that SDN can determine each individual packet flow's path through the network and it can ensure it traverses every functional appliance (VNF device) that it is required to pass through.

Furthermore, SDN can determine and provision these paths on a per-client and –service basis, as shown in Figure 29-2. For example, Client A, who requires FW and AV, will travel a different path through the network than Client B, who requires NAT, IDS, and FW, and similarly Client C will follow yet another path to receive IDS, AVS, and CF, even though they are all destined for the same destination.

SDN and NFV allow the traffic to be intelligently routed through the network so that the packets pass through the required functional services, and only those devices, on a per-customer basis. By enforcing the client's service policy via SDN's own automated provisioning of the traffic flow tunnels, SDN can automate the provisioning of functions and services on a per-customer or –client basis. This enables multitenancy. (For example, SDN will introduce tunnels that virtually segregate each client's traffic.) What's more, it will introduce the capability to support different service chains for different clients all traveling on the same network without inducing unnecessary latency and overprovisioning of appliances by situating them at traffic aggregation points.

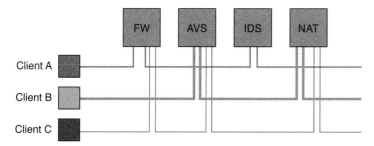

Figure 29-2   *In a programmable network, service chaining can be customized on a per-client basis.*

SDN has the potential to reduce the complexity of provisioning functions to each customer via service chaining because it can do it dynamically. SDN can create and provision the best path per customer's service chain automatically and therefore can bring flexibility and agility to service deployment. With SDN handling the provisioning of packet flows per customer, products sold as services will be dynamically provisioned and deployed to the customer's profile in minutes rather than days on an SDN network.

Service Chaining

Service Chaining is a Term for Stringing
Together Network Services

IN THE GOOD OLD DAYS:

Each client got all services even if they didn't want them. This was very inefficient.

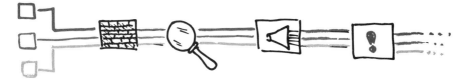

POLICY BASED ROUTING:

PBR enabled network admins to program services on a per tenant basis.
This was slow and complicated.

SDN SERVICE CHAINING:

All the benefits of PBR but much, much easier to program, because you have to only program
the controller—which automatically programs the network. Changes are easy, too.

NFV: What Happens to All the Network Appliances?

With the advent of network functions virtualization (NFV), many of the purpose-built network appliances are likely to go away. So, what's going to happen to them? This is a good question, and one that this chapter will attempt to answer. However, to understand this outcome of NFV, we must first consider what the goals are, for they differ from server and application virtualization. Let's consider first why server and application virtualization was such a success.

How Network Appliances Are Different

The great advantage of virtualizing applications is that administrators could host applications as virtual machines (VMs) running on a host server. Server administrators typically installed one application on one dedicated server. This was very inefficient because one application rarely used anything approaching the server's potential, and underutilization of resources was very wasteful. By consolidating smaller applications on VMs hosted on one larger server, IT teams achieved greater efficiency and reduced the server sprawl throughout the data center. By applying server virtualization, a data center could reduce their server count (and overall costs of the data center) considerably. This was an obvious and easily realized benefit of server virtualization. For example, a network administrator could realistically reduce the server headcount by 50 percent simply by optimizing the location of applications onto underutilized servers.

However, network functions virtualization is somewhat different depending on the model applied. This is where NFV becomes more complex. The issue is that network virtualization is not about consolidating network appliances; it is actually quite the opposite. NFV is about creating cheaper appliances that can then be deployed in the network where they are required. This is an important point with NFV: It doesn't necessarily replace existing appliances. There are use cases where they do, of course, such as the virtual customer premises equipment (vCPE) model, but even then it will be on a one-to-one basis. NFV is more about distributing functionality rather than consolidating it.

The reason for most consolidated network functions is that it is much easier to use virtualization concepts and apply them to applications and servers than it is to network appliances. For example, a software application's performance is based on the number of clock cycles per second (the number of instructions it can run per second) and will require a minimal physical configuration such as processor speed and type, OS, and memory requirements to run optimally. An administrator could then check the server utilization figures for the application and determine its maximum usage of the host server's resources. With this data in hand, the administrator could then consolidate servers by moving applications, as VMs, onto one larger server, thereby maximizing the efficiency of the server's resources.

However, this model doesn't quite work with network appliances. This is because the software requirements and resources they consume do not form the criteria for judging and sizing a network appliance. For example, to run a firewall application, on even a home PC, consumes hardly any system resources because it is not complex software, especially if it is dealing with one user and minimal traffic. A network firewall appliance, however, running similar software has to deal with potentially hundreds or thousands of users and process 10-Gbps traffic at wire speed. This is why vendors of network equipment go to such great lengths to optimize the platform on which the software runs. Typically this requires specialized application-specific integrated circuit (ASIC) chips and hardware designs that focus on maximizing performance under loaded conditions. Because of this, you achieve nothing by replacing that special-ized appliance with a COTS (commercial off the shelf) server running the same software as everything else on the network, let alone trying to consolidate several firewalls onto the same COTS server to save space.

Replacing Big Hardware Appliances with Many Small Virtual Appliances

If you look at a conventional network, you will see strategically placed network appliances, typically located at traffic aggregation points. This strategy relies on a few expensive and overprovisioned appliances being located at key locations within the network. The problem here is that all traffic has to pass through those few appliances to ensure all traffic is processed. In the preceding chapter (on service chaining), you saw the drawbacks with this model. Although consolidating a few network appliances in the network is efficient from a cost and management standpoint, it can be devastating to performance and optimal traffic flow. Replacing those expensive appliances, which can handle vast traffic throughput due to custom ASICs and purpose-built hardware, with software-based COTS servers is not going to help the situation.

The misunderstanding with network functions virtualization (NFV) is that it is often referred to as a capital expenditure reducing technology. It actually is, just not in the same way as server virtualization. Where NFV reduces capital expenditure is not in the consolidation of network appliances or even their reduction in numbers but in the savings made by replicating them and then distributing the functions as software throughout the network. If this were done with hardware, it would require expensive equipment expenditures. This is the distributed function model whereby you do not consolidate the functions centrally, but instead you distribute them as smaller entities. Although the virtual versions of these appliances have much lower throughput and processing capabilities, there are many more of them, and because they are distributed, the traffic burden on any one appliance is greatly reduced. For example, NFV could be used at key network borders in a layered security model so that instead of having one expensive appliance as a gatekeeper for an entire section of the network, you could distribute the firewall functions to several COTS servers at specific locations in the network adding granularity. The capital expenditure savings here do not come from replacing existing equipment because you could end up with more stuff in the network, but on the saving made from purchasing several COTS servers instead of very expensive purpose-built appliances.

That's a key to NFV: The benefit does not come from consolidating appliances but rather from the cost-effective distribution of network functions. The importance of this strategy becomes clear when you consider applying network functions and services in multitenant networks.

In a cloud or similar multitenant network, customers have different policies. Applying all policies on one appliance would be an extremely risky and an onerous task (and probably not allowed by certain customers who are heavily regulated [retail, healthcare, and so on]). However, by separating the functions as software from the underlying hardware, you can apply individual policies much more efficiently by applying a virtualized network function to VMs as chained services matched to each customer's profile.

When Not to Get Rid of an Appliance

In addition, let's look at why you might not want to replace your expensive vendor appliance with a COTS server. With server virtualization, it takes little skill to virtualize a Linux or Android operating system onto your Windows laptop. You can also buy VMware Fusion or Parallels and run a fully capable Microsoft operating system on your Mac device. It's also pretty easy to set up just about any program as a VM on Amazon Web Services (AWS) or other cloud-based service.

Network functions virtualization (NFV) is completely different, however. Most equipment vendors will supply you with software versions of their network appliances that you can load onto a COTS server for a price (no open source here). The pain point here is not in the set up or even the performance (assuming you have the distribution set up correctly). The hard part is actually in the coordination. Reengineering network traffic to ensure that all traffic is processed (especially in the case of security) is critically important. This brings us back to the previous chapter on NFV, which brings up the earlier topic of controlling the network. If the firewalls and security appliances are generic servers on the network, who is responsible for them? The security team or the network team?

Another consideration is that maybe you don't need to throw out the expensive appliances. You could capitalize on their worth by strategically placing them where they are most advantageous. A COTS server, for example, will struggle to equal the performance of a vendor's custom appliance.

To illustrate that point, studies have shown that appliances are typically rated at 95 percent of advertised performance, whereas virtualized software-hosted appliances (NFV) sitting on a high-end x86 server managed only 64 percent out of the box. After considerable tuning, replacing the vSwitch and hypervisor, the results climbed to 85 percent. It might not seem like much, but a 95 percent to 85 percent drop off is huge, and the performance differentiator is down to the bottlenecks in the software vSwitch and hypervisor. Think twice before you throw out that Cisco box because the CEO read an article on how awesome NFV is.

Security
The Security Thing

Where's My Data, Exactly?

With the advent of the cloud in the late 2000s, the question, "Where's my data, exactly?" crops up time after time when discussing the possibility of deploying applications to a cloud service provider. Businesses are rightly skeptical about passing and storing confidential, sensitive, or valuable data on a network outside of their own jurisdiction. This question is often posed by those who are either against the use of a third-party cloud or by those who lack a technical understanding. It is important to ensure data is secure, but the issue of exactly where the data is located is inconsequential. To understand why specific location is not a big issue, we need to look at storage virtualization—how it has evolved from the PC's local hard drive into today's cloud storage structures.

NOTE   The focus of this chapter is on data virtualization. There is a legal concept called *data sovereignty*, which is legally required by some countries. This concept holds that specific types of corporate data created within a country cannot be stored outside the country. This will be discussed at the end of this chapter.

Storage Virtualization

Storage virtualization has been around for a very long time. It is such a complex process that it necessitates us abstracting the technicalities from the user. For example, consider a PC's hard drive. In the old days (prior to the advent of solid-state storage), hard drives were simply a platter of magnetic disks that were formatted into cylinders, heads, and sectors (CHS). Data was stored in binary format within those tracks. However, the number of cylinders varied per drive, and hence the different hard drive capacities. Therefore, an addressing system using CHS was not feasible, as the specific parameters changed with every hard drive. The solution was to get the drive's firmware to virtualize the CHS address by numbering each consecutive slice of CHS, a process termed *logical block addressing* (LBA). In addition to LBA, the drives used a file allocation table to keep note of where each file was stored on the physical platter. Obviously, the user did need to know any of that low-level intricacy, so this was abstracted by applying the physical hard disk a label (for example, C:). This meant the user could access their data using the label and the directory path; i.e., c:\user\filename.

Basically, that was local storage virtualization. Network storage virtualization is much the same. When using LBA, the virtualization process manipulates a single disk to form a consecutive list of LBA addresses. With block virtualization, the goal is to take several physical disks and present them as a single large logical drive. The idea behind this is to aggregate the address blocks of all the participant drives to create a logical drive that appears to the operating system as one single large drive. Block aggregation works because the storage consumers, which are the applications, do not care about the physical aspects of data storage, such as the number of drives or arrays. Instead they have simple requirements:

- **Capacity:** Can the storage area store all the data generated by the application? How big is the storage?

- **Performance:** Can the storage area meet the application's response times? How fast is it?

- **Availability:** Can the storage area meet the reliability requirements of the application? How reliable is it?

With network storage virtualization, the user is connecting to a storage area, perhaps on a server's hard drive in a data center. This drive will be part of a storage array that consolidates smaller dives into one larger drive "space." Again, the virtualization here is supposed to abstract the complexity of the network path to the data for the user or application. The user will simply access his data using a label (for example, G:\), and he will save and retrieve his data using G:\user\filename, without any need to know the physical underlying structure or where the data is actually stored.

Storage-Area Networks

As network storage evolved, it grew in complexity, and even larger drives were being aggregated into storage arrays to support enterprise levels of data that required dedicated storage-area networks (SANs). The SAN (see Figure 31-1) might not necessarily be in the user's local data center, but instead be hosted in a regional data center, but again this was not something the user was aware of, or was interested in knowing.

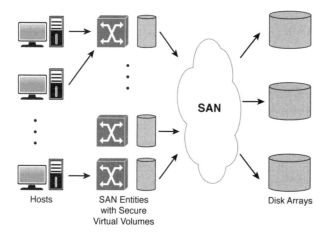

Figure 31-1 *Storage-area network diagram*

Furthermore, as the complexity of SAN administration grew, so did the need for dynamically configurable storage areas that could grow and shrink as required. There was also ever increasing demand for higher performance and availability of data storage. An administrator typically addresses performance by striping data across logical unit numbers (LUNs) from multiple arrays. Similarly, they use data mirroring and replication techniques to mitigate availability issues through storing data in multiple locations in order to aide parallel processing and support business continuity. Indeed, storage mobility became a requirement with the advent of virtual machines that could dynamically move from server to server, so too could LUNs in virtual storage. Therefore, the actual location of data is transparent to all outside of the administrator's management console. This is because LUNs move about the SAN depending on their resource requirements. Virtualization has abstracted the actual storage location from not just the user but also even the storage administrator's view.

Therefore, where exactly the data so stored is not a technical issue (well, not in huge enterprise networks), because we don't really know. Of course, we know which data centers store the data, but not specifically on which storage area element or drive array because it will be located in several locations for performance, availability, and backup.

Data Location and Security

Users don't need to know the location of their data as long as they have confidence and trust in the storage administrators (the company) to store their data with regards to the three tenets of security:

- Confidentiality
- Integrity
- Availability

These three attributes are commonly referred to as the CIA triad and are shown in the diagram in Figure 31-2.

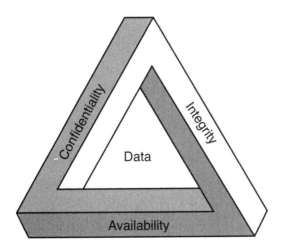

Figure 31-2   *The CIA triad is a broadly used concept describing the self-reinforcing concept of data security with regard to confidentiality, integrity, and availability.*

Typically, that confidence and trust is a given in enterprise network scenarios. However, it is interesting to see what happens when we scale up from enterprise networks to global service providers that have both businesses and the public as their customers. How does the customer build confidence in both of these scenarios?

With regard to the public, knowing where their data is stored has typically never been an issue. They have used global email service providers for decades without ever questioning the location of their mailboxes, because their email providers have met their performance and security expectations. Similarly, the public has rushed to adopt cloud services for data storage, such as Dropbox (as have many businesses, or more accurately individuals who use services like Dropbox for business purposes outside of the control of IT). Seemingly with the public, convenience—especially if it's free—trumps security. However, what about business users? How do they feel about where their data is being stored?

IT security has been against the use of free anonymous email since the beginning, and they have considered hosted email solutions as being little better, sometimes even worse. Their compliance revolved around the ambiguous storage of company data, regarding not just storage location, but with regard to data ownership and other legalities. Nothing has changed in the meantime. IT security teams are still concerned with locating data on the public cloud, not so much for technical reasons but more for the political and legal concerns.

So What Are the Nontechnical Issues That We Need to Address?

The issue is that the big cloud providers (Google, Amazon, and Microsoft, among others) all have global networks and could be (and probably are) storing your company data in any part of the world. Other smaller cloud providers may not have the scale of these behemoths but are just as oblique in their storage policies. After all, these providers are storing your private and confidential data on proprietary cloud storage networks in locations you perhaps cannot verify and that you will have little chance of auditing. Figure 31-3 shows a diagram of AWS storage, which does not guarantee a specific location for their customers' data.

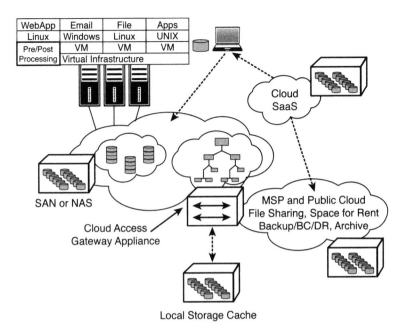

Figure 31-3 *A block diagram of AWS storage. AWS does not guarantee that it can or will provide details on the exact physical location of customer data.*

Summary

Hopefully, this chapter has made the case as to why individual users don't or shouldn't care about where their data is stored as long as the storage provider maintains a suitable level of confidentiality, integrity, and availability. However, for a business, there are legal issues and requirements as to where and why they would want to store their data. For instance, in the European Union, there is a higher emphasis in data protection on privacy than there is in the United States (at least at the time of this writing). There is also a greater burden of proof required by law enforcement and the authorities in the EU to access stored data. Therefore, companies registered in the EU would be very reluctant to store their data in a location within the United States. (The Safe Harbor Act has gone some way to try to remediate this issue.) That is just one example of why companies might be reluctant to store data within the borders of even friendly nations, let alone those with diametrically opposed political perspectives.

NOTE As of October 2015, the EU courts have overturned the EU Safe Harbor Act. Anyone who does business across the U.S. and EU regions should contact their IT organizations and legal counsel regarding any changes in the laws.

Cloud providers such as Amazon and Google have truly global footprints and data centers around the world; therefore, where your company's data is being stored is of concern to not just IT but also to those involved with corporate governance and compliance. After all, acts such as Sarbanes-Oxley (SOX) demand that the company complies with data handing and auditing practices and processes. But how can that be so when the company is storing their data in the cloud? Can a company really audit Amazon or Google's data handling processes to SOX standards?

Some cloud providers, such as AWS, do provide frameworks to do compliance auditing, but they may or may not align exactly to your internal IT processes for auditing.

In later chapters, you'll see how a company can secure their data in the cloud at least, even if they cannot fully audit it or even ascertain where it is. However, for now, this chapter will close with a final example of why you might want to know where your data is exactly.

The legal requirement of storing data within a country's border is something of a legal antiquity, the practicalities of which became redundant with the advent of the cloud. However, in many countries, the law still exists because the community adopts disruptive technologies such as the Internet and the cloud far quicker than lawmakers can react. As a result, there are still several active and in-force laws ("data sovereignty") with relevance to where data is created and stored. This means that wise companies take legal advice to ascertain their position with regard to the law when deploying applications that generate, store, or consume sensitive data in the cloud. Therefore, the question, "Where is my data, exactly?" is more of a legal and governance concern than a technical or security one.

Where's My Data?

3rd Party Cloud

1

Data in the cloud is not just on one server or even in just one data center. It's in a lot of places and through a technique called sharding, it's broken up in a way that makes it really safe.

2

A good analogy for sharding is the broken plate concept. Imagine your data set as a plate. Then, imagine that you drop the plate, which causes it to shatter in to many random pieces.

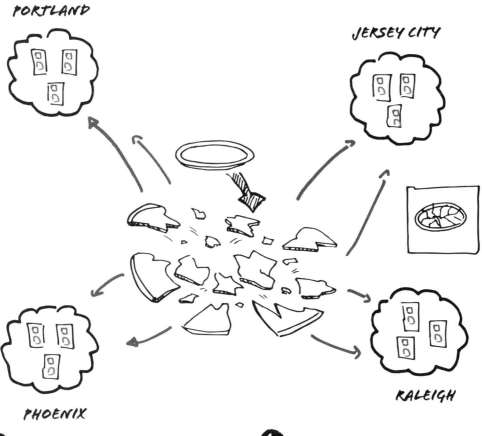

PORTLAND

JERSEY CITY

PHOENIX

RALEIGH

3

These random pieces are then distributed to many different places—and because the data is now random, even if one data center was compromised, the data is not very useful.

4

The key to making it work, of course, is that the cloud provider has to be able to put all the pieces together. This can cause some performance issues, but it's a good trade-off for the security that it provides.

Preventing Data Leakage

In the preceding chapter, you learned that it is not always possible to know where your data is being stored when you use a cloud service provider. This is usually okay for most companies, but it could be a legal conundrum for regulated businesses. Although the specific location of data in the cloud is not a serious concern, there are grave issues with regard to what data is being stored and who is storing it and who has access to it.

Unauthorized removal of data from businesses has long been a problem, especially with the advent of high-capacity removable storage such as laptop hard disks and USB thumb drives. However, with the advent of the Internet and its associated technologies such as private email, mobile wireless devices, and cloud storage, it has never been more difficult for IT security to secure the company's data. Recent business initiatives such as bring your own device (BYOD) and worse bring your own cloud (BYOC) have almost given employees free rein to transfer data outside of the business on personal devices and even to store company data on personal storage clouds such as Dropbox. Note that this is not meant to imply that rogue employees with the intent of stealing data are the main issue here. That is a problem, of course, but in the main, data leakage is usually caused by well-meaning employees who are simply trying to work more efficiently. They reason that by replicating their office ecosystem into the cloud they can work more effectively; what's more, they can work from anywhere and at any time. Although this is true, when employees do this on their own, using a non-company-controlled cloud, they are inadvertently causing a huge security problem and most of the time are not in compliance with information security policies.

It is for this reason that data leakage is a major concern—not surprising given that for most companies data is a major asset with intellectual and financial value. In some businesses, such as financial services, regulatory bodies set standards and rules for how the company manages sensitive data. These are legal responsibilities, and the onus is on the CIO and CFO to apply governance to ensure compliance with these regulations or risk heavy fines.

Furthermore, it is the responsibility of IT security to ensure that data is stored securely, maintaining the confidentiality, integrity, and availability of information within the company's borders. However, herein lies the problem: IT is charged with securing the company data while at the same time permitting, in the spirit of BYOD, the free flow of data out of the business on personal devices or on personal cloud storage.

The problem is further exacerbated by there being so many ways that data can casually leak from the organization. Employees can send files using private email, or store them in the cloud on Dropbox. They can also save files to their smartphone or tablet or even replicate the company's business computer in a virtual machine (VM) stored in their personal cloud environment. In addition, because the employees are doing all of these practices without any malicious intent, they are genuinely unaware of the potential dangers of transmitting and storing data in the cloud. To them it's just as if it were another virtual drive on their work PC. Clearly, security has to do something to prevent this leakage of data from the company, but their solution cannot be detrimental to employee efficiency and mobility.

Consequently, if you cannot stop or even hinder the BYOD or BYOC initiatives, something has to protect the data itself rather than prevent the methods for its transportation. Unfortunately, the industry has to face the unpalatable fact that companies are always going to lose some data through leakage.

Minimizing Data Loss

The goal, then, is to minimize data loss, because 100% prevention is all but impossible (or at least not worth the price that most companies are willing to try to achieve it). Consequently, IT should try not to "boil the ocean" in their attempts at applying controls to all of the data. Instead, taking a practical approach to protecting valuable data is the smarter play. Subsequently, there are two key steps in minimizing data loss:

1. Apply the risk formula for data loss (Risk = Impact × Rate of occurrence). This differs from the standard security risk formula because data loss is inevitable, unintentional, and (importantly) it can be measured and mitigated.

2. Apply the 80:20 rule of data loss to identify where you are likely to experience a high impact data breach.

To understand how to approach data loss prevention, organizations need to understand and identify the type of data they are trying to protect:

■ Data in motion (traveling across the network)

■ Data in use (being used at the endpoint)

■ Data at rest (sitting idle in storage)

Second, identify data as described or registered:

■ **Described:** Out-of-box classifiers and policy templates, which help identify types of data. This is helpful when looking for content such as personal identifiable information.

■ **Registered:** Data is registered to create a "fingerprint," which allows full or partial matching of specific information such as intellectual property.

To apply your efforts to the most likely high-impact breaches, use the Pareto 80:20 rule to find the 80% of the record and files compromised by the 20% of breach vectors (hack, cloud uploads, data being transferred to removable media, BYOD devices). Because most data loss is via cloud uploads, data transferred to removable media, and BYOD devices, we need to apply our efforts to the network and to data in motion and data in use.

You might wonder why this approach does not focus on data at rest, because that would be the logical starting point. However, there are things to consider when protecting data. First, you don't know where all your sensitive data is located. Second, the sheer volume of data at rest makes searching, identifying, and classifying every file in storage nearly impossible and is unlikely to reduce risk significantly. Third, it is easier and makes more sense to identify and classify files in use and files in motion, because they are the ones currently at risk. This is where data loss prevention (DLP) technology comes into play.

Data Loss Prevention

There are two basic types of DLP:

- **Full suite DLP:** A dedicated system that works exclusively on DLP. A full suite DLP solution covers the complete spectrum of leakage vectors, from data moving through the network (data in motion), data at the computer or endpoint (data in use), to data stored on the server drives or in a storage-area network (SAN) (data at rest). Equally important, a full suite solution addresses the full range of network protocols, such as HTTP, HTTPS, FTP, email, and other nonspecific TCP traffic.

- **Channel data loss prevention:** A DLP function on a multifunction system. Channel DLP is typically designed for some other function but was modified to provide visibility and DLP functionality. Examples include email security, web gateways, and device control.

The earliest DLP solutions used deep packet inspection (DPI) to perform pattern detection—in a similar manner to intrusion detection systems (IDS), which detect malicious patterns known as signatures in files. DLP used these techniques to identify patterns such as account numbers or credit card information. However, these methods were not hugely successful, and today most DLP solutions use a technique called data fingerprinting. The DLP uses the fingerprinting process on data in the database (structured data) and on data in files and documents (unstructured data). The fingerprinting process creates a one-time hash of the structured and unstructured data and stores it in a database as a unique reference.

DLP uses these data fingerprints to identify files or partial files as it scans them looking for sensitive information, and then DLP can block them from leaving the network. However, DLP is not always about prevention, despite its name; many companies prefer just to detect the movement of data out of their network, because they fear that blocking data flow could have a detrimental effect on business processes. Blocking can be performed on email and web mail access. For email, the DLP will act as a mail transfer agent, which will provide the technological means to selectively block or allow individual email messages. However, blocking other protocols is not so easy and requires that the traffic crossing the wire be analyzed in real time using DPI. Another method commonly used is to implement an Internet Content Adaptation Protocol (ICAP) proxy server to filter all HTTP, HTTPS, and FTP request at the gateway and redirect them to the DLP for analysis and inspection of traffic for violations.

Implementing DLP in the corporate network is fraught with technical issues, but is relatively straightforward from a governance perspective, as long as you follow some general guidelines regarding data privacy and data monitoring:

- Employees do not lose their privacy and data protection rights at the office door. This means that a country's privacy and data protection laws likely apply to workplace monitoring.

- Any limitation on the employee's right to privacy should be proportionate to the likely damage to the employer's legitimate interests, or, conversely, monitoring must be proportionate to the risks confronting the employer.

- Employers should be clear about the purpose for monitoring and satisfied that the particular monitoring arrangement is justified by real benefits that will be delivered.

With a cloud service provider, however, it is not as simple because they must comply with privacy laws and data protection legislation. After all, it is not their data, or is it? DLP is just one of several technologies that potentially breach data privacy laws, so cloud service providers go to some lengths to blur the distinction of ownership of the data. Therefore, it is important to read the small print in the contract when considering using the services of a cloud provider.

Preventing Data Leakage

1

Your data exists in a lot of places, and most of them are pretty safe.

3

A big problem today is that employees often use third-party cloud or data sharing sites to make collaboration easy. It works great, but it's a major source of data leakage as company data is now stored on external servers that they do not own and often don't have direct access to.

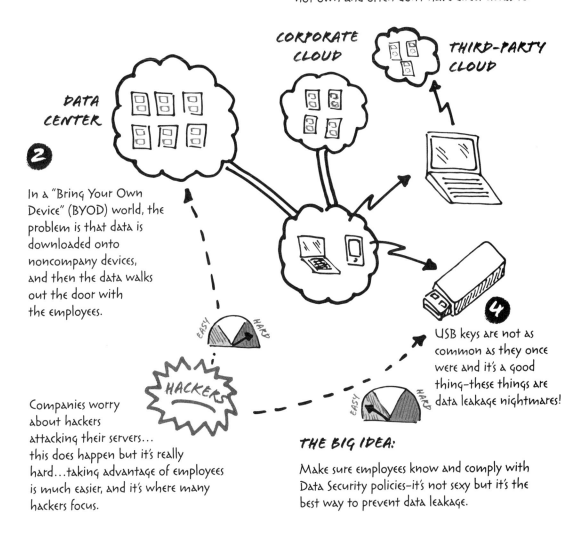

DATA CENTER

CORPORATE CLOUD

THIRD-PARTY CLOUD

2

In a "Bring Your Own Device" (BYOD) world, the problem is that data is downloaded onto noncompany devices, and then the data walks out the door with the employees.

EASY   HARD

HACKERS

Companies worry about hackers attacking their servers... this does happen but it's really hard...taking advantage of employees is much easier, and it's where many hackers focus.

4

USB keys are not as common as they once were and it's a good thing–these things are data leakage nightmares!

EASY   HARD

THE BIG IDEA:

Make sure employees know and comply with Data Security policies–it's not sexy but it's the best way to prevent data leakage.

Logging and Auditing

One of the biggest issues with cloud computing, as discussed in an earlier chapter, is that you are never quite sure where your data is being stored. You have no idea whether the provider is replicating your data. You may have few assurances that they are actually securing your data on their network. You should be able to be confidently assured that your data is being safely handled. After all, even though you have subcontracted the storage to a third-party cloud provider, you should be able to ensure the confidentiality, integrity, and availability of your data, because it's still your data. You may outsource responsibility, but you cannot outsource accountability.

This is one of the big issues with the cloud. In many ways, it is a black box, where, to the consumer, nothing inside the cloud is actually visible. Furthermore, consumers of cloud services have little or no idea how providers handle their applications or data within a cloud. They must just accept that the cloud provider is honest and competent. Also, they must hope that the provider's staff have no malicious intent and will not tamper with their data or violate their privacy.

This, of course, is a massive concentration of risk as potential losses of data through leakage can be significantly larger than in a conventional data center. There is also a concentration of other cloud users, which directly relates to higher concentrations of potential threats. The reason for this being that although the consumer of the services will upload and communicate with the provider's cloud using encryption—HTTPS or SSL/TLS—to protect the data as it traverses the Internet, most cloud providers will terminate the encryption session at their gateway. Consequently, all the consumer's traffic goes through the provider's multitenant network unencrypted. In other words, traffic is encrypted to the cloud, but not through the cloud. Because of this, some security experts consider this to be only slightly more secure than the Internet. Before going deep into why you need to audit and log events in the cloud environment, you first have to understand why companies use the cloud despite the inherent risk.

Cloud service providers have three conventional business models:

- **SaaS (software as a service):** The applications and data reside with the service provider.

- **PaaS (platform as a service):** The provider supplies software development languages and tools as a development platform.

- **IaaS (infrastructure as a service):** The provider supplies a virtual network infrastructure of servers, storage, and high-capacity networks, which is charged on a usage basis. This is the most conventional use of cloud services for business.

Each of these models has different security issues. With software as a service (SaaS), the business is wholly reliant on the software supplier to provide confidentiality, integrity, and availability of the service. Platform as a service (PaaS) is a developer platform where a multitenant environment can impact security if all traffic goes unencrypted through the provider's network. Infrastructure as a service (IaaS) has many potential issues due to the number of consumer configuration points.

Whatever business model the cloud provider delivers—for example, Azure specializes in PaaS, Salesforce in SaaS, and Amazon in IaaS—they must all provide adequate cloud security. They do this by providing a broad set of policies, technologies, and procedures (controls) to protect data, applications, and the associated infrastructure, and this is where the cloud provider must adhere to auditing and data security compliance regulations. They must also allow independent and recognized auditing companies to audit their service to ensure it meets regulations compliance. These regulations include Health Insurance Portability and Accountability Act (HIPAA), Sarbanes-Oxley (SOX) and the Payment Card Industry – Data Security Standard (PCI-DSS), depending on the industry, which means providers may supply their services in community or hybrid deployment modes to ensure that they meet specific industry regulations. Instead of offering a one-size-fits-all service, they instead offer industry-specific services that meet the relevant regulatory compliance.

There are several audit certifications for cloud providers:

- **SSAE 16:** The standard put forward by the Auditing Standard Board of Certified Public Accountants

- **SA 300:** Planning guidelines for an audit of financial statements, which takes into account the effect of IT on the audit procedures, including the availability of data and the company management's commitment to the design, implementation, and maintenance of sound procedures.

- **SA 315:** Concerns itself with occasions when IT is used to initiate, record, process, or report transactions or other financial data for inclusion in financial reports

It is the duty of the business consuming the cloud service to ensure that their cloud service provider is certified to meet their specific business's industry regulations. However, it is not quite that simple, because the cloud holds a greater risk than storing your data in a local data center. For example, what happens if the service provider goes out of business? How is the company's data protected from big data mining algorithms? Who is responsible for complying with regulations if the provider subcontracts storage to a third party? Also, how can you protect the vulnerable data link between the company and the provider (because this will be a prime attack vector for any malicious attacker)? These are all considerations that must be investigated as part of the audit procedure.

Where Logging Matters

A conventional audit procedure should take a risk-mitigation-based approach and identify both inherent risks that arise naturally and controllable risks that arise due to insufficient controls. The audit should also identify controls that are in place to treat identified risk and perform sampling of controls to determine effectiveness.

However, herein lies one of the big problems with cloud security auditing. It is very difficult to audit a provider's controls on your data while it's being held in the cloud provider's network. Yes, they have to allow respected industry auditors to validate their services if they want to gain certification, but they are not going to let customers perform ad hoc audits on data and infrastructure controls. This is where logging comes in.

If consumers cannot audit their data, they should at least be able to log access to what actions occurred, when they occurred, where they occurred, and who did it. After all, a multitenant environment can provide a perfect attack zone; instead of attackers having to scan the whole Internet looking for victims, they have a much smaller but more valuable target. Of course, to the cloud providers, this was a monumental challenge. The solution, or at least part of it, involves identity management.

To log access and record activity effectively, a service provider (or an application) must be able to tell the difference between users and then document their activity. One of the problems early cloud providers faced was that not only was it a problem segregating thousands of tenants, they now had to track the movements of tens of thousands of subtenants and somehow identify them.

Another issue with logging is that much of the data is mobile and the locations are virtual. So, where you store the logging information is in question as it could be stored on many different servers. This means that you need to consolidate logging reports within one user report. Furthermore, in a dynamic environment such as the cloud, you need to determine how long you should store historical data. This is one of the key elements to log management in the cloud; the consumer must challenge the provider, with regard to what is logged, where it's logged, and how long the logs are kept. It's also important to ensure the provider has security and event management system (SIEM) automation that processes the logs and raises alerts.

It should be obvious why a business would want to have access to logs on their local network. Reasons include the following:

- The ability to detect and/or track suspicious behavior

- Providing support for troubleshooting, maintenance, and operations

- Support for forensic analysis

Unfortunately, these are not so effective in the cloud, where infrastructure and application data's location is blurred. Fortunately, most businesses deploy IaaS as their cloud platform, and logging is very similar to normal enterprise log management—the big exceptions being where the logs are stored and where (and to whom) the alerts are sent. The most common solution is to set up a virtual machine as a log collector. The log collector aggregates and analyzes the logs generated within the IaaS platform. Alternatively, you could have each virtual machine in the IaaS cloud send back its individual logs to the company's data center for aggregation and analysis. This keeps it all "in house," but it creates a lot of traffic. Another option is to send the log traffic directly to a managed security partner or, as shown in Figure 33-1, to a third-party auditor (TPA) and have them deal with it all. This works well because they do all the auditing and collect auditing proof. When desired or required, the client can then retrieve that info from the TPA. This, of course, is only an option if you are allowed to outsource security management (not all companies are).

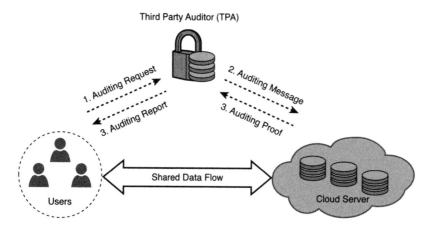

Figure 33-1　*TPAs manage ongoing auditing and logging. The client (users) can then gather that data as needed.*

Using PaaS and SaaS is more difficult because many cloud providers still do not support log management for these platforms. The bottom line is that with PaaS and SaaS, customers need to verify that application logging is an option and weigh that in their purchase decision. If a company is bound by either an internal or external requirement, some providers may not be an option.

That said, pressure is increasing for providers to figure this out with every development or application migrated to the cloud. As a result, this problem is likely to be solved soon because application and in-house developers' logs are much harder to parse and interpret than OS or network logs.

Ultimately, log generation in the cloud for organizations requires the same considerations and resources that are already employed for local data center logging. There will be storage and processor overheads, which will add to the cost of cloud storage and the problem of safely transporting the logs back to the company's data center.

Summary

To conclude, auditing and logging can be challenging in most cloud environments but the major players, such as Amazon, Google, and Azure, have recognized this deficiency, and all have developed and released auditing and logging portals.

Audit and Logging

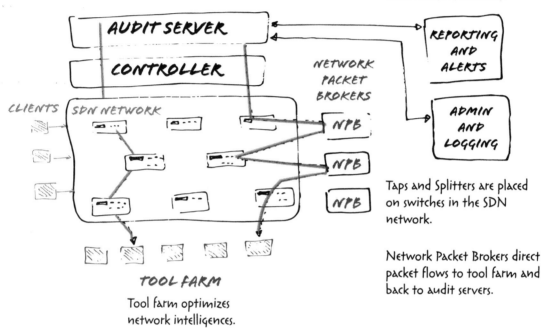

Audits should be kept separate from admin functions.

AUDIT SERVER

CONTROLLER

NETWORK PACKET BROKERS

CLIENTS SDN NETWORK

NPB

NPB

NPB

REPORTING AND ALERTS

ADMIN AND LOGGING

TOOL FARM

Tool farm optimizes network intelligences.

Taps and Splitters are placed on switches in the SDN network.

Network Packet Brokers direct packet flows to tool farm and back to audit servers.

In addition to being required for most regulated industries, audit and logging provides:

- The ability to detect or track suspicious behavior
- Support for troubleshooting, maintenance, and operations
- Support for forensic analysis

In cloud environments, auditing and logging can be challenging, but major players such as Amazon, Google, and Azure have recognized this problem and all have developed and released auditing and logging portals.

Encryption in Virtual Networks

Companies that have adopted the cloud and software-defined networking (SDN) are finding that although they bring many benefits in terms of large financial savings and reduced network complexity, there is a downside when it comes to data security. The security challenges that the cloud and SDN present are formidable, and organizations should not be taking them lightly. Prior to the cloud and SDN, companies mostly moved and stored their data locally within their secure network-edge perimeters. However, recent IT trends such as cloud, mobility, and bring your own device (BYOD) have made the hard network perimeter a thing of the past. Networks now have myriad access points to secure, so it has become more practical to virtualize the network in the cloud. By shifting the responsibility of the infrastructure to an infrastructure as a service (IaaS) provider, an organization can focus on protecting the data rather than the infrastructure. The best option for protecting data is to use encryption, but encryption can sometimes raise more issues than it addresses.

Encryption solves the biggest issue with moving and storing data beyond the organizational boundaries, by ensuring confidentiality and integrity. You can further break this down by considering the two states of data in the cloud: data in motion and data at rest.

Data in Motion

With data in motion, the client is typically concerned with how they will encrypt their data while it traverses the Internet on its journey to the cloud provider's network. This is not normally an issue with secure protocols such as Secure Sockets Layer/Transport Layer Security (SSL/TLS) used to encrypt the HTTP traffic. SSL encryption is great because it's generally secure enough and the user does not have to do anything special to make it work. It's easy to find info that suggests SSL is not secure, but the reality is that it's secure enough for the vast majority of organizations. SSL is only a web-based solution, which means unless you have a web-based applications it does not work.

For cases when applications are not web based, an encrypted (virtual private network [VPN]) tunnel is a great solution. However, as shown in Figure 34-1, the cloud provider usually terminates the tunnel (that is, they decrypt the traffic) on their Internet gateway at the edge of their cloud. This means that the data is unencrypted within the cloud.

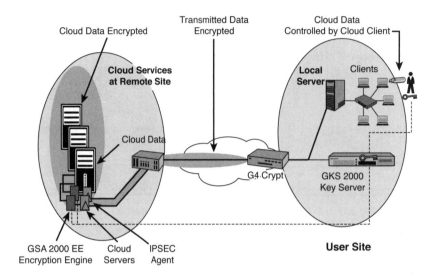

Figure 34-1 *IPsec VPNs are a good way to encrypt data over the WAN, but the encryption terminates at the cloud edge, leaving data in the clear within the cloud.*

Data at Rest

It is extremely important that if a business has sensitive or valuable information stored in the cloud, that it is stored securely by being encrypted. If IT follows this rule and encrypts data within the host's cloud network, it doesn't matter if the cloud provider suffers a security breach or even if they are compelled to disclose the data they store to the authorities. If the data is encrypted, it will remain unreadable. (Yes, the NSA can probably crack it, but a scenario where they want to crack your data is unlikely to the point of it being a border case.) However, this security applies only if the organization retains its own encryption keys (rather then handing them over to the cloud provider). This is the first dilemma encryption raises: Who retains the encryption keys?

This might at first seem obvious: that if a company bothers to encrypt the data before uploading it to the cloud, the company would also retain control and be in sole possession of the keys. However, there are a couple of problems with that. For example, if the client encrypts the data and then stores it within cloud storage, it will only be accessible to devices that are already in possession of the keys. This might seem like a good idea, but IP mobility and bring your own device (BYOD) are making the requirement of availability and access to data from anywhere and any device the norm. These BYOD devices may (rightfully) download the encrypted data, but it will be useless, because these devices would likely not have the decryption keys installed.

One additional consideration of encrypting data at rest is that encrypted client data is invisible to searches, sorts, audits/reports, or other common cloud administrative functions. This can impact a cloud provider's service level agreement (SLA) or prevent it from performing other value-added services. The upside here is that encryption also renders data free from snooping big data algorithms and provider analytics.

The alternative to client-side encryption, whereby the client encrypts the data and manages the keys, is provider-side encryption. In this model, which is favored by Microsoft, Google, and Yahoo!, the service provider is responsible for encryption of the client's data and will manage the decryption keys. The upside here is that IP mobility and BYOD devices can download the data decrypted and in a usable format without having to hold the decryption keys on the mobile device. This is much more practical for data that is regularly in motion or in use. The downside is that clients have to place all their trust in the cloud provider to manage and keep the data and the keys safe.

Placing the responsibility for encryption does have its drawbacks, though. The first is that the client makes the cloud provider a potential source of a breach. Whether it's a rogue employee who steals data, or a federal subpoena that forces the cloud provider to hand over the data (and the keys), the fact remains. When you hand over both the encrypted data and the keys to a third party, it's the same as not encrypting the data at all from a risk perspective.

The second consideration is that if you outsource encryption to the cloud, the provider will charge for the service. In this case, the provider supplies an encryption service (encryption as a service [EaaS]), which they bill the client for based on the client's usage. Therefore, it is imperative that to manage costs, the client identifies what data actually needs to be encrypted and what doesn't.

While using blanket ubiquitous encryption on all data can be convenient (if affordable), it will directly affect not just application performance but can also impact the integration of other cloud services. This is an important consideration because developers are building cloud applications using a building block approach whereby they use micro-services and application programming interfaces (APIs) from other cloud service providers (platform as a service [PaaS]) to build complex applications. Therefore, a more selective and discretionary approach to encryption is often the better choice.

Another important factor when deciding what to encrypt is to ensure that corporate security policies are being followed. Not only will this prevent an organization from having to start the categorization and classification process from scratch, it will also highlight not just sensitive files but also those internal and external files required for compliance to the regulatory bodies relevant to the business.

Automation-ready encryption is another option organizations can investigate when considering the encryption dilemma of which data to pass to the provider to encrypt. With this technique, IT preclassifies network data as to whether it is sensitive and in need of encryption. When a file is in motion, the software analyzes the packets and determines whether they should be physically encrypted when leaving the network on the client side or just tagged as such, which will allow the cloud provider to identify data it is to encrypt on the provider side. This technique can automate the identification and classification of sensitive content within the network and act to mitigate the potential for data leakage. It's not just about clicking a button, though; someone has to program the logic regarding what constitutes sensitive data.

The big takeaway here is that when it comes to the cloud encryption, no one doubts the importance of encrypting data in the cloud at rest and in motion. The real is issue is who manages the keys.

Key Management

Key management is not just a cloud issue. It's also one of the most important tasks that an IT manager has within a conventional network. Making sure that the keys are stored on a separate isolated server from the data and, preferably, on a separate storage block is essential. The IT manager must also ensure that the encryption keys are backed up and that the backups are stored in another secure remote location. However, the real problem IT managers have to deal with is key refresh, certificate revocation, key rotation, and destruction (for data-at-rest encryption). This is because most keys expire automatically and then have to be archived in a way that matches historical data and backups. This is a potential nightmare for some companies that have a need from time to time to access archived encrypted data. If the keys are not stored correctly, getting access to that data can be a painful and expensive process. This is hard enough on a conventional network, but since the shift to the cloud and the explosion of the volume data being stored there, a different approach is required.

Clients should consider, especially if they are hosting mobile applications and the data they produce within the client's virtual (IaaS) infrastructure, having their service provider or a third-party proxy manage the encryption keys on their behalf.

The key to this (no pun intended) is that the client must believe that the provider is better at securing and managing the keys than they are, and that they are as vested and will demonstrate the same diligence in protecting the data as the data owners. This is important because cloud providers are not subject to the same breach disclosure laws as are other regulated businesses. In the scenario where a cloud provider suffers a major data breach, it is not the cloud provider but the company that owns the data that the regulatory authorities will hold accountable. The client is also likely to receive the majority of the negative publicity if its customers' data is breached, even if it held that data in yet another company's cloud. The point is that the client retains the accountability for protecting its data wherever and however it is stored or processed.

Best Practices

There are a lot of options and considerations when it comes to data encryption in the cloud. What follows are some best practices and least recommendations, which are diagrammed in Figure 34-2:

- Encrypt data for privacy using approved algorithms and long random keys.

- Encrypt data before it leaves the client network and as it travels the network using SSL/ TLS or encrypted VPN tunnels for non-web-based applications. Note that not all VPNs are encrypted.

- Data should remain encrypted in transit, at rest, and when in use (on a device).

- The cloud provider and its staff should never have direct access to the decryption keys.

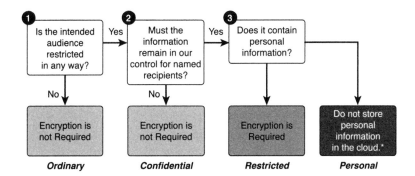

Figure 34-2 *Not all data needs to be encrypted. Companies should have some process to determine what types of data need extra security.*

Note that the final recommendation does not suggest that the cloud provider or a third party should not manage the keys on behalf of the client, just that they should not be able to have visibility to the keys.

The general rule is that sensitive data should be encrypted at rest and in motion and should only be decrypted at the very point in time it is required, and then must only be in the clear within protected transient memory space. Also, there should be no record of either the keys or the clear-text data in static memory, logs, or being written to disk or RAM caches.

Clients that run IaaS should look seriously at provider-side encryption because it allows the client to manage the encryption within the provider network much more effectively in the case of applications and their data (in motion, in use, and at rest). For clients using only cloud storage for backups and archiving, maintaining client-side encryption and key management is fine because they are dealing only with data at rest. However, for a belt-and-suspenders (extra cautious) method, a client might want to look at a third-party key management company, bearing in mind that although that will provide added reassurance, it will also add an additional layer of cost and complexity.

Encryption

IN MOTION

Encryption in motion is REALLY easy for web-based applications. It's great, because SSL encryption goes all the way from the web server to the user's browser, AND the user does not have to do anything extra to set it up.

Encrypted tunnels work great for non-web-based traffic, but be aware that the encryption tunnel terminates at the cloud gateway, which means your traffic is in clear text within the cloud. If this is a concern, don't use a third-party cloud.

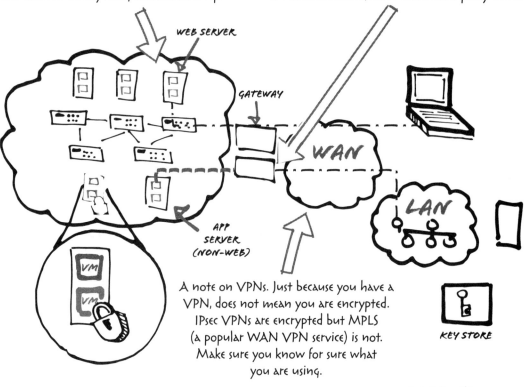

WEB SERVER

GATEWAY

WAN

LAN

APP SERVER (NON-WEB)

VM
VM

KEY STORE

A note on VPNs. Just because you have a VPN, does not mean you are encrypted. IPsec VPNs are encrypted but MPLS (a popular WAN VPN service) is not. Make sure you know for sure what you are using.

LEGEND

- - - ENCRYPTED TRAFFIC

— — UNENCRYPTED TRAFFIC

AT REST

Encryption is pretty straight-forward even in third-party clouds.

The key to encryption (pun intended) is to make sure that your keys are not stored or owned by the same third-party where your encrypted data is stored as it leaves you open to security breaches or other nasty surprises (like government snooping).

Everything Old Is Now New Again

Consider the following generic definition of the cloud that some technologists use: The cloud is a large compute resource that we can dynamically provision and make available to clients as virtualized infrastructure, which you can support with security and management controls. Although not the most exciting definition, it is correct, but here's the interesting part. This is very similar to the description of mainframe computers back in the 1970s. It appears that we've come full circle.

How We Got Here

With that in mind, let's take a look at the six computer models that have brought us from the mainframe's heyday in the 70s and early 80s to today's cloud paradigm three decades later.

The Mainframe Model

The mainframe was a centralized compute, storage, and network model that relied on massive computer and storage. (*Massive* at that time was less compute power and storage than what first-generation iPhones had, and yet these things filled a room.) The main mainframes were accessed via distributed dumb terminals (referred to as *green screens* because of the luminescent green text on the screen). Later, some very limited graphic terminals became available, but regardless the processing intelligence all resided on the centralized mainframe. The mainframe, because of its vast expense, could be multitenant, with the owners renting out a virtual mainframe by creating logical partitions. Each partition was a mainframe in its own right with its own segregated share of compute, memory, storage, and I/O. Also, the operators could dynamically provision the mainframe partitions, and security and management were intrinsic to the mainframe's design.

The Personal Computer Model

In the early 1980s, IBM delivered the IBM PC, and this heralded the era of the PC. These personal computers gradually replaced the mainframe terminals, and they soon became powerful enough in their own right to support most users' computing needs. Soon after, they became affordable to the point where many office workers (even those only doing word processing) had their own. This was a deliberate move away from the centralized model to a distributed, autonomous model.

The Networked Model

Once most workers had a PC at work, it became clear that some resources were better shared, such as mass storage devices for backups, printing, and application servers, and file servers to store and share files with colleagues. The solution was to network the PCs together on a local-area network (LAN) and to use larger computers called *servers* to host common applications and to be a central repository for files and data.

The Internet Model

LANs were soon connected together via routing protocols, routers, and wide-area network (WAN) links to other networks to share information and to allow global connectivity; the Internet became a network of networks.

Grid Computing Model

This was another distributed model, but only for very specialized applications that needed aggregated power and performance by having several or tens of thousands of distributed computers networked to collaborate and share the workload.

Cloud Computing Model

This is the present-day shared resources paradigm, whereby large service providers make available, on a charge-by-the-usage basis, parts of their vast networks to companies that either do not have a network or require additional resources for only a short time. Clients use infrastructure as a service (IaaS), software as a service (SaaS), or platform as a service (PaaS), or a combination, to enable them to take advantage of the provider's economies of scale to rent infrastructure, a development platform, or web-based (shared) applications much more economically than they could if they were buying their own. The provider can dynamically provision the client resources in compute, storage, and networks and bill only for the time they use them. Furthermore, the provider can dynamically shrink and stretch (elastic) the resources to meet the client's demands on resources and reclaim the resources automatically at the end of the agreement.

What We Have Learned

Looking at the earlier descriptions, there doesn't seem to be a lot of difference between the mainframe model of the 70s and today's cloud model. They both seem to serve the same purpose, albeit with today's vastly more powerful technology. However, with closer inspection, we can find a few important differentiators:

- A mainframe offers finite resources and performance, whereas the cloud offers almost infinite power and capacity.

- The mainframe terminals were simple keyboard and screen input/output devices that interfaced with the mainframe, whereas today clients' input devices are powerful PCs, laptops, smartphones, and tablets that can process information and execute local applications in their own right.

- The controller environment of a mainframe, which is the basis of its security and management typically, will require an administrator to provision computing power to clients, whereas the cloud runs on x86-based distributed architectures, where a key attribute is that provisioning in the cloud is self-service.

- The mainframe ran on specialized, proprietary hardware and used proprietary operating systems. This limited the types of applications that could be built, and the pace of innovation versus the x86 and open source options that exist to developers today.

Therefore, we can see that although there are many similarities between the two computer paradigms, the mainframe is not actually a private cloud, or even a cloud in a box. This is despite the fact that modern day mainframes can run Linux and virtual machines (VMs), and have been handling virtualization for the past 30 years. It is the lack of self-service provisioning, which is one of the five characteristics of a private cloud, that a mainframe just doesn't meet.

Table 35-1   *Comparing Private Clouds to Mainframes*

Feature	Private Cloud	Mainframe
Scalable (High levels of utilization through virtualization)	Yes	No
Accessible (Users can self-provision resources)	Yes	No
Elastic (Stretch and shrink resources on demand)	Yes	Yes
Shared (Capacity is pooled, workloads multiplexed)	Yes	Yes
Metered consumption (Billed for usage or resources)	Yes	Yes

Therefore, even if it appears we have gone full circle with the computer paradigm and architecture, we haven't quite; there is still some work required on today's mainframes for us to define them as private clouds. However, that doesn't mean that mainframes like the IBM z-series cannot be part of a cloud hardware infrastructure. They certainly can be and are used by many service providers and enterprises in building private cloud configurations.

Retro Security Considerations

So if we now acknowledge that not everything old is new again, when discussing the differences between clouds and mainframes, it's worth taking a look specifically at security. In many ways, the difference is in both the number of external players today but also in that so much of your personal life and business secrets are stored on servers that are externally accessible. This, of course, was not the case 40 years ago.

Surprisingly, though, the most notable threats to arise in 2015 are not new threats. Bad ads, crypto-ransomware, and macro malware are known to all antivirus software houses and are well-known threats from the past. The interesting thing here is that to achieve their latest prevalence and success, these old threats have been reengineered to succeed against the security controls that once identified and contained them.

Ransomware, for example, had dropped out of site and off the AV software houses' radar for several years before the most destructive and dangerous form of crypto-ransomware's sudden resurgence in the early months of 2015. Similarly, bad ads (malvertisements—which is a term for when attackers subvert third-party ad servers to serve up malware to trusting and legitimate websites) made their own vengeful return by targeting zero-day vulnerabilities using new exploit kits. Although neither bad ads nor zero day vulnerabilities are new threats and were well under control, bringing them together using the latest exploit kits has provided them a new lease on life.

However, the reemergence of crypto-ransomware and malvertisements after a few years pales into insignificance when we consider the third threat to make its spectacular return, the 29-year-old macro malware. If ever the saying "everything old is new again" holds true, it is with the reemergence of this threat. One lesson we can take from this is that threats are never fully eradicated; they can always be reevaluated, reengineered, and reapplied to suit new technologies and defeat aging security appliances.

If we consider that three previously vanquished threats returning as the top three threats of early 2015 and defeating state-of-the-art firewalls and antivirus protection is a bit worrying, what are the ways to remediate these threats in the cloud? The answer appears to rely on another equally old technique: logging. The cloud now holds the potential to aggregate and analyze logs in real time, so that instead of trying to recognize a malicious file by its signature (which can be masked or changed to make it effective for a short time before it's reclassified), we can instead track anomalies in its behavior. We can now achieve this by using big data mining techniques to shift through vast quantities of good old-fashioned event logs generated in the cloud, analyzing them in real time or close enough, and this can shorten response times in the event of a breach. This was the way it was done, albeit manually, years ago when security parsed logs daily looking for anomalies and evidence of malicious behavior. Now the technology exists to parse the logs—and far greater quantities of them—much more efficiently and in real time.

Another security technique that has reemerged to great effect in the era of the cloud and virtualization is encryption. IT departments have realized the potential privacy issues that exist in the cloud and multitenant virtualized platforms and networks, and have begun in earnest to encrypt their data. IT now sees cryptography as the old-school solution but also as the key to success to mitigate the new threat that mobile apps, cloud, and big data now present.

Recycled Ideas on Mobile and Web Apps

A final example of where "everything old is new again" is in mobile and web apps that are being developed and delivered in the cloud and where recycling of failed ideas can prove lucrative. Just because an idea bombed a decade ago—before cloud infrastructure was mainstream and start-ups still relied on conventional networks—doesn't mean that it won't work now. With all these scalable resources and unlimited CPU, storage, and network, it probably will. Many new and successful mobile and web apps are recycled ideas from five or six years ago, where the idea was great but the technology just did not exist at the time to deliver it. Cloud infrastructure, IaaS, and PaaS have provided start-ups developing software with the infrastructure and platforms to succeed where others previously failed. For example, the Facebook messaging platform, hailed as a major initiative, is simply a variation of an idea many companies were trying to implement back in the early 2000s. Other examples are the video streaming products Meerkat and Periscope, which are highly successful applications that have benefited from cloud deployment, sophisticated mobile phones, and 3G/4G networks. This technology simply wasn't around when Qik and Flixwagon attempted the same idea back in 2007. Let's not forget the huge failure that was Newton from Apple back in 1998, as compared to the runaway success that the iPad was when launched in 2010.

Recycling and reuse is all around us as we enter the new era of SDN virtualization, and whether we call it service-oriented architecture (SOA), virtualization, or simply the cloud, the present isn't looking too different from the past.

Data Center Evolution

Early computers were big room-filling machines. All the computing power (limited as it was) was in the data room.

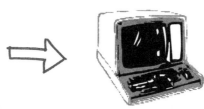

Data was accessed via a "Dumb Terminal" —all it did was present information or accept keystroke commands.

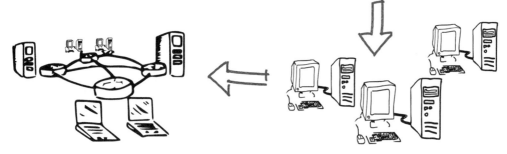

Computer networks connected machines and people together like never before, but now the servers were hard to support and manage.

The PC revolution put a computer on or under every desk so that everyone could be more productive but collaboration was difficult.

1000'S OF SERVERS IN DOZENS OF BUILDINGS SPREAD OUT ALL OVER THE WORLD ACT LIKE ONE BIG COMPUTER.

Modern data centers made SW support and control much easier, but the data centers got really big and were inefficient.

Virtualized data centers are now massive collections of virtualized machines with users accessing data from a browser —and all they do is push and pull data. This is very similar to the old "dumb terminal" days (but on a global scale). In some ways, all this technical progress has come full circle.

Visibility

PART **9**

Overlay Networks

It was not too long ago that people just spoke about the network without qualifiers. Today, however, you typically hear about the network in terms of an overlay network or underlay network, especially with regard to the data centers and clouds. In cloud-based data centers, overlays act as independent networks that sit on top of the physical infrastructure, which is the underlay network, but they also provide the means to provision and orchestrate networks alongside other virtual resources.

This all starts to sound like software-defined networking (SDN) or network virtualization (NV), but you must be careful not to confuse terms, because overlay networks are not necessarily either of these technologies. For instance, a network overlay can simply be a computer or storage network built upon the physical network using virtual links and will be transparent to the underlying infrastructure. Other overlay techniques, which are neither SDN nor NV, are virtual LANs (VLANs), generic routing encryption (GRE) tunnels, and Multiprotocol Label Switching (MPLS). These tunnel techniques are all forms of virtualization because they segment the physical network into smaller private segments that look and act as autonomous networks. This is where it's important to understand that the term *overlay* is a logical set of network connections running or overlaid on an existing (physical) network, rather than being a network itself. Therefore, the word overlay can be a bit of a misnomer and confusing. It is not another network built atop of a base network, but rather a series of logical tunnels drilled through the existing infrastructure.

MPLS: The Original Virtual Network

MPLS is very similar to the modern concept of network virtualization because it abstracts the complexity of the underlay physical network by creating tunnels (label switch paths) between the customer-edge end nodes, which effectively abstract the underlay physical Layer 2/3 routers in the network. What this means is that network administrators do not have to configure every node on a path from customer site A to customer site B; they only need to configure the respective tunnel endpoints. In addition, the tunnel provides traffic segregation, and if the administrator configures MPLS as an L2VPN, they effectively create a private wire or LAN between the customer's sites. As shown in Figure 36-1, you can logically separate traffic from different users or companies on a shared network by labeling the traffic. The network makes forwarding rules based on the labels. If the administrator wants, he could create a Layer 3 VPN—using virtual routing tables and route distinguishers. In either case, the tunnel facilitates the segmentation of the backbone physical network to deliver independent subnetworks that accommodate multitenancy and the use of shared IP subnets between customers.

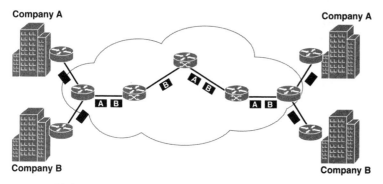

It is important to note that MPLS only provides logical separation—the data is not natively protected (encrypted).

Figure 36-1   *In MPLS, traffic is tagged with labels, and then forwarding rules are based on these labels, effectively segmenting them and making them "virtually private."*

Large-scale network virtualization, however, takes the MPLS overlay a step further by using software-defined networking (SDN) to automate the provisioning of the tunnel overlays. This is very important in virtualized server environments where virtual machines (VMs) need to connect and communicate with VMs located on other servers within the data center. The importance of this is that for VMs to perform most of their advanced and desirable features, such as mobility, requires sharing a Layer 2 switched broadcast domain. The VMs require this Layer 2 adjacency so that they can communicate or move—while still active—from one server to another without changing the IP address of the VM. This is fine if the VMs want to relocate to a server connected to the same top-of-rack (TOR) switch in the same subnet. In that scenario, the servers share the same Layer 2 domain. However, to communicate with a VM hosted on, or to relocate to, another server across the Layer 3 physical network would require the administrator to reconfigure VLANs, trunking, and Layer 3 routing, which is not feasible.

Virtual Layer 2 Designs

The initial reaction to solving this problem is to reengineer the architecture to be a flat Layer 2 network. This would certainly assist in VM east-west communications across servers and racks and remove any obstacles that prevent VM mobility. Unfortunately, there are some fundamental problems with this plan. First, companies are reluctant to reengineer their data centers, because of high costs and risk. Second, there are good reasons why data center networks were designed in a hierarchical topology. The most relevant reason is that flat Layer 2 networks have major issues in scaling. This is because in the data layer, hosts communicate using MAC addresses they learn through Address Resolution Protocol (ARP) broadcasts, and that technique does not scale well. There are, of course, VLANs that will segment the broadcast domains into many smaller manageable broadcast domains, and that can be fine for small data centers. For large-scale networks, VLANs are not an option because they are limited to a max of 4096 instances—and often a lot less than that in practice—which in a service provider-grade network is not nearly sufficient.

Another issue with Layer 2 networks is that switches need to remember the MAC addresses and switch port mappings, so that they do not have to continually broadcast ARP requests onto the wire. The problem is in large-scale networks, that can mean millions of customers' MAC addresses are being stored on the data center core switches.

However, the biggest single issue with flat Layer 2 network scalability is loops. It is very easy when designing Layer 2 switching networks to inadvertently introduce a loop. Loops can cause massive disruption on a switched network because Ethernet frames do not carry a time-to-live (TTL) counter. Because of this, the frames will loop continuously and multiply (very quickly), resulting in what is known as a "broadcast storm," which will eventually consume all the available bandwidth and bring the network down (and it can happen in the blink of an eye). Modern switches have techniques to mitigate the effects of a broadcast storm, and administrators can prevent loops in the network using protocols such as Spanning Tree Protocol, but that can often be a case of the cure being worse than the disease.

Of course, this is not a practical approach when considering large-scale data centers; hence, the traditional Layer 2/Layer 3 hierarchal network because Layer 3 is eminently scalable and avoids the horrors of spanning tree (an effective but inefficient protocol to prevent loops in Layer 2 networks). As a result, network virtualization falls back on the old trick of overlaying a web of Layer 2 tunnels through the physical underlay Layer 3 network, as shown in Figure 36-2. Individual VMs or physical switches (if they have VXLAN Tunnel Endpoint [VTEP] software installed) can act as tunnel endpoints. By provisioning these tunnels through the existing network infrastructure, the administrator can provide connectivity between Layer 2 subdomains separated by a Layer 3 network. Consequently, VMs can migrate from one server to another as if they all reside on the same flat Layer 2 network. Also, one important point is that any tunnel that the administrator creates, edits, or tears down has no effect whatsoever on the existing physical network's configuration.

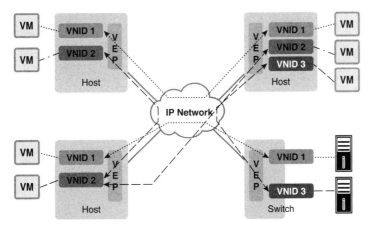

Figure 36-2 *Layer 2 tunnels allow you to connect Layer 2 (switched) domains over Layer 3 (routed) networks.*

Enter SDN

Where SDN comes into play is that it can orchestrate the provisioning of these tunnels dynamically on demand, thereby relieving the network administrator of the burden. What this means is that if VM1-192.168.1.50 on server 1 wants to communicate with, say, VM2-172.16.10.1 residing on server 2 (in a different Layer 2 domain), SDN will provision the tunnel on demand, and VM1 and VM2 can communicate as if they shared the same vSwitch. Similarly, if VM1 requires relocating from server 1 to server 2 located in another part of the data center, due to say an unexpected increase in the workload, or a lack of server resources, it could move to server 2 using VM mobility (vMotion) as if it were crossing a common Layer 2 LAN and yet still retain its original IP address.

Overlay networks are therefore hugely important when considering large-scale networks, because they alleviate many of the problems by providing Layer 2 connectivity regardless of a switch's or VM's physical locality or the underlay network topology. Overlays use encapsulation techniques to package traffic inside IP packets that are able to traverse the Layer 3 boundaries in the network, thereby removing the need for manually preconfigured VLANs and trunks. Furthermore, the encapsulation method is transparent and done behind the scenes, so is independent of the application. In addition, the overlay technique removes the dependence on the underlay physical network's configuration, and as long as there is IP connectivity, the overlay will work.

Common Encapsulation Techniques

The way that overlays work is through applying one of the three common encapsulation techniques to the traffic. The three commonly deployed methods are as follows:

- Virtual Extensible LAN (VXLAN)

- Single spanning tree (SST)

- Network virtualization using generic routing encapsulation (NVGRE)

The basic technique that the VXLAN and NVGRE encapsulation methods use to improve on VLAN is to increase the address space from VLAN's 12-bits Vl tag, which allows a max 4096 instances, to a 24-bit virtual network interface device (VNID), which allows 16 million instances. SST uses an even larger 32-bit VNID, which provides a huge pool of potential tunnel instances. As shown in Figure 36-3, this allows us to run multiple virtual networks over a single physical network.

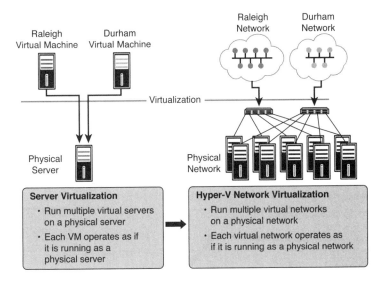

Figure 36-3 *Server virtualization versus network virtualization*

The tunnel protocols themselves work in a similar manner, insomuch as the process identifies the tunnel endpoints and assigns them a virtual network ID (VNID) unique to that tunnel. The endpoints will belong to the virtual network regardless of where they reside on the underlying physical network. The endpoints on each host, a VM, or switch, which are identified by their VNID, are attached within the host to a virtual endpoint (VEP), which is a vSwitch, which can encapsulate/decapsulate traffic for its client virtual networks (tunnels). Each host can have one or more VNIDs operating on it, and each workload assigned to a given VNID can communicate with other workloads in the same VNID, while maintaining separation from workloads in other VNIDs on the same or other hosts.

VEP can run in virtualized VM environments, but it can also run in hardware such as switches; so, servers, switches, firewalls, and other network appliances can be added to the virtual network overlay. In addition, network overlays provide for multitenant support over shared IP networks, and deliver the flexible and rapid provisioning required by today's service providers. By using overlays, a network administrator can ensure that applications and services are added, moved, and expanded without the need for manual configuration of the underlying network infrastructure.

Overlay Networks

Enterprises see two big issues with SDN:

1. They have a lot of investment in their current infrastructure and want to maximize their investments.

2. SDN blurs the lines between networking, IT, and storage groups—so who gets to be in charge?

Overlay networks are a good solution, because they allow many SDN benefits on the network that is in place now.

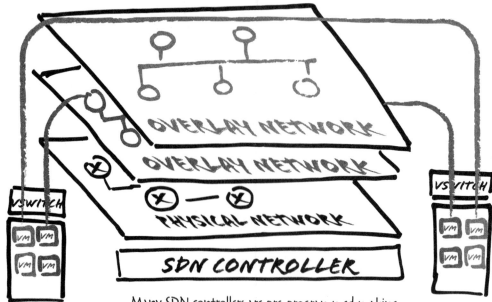

OVERLAY NETWORK

OVERLAY NETWORK

PHYSICAL NETWORK

SDN CONTROLLER

VSWITCH

VM VM
VM VM

VSWITCH

VM VM
VM VM

Overlay networks are created by creating tunnels that connect VMs via Vswitches.

Many SDN controllers are pre-programmed making it easy to set up overlay networks on existing infrastructure. The type of controller you use depends a lot on your needs and your talent.

WHO TO CHOOSE?

CISCO ACI

Cisco's Application Centric Infrastructure (ACI) is great when there are hard divisions between networking and IT teams and when the networking team has expertise on Cisco infrastructure.

VMWARE NSX

Great when networking expertise is limited or when IT team control is preferred over network team control.

Network Management Tools

You can look at software-defined networking (SDN) as being a new method of designing, building, and managing networks achieved through the separation of the control plane from the underlying forwarding data plane on devices within the network. To make this actually work and to prevent SDN from becoming a multitude of autonomous network applications and monitoring tools, SDN offloads control to centralized network control computers. Consequently, these controllers need a method of communication with the forwarding data planes of the distributed devices in the network. This SDN design setup allows great flexibility and tight management control by:

- Forwarding data flows along the most optimal path (which is not necessarily the shortest path).

- Applying quality of service (QoS) policies to data flows to dictate how network traffic is handled and prioritized.

- Providing a mechanism for feedback control to the forwarding path device so that it relays information about its own current state back to the controller. This application of feedback from the forwarding plane to the central controller allows the software to effectively adjust its own future decisions based on the results of its previous actions.

These inherent features of SDN are part of what makes SDN so attractive to network engineers and designers. By having such a high level of programmable control, the controller can make intelligent decisions as to how network traffic and data flows through and across the network, and changes/optimization can be done in real time. However, having these traffic control capabilities does not negate the requirement of real-time traffic monitoring. If anything, it can be argued that automated systems require more, not less, monitoring and analysis.

SDN brings improvements in the way that networks are designed, built, managed, and scaled within the data center while simultaneously introducing automated provisioning processes to mitigate the risk of human error. However, there is one drawback. By abstracting the underlying network's applications and protocols at OSI Layers 4 through 7, SDN actually reduces network visibility into the traffic flows. Having visibility into data flows that are crossing the wire is critical for administrators tasked with analyzing data network traffic for the purpose of securing, optimizing, and troubleshooting the virtual and physical networks. Therefore, for network administrators, it is imperative that they and their network and application management tools have complete network transparency.

What's in the Tool Bag?

For administrators to manage, secure, optimize network traffic, and stay compliant with regulatory bodies and the law, a variety of test and monitoring tools are used:

- Network analyzers

- Data leakage protection (DLP) systems

- Intrusion detection and prevention systems (IDS and IPS)

- Tools for network security, compliance, and policy assurance

- Lawful interception taps

- Content filtering applications

- Computer forensic analysis and data capture tools

One issue that network admins are running into is keeping up with increasing network speeds. Networks are getting faster and faster. Today, many data centers are running 10-Gbps links throughout and using 40/100-Gbps aggregation links. With network speeds increasing, capturing, inspecting, analyzing, balancing, and filtering network traffic at wire speed is becoming difficult, especially from a budget perspective. Network admins are often under intense pressure not only to manage the network but also to do it within a budget. This is especially difficult when, for example, a department invests in a 10G analyzer one year only to find that the networks are running 40G traffic the next year. Businesses typically expect to achieve five years of usage out of this type of equipment. Overprovisioning is one solution, but it's equally difficult to justify the increased cost of a 40G tool when most traffic is still at 10G.

Tapping In

The conventional way to connect network-monitoring equipment to switches was through the use of Switched Port Analyzer (SPAN) ports on an access or aggregation layer switch. These were convenient traffic aggregation points for connecting a network analyzer to capture all the traffic passing over the switch ports of interest. A network analyzer could then apply filters to the traffic flow to separate traffic of interest by applying one of a multitude of filters such as IP address (src and dst), VLAN, protocol, TCP flags, or application type. This is still a method that network administrators use in small and medium-size business (SMB) and enterprise LAN networks, because it is quick and convenient to deploy when troubleshooting network traffic issues. However, in SDN data center and clouds, where data traffic visibility is much more opaque, administrators use test access points (TAPs) to passively collect network traffic from specific endpoints.

Unlike other network capturing methods such as SPAN ports, which use a single network cable connected to a port on a switch, TAPs are connected between two switches. A pair of cables connects the TAP device to the relevant endpoint ports on each switch. A complete copy of the network traffic is sent through the endpoint ports and across the TAP without interruption to the flow of traffic across the wire. TAPs provide for passive monitoring, data access, and network visibility and can operate at data center wire speeds of up to 100 Gbps.

Several types of TAPs are used in data center environments, and they are classified as follows:

- **Network bypass TAP:** The purpose of the bypass TAP is to provide a fail-proof path for connection of in-line network monitoring or security appliances. As shown in Figure 37-1, by providing a separate path and a cloned copy of all the network traffic flowing between the two endpoints, the network is protected against any break in service from the appliance such as hangs, reboots, or fails.

- **Aggregation and regeneration TAP:** These devices provide a safe and convenient way to capture and then reproduce network traffic, which is presented on several monitoring ports. This enables network monitors, analyzers, or security devices to have visibility and connectivity simultaneously without any detrimental effect on network performance and throughput.

- **Network breakout TAP:** This type of TAP is used in data center monitoring to passively collect and copy 100 percent of the network traffic crossing the wire, and they can work at speeds up to 100 Gbps unidirectional or 40 Gbps bidirectional.

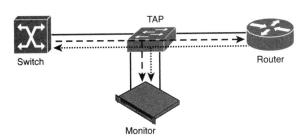

Figure 37-1   *Network bypass TAPs clone traffic to allow monitoring without disrupting traffic flows.*

The benefit of using TAPs instead of the conventional SPAN port method is that mirroring ports of interest to a SPAN port on a switch presents the real risk that the aggregated traffic will swamp the span port, resulting in lost data and therefore inaccurate analysis.

Gaining Visibility

To get the most out of deploying TAPs for monitoring network traffic, the goal is to create a network *visibility layer* within virtualized networks that will allow monitoring equipment to have complete transparency into all the data flows crossing the network. SDN does not remove that requirement; indeed, administrators still need a way to connect and have visibility into what is going on within the virtual and physical networks, and hence the importance of creating a visibility layer.

The concept of a visibility layer comes about because of the uncertainty that the conventional method of connecting applications to a network, via network packet brokers (NPBs), will be as effective in a virtualized network or even if they can be virtualized. The way packet brokers conventionally work is that they control the flow of traffic and make it possible to capture data and provide a method to interface monitoring devices and applications in 10/40/100-Gbps data centers or, as shown in Figure 37-2, to "tool farms," where traffic is aggregated and then replicated so that all tools see all traffic without impacting performance. Consequently, there has been interest in the virtualization of packet brokers via network functions virtualization (NFV). OpenFlow Version 1.4 includes as a use case a feasibility/tutorial study for configuring switches to have NPB-like functionality, which would be a step forward toward virtualized network visibility if it were production ready.

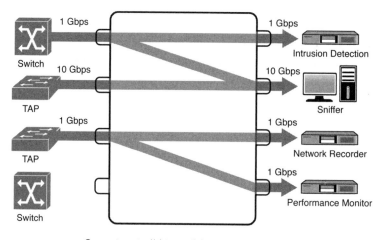

Connect any tool(s) to any link at any time without
affecting the producation network

Figure 37-2 *TAPs allow traffic to be collected and sent to tool farms for monitoring.*

Despite this uncertainty over the suitability of NPB as a virtualized network function (VNF), it remains that a TAP is a fundamental and essential requirement for network monitoring in an SDN or virtualized network environment. This is simply because TAPs provide a real-time, uninterrupted view of the underlay physical networks to the monitoring and analysis equipment. Furthermore, and most important, in an SDN virtualized environment, TAPs provide the means for full network visibility to the SDN controller software.

Of course, not all virtualized networks are SDN, and here is where we encounter another problem with conventional network monitoring systems (NMSs): virtual overlay networks. In summary, virtual overlays are actually tunnels provisioned through the underlay physical network and hence are dependent on the underlay network for IP connectivity.

Consequently, we know the virtual tunnel endpoints (VTEP) and can terminate these tunnels with entities, such as virtual machines (VMs) or physical switches that have VTEP enabled through their firmware. However, between the endpoints, we have no idea what path these packets take along their way to the corresponding tunnel endpoint. Furthermore, with conventional network monitoring equipment, we are blind to these encapsulated packets passing through the tunnels. To the monitoring software, there is no tunnel, and the packets look just like any other IP packet.

In addition to the poor visibility that network monitors have with regard to the tunneling issue, there was/is sometimes an even bigger issue at the tunnel endpoints. The potential issue here is that older hypervisors had primitive software vNICs and vSwitches. These software implementations did not support many traffic monitoring features, which made intra-VM-to-VM traffic invisible to conventional network monitors. This was because intra-VM-to-VM traffic never left the host physical server's memory, let alone went onto the wire on the physical network interface card (NIC). Furthermore, network monitoring and traffic analysis was hampered by the lack of SPAN port features, VLANs, and quality of service (QoS), which made network monitoring difficult. Later versions of vendor hypervisors remedied most of these legacy issues, and now if using a licensed enterprise edition or a new release of an open source version of a hypervisor, you will have vSwitch traffic management features, QoS, multi-VLAN, and SPAN to match modern physical switches. This topic is covered in detail in Chapter 39, "Monitoring Traffic Between Virtual Switches."

However, before delving into the intricacies of vSwitch-to-vSwitch monitoring, in the next chapter we look at another aspect of virtual networking that is highly relevant to network monitoring: measuring and meeting the customer's or user's quality of experience (QoE).

SDN Monitoring

With the massive growth in virtualized traffic within the data center, providers and clients face a big challenge when it comes to monitoring virtual traffic for application, network, and security analysis.

Virtual monitoring solutions provide intelligent filtering technology that enables virtual machine (VM) traffic flows of interest to be selected, forwarded, and delivered to the centralized monitoring tools for analysis.

Network Packet Brokers (NPBs) are network devices that gather and aggregate network traffic from switch ports or network TAPs.

NPBs then split or duplicate that traffic to enable the more efficient use of network security and performance tools.

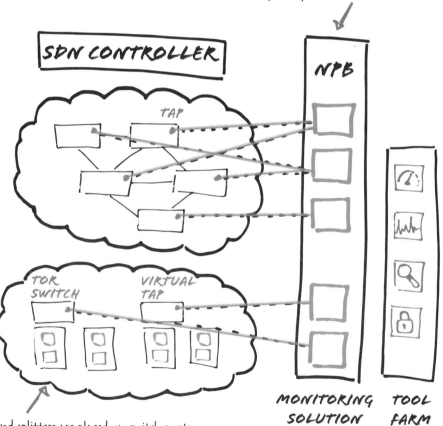

Taps and splitters are placed on switch ports throughout the network. Virtual taps are available for VM traffic visibility. This is key as VM-to-VM traffic can be otherwise undetectable.

Quality of Experience

Service providers have for many years searched for the solution for providing satisfactory customer end-user quality of experience (QoE). It is the holy grail of customer service, which is delivering the level of service that consumers believe they should receive. Delivering QoE to the customer reduces churn and enhances the provider's reputation. Despite this, many providers have failed to deliver satisfactory QoE with their network services or personalization to the customer, in comparison to other industries such as retail and banking. There are many reasons for this occurrence; one is due to the rapid turnover in services and applications, and second, the prominence of virtual network overlays in the data center, where there is a lack of visibility between the virtual and the physical networks. This decoupling of the virtual and physical networks tends to make the overall network monitoring and management a problem and hence the lack of visibility into the customers' QoE.

In spite of this, over the past few years, virtual network design has proliferated throughout the data center, and consequently the capability to monitor traffic passing through virtual and physical interfaces has developed to the extent that monitoring equipment can now accommodate monitoring data traffic through virtual overlays and even match their correlation with the physical underlay network.

Virtualization, cloud, and mobility are all major themes in the modern networks. Users are adopting bring your own device (BYOD), and they are demanding access to their applications and data from anywhere, at any time, and on any device. The problem is that today, applications and data are also mobile and they can shift from server to server throughout the data center, or even globally. Consequently, while virtual machine (VM) mobility is driving IT, it is also making the virtualized IT data network very complex to monitor. It's also all but impossible to predict at any given time where users will be when they access the network, and to a lesser extent where the data will be when they access. This means that guaranteeing a high QoE is very difficult—certainly much more difficult than it was a few years ago when the location of both ends was relatively fixed.

As a result, in a dynamic virtualized environment, it is becoming difficult to determine whether a user, an application, or the underlying infrastructure is performing as required. Therefore, monitoring of traffic flows across the network is crucial to determine whether the security, compliance, and audit requirements are being fulfilled as per company policy. Similarly, the cloud initiative is changing the way IT and their consumers think about compute, storage, and connectivity.

The cloud and software-defined networking (SDN) have changed the previous upfront business *capital expenditure* (CAPEX) model, which required that small and medium-size business (SMB) or enterprises front-end capital investment to build infrastructure, and has gravitated toward a new business-driven operational expenditure (OPEX) model (rent, not build/buy). The cloud also introduced a new technology model where applications could grow or shrink with elasticity of compute, storage, and network to meet real-time demand. In this model, applications or an SDN controller determine the available resources applications require, which they add and remove on demand based on the applications' dynamic capacity requirements.

Although cloud deployment makes application deployment very easy, it also makes it trivial to adjust resources to meet individual applications' demands without prior capacity planning. For example, when building traditional networks, designers would calculate the expected resource capacity for an application based on visits per second, throughput, bandwidth, CPU, and storage, among other criteria. Subsequently, they would then build into their design that capability with allowances for overhead. However, the advent of mobile apps and web-scale applications has meant that predicting usage is a problem. The designer might allocate a certain amount of resources based on expected uptake, only to find that the application has gone viral. In a traditional application deployment, suddenly meeting this boost in traffic would require reengineering the entire infrastructure (that is, adding more web servers and load balancers). In a cloud environment, that is unnecessary; because the applications can demand of the network the resources they require, the availability of resources shrinks or grows per demand, and in real time. This assumes, of course, that the cloud provider has ensured capacity. There is always an upper limit on physical resources.

However, this network flexibility also makes it very challenging to monitor traffic flows as the application's new capacity requirement is fulfilled though spinning up a new VM instance of the application on the server or relocating the VM to a different server that can meet the required resource contract. This is the huge benefit of virtualization; VMs and their applications can be spun up or down to meet the fluctuating capacity requirements of applications, and that is often done dynamically, transparently, and without any loss of service.

What is more, the VMs hosting the application may be required to move to other physical servers, those that can meet the application's resources demand within the data center. This makes monitoring customer flows problematic with traditional network monitoring system (NMS). The reason for this is that NMSs are conventionally designed to track, among other things, packets, protocols, subnets, and virtual LANs (VLANs). Telling an NMS to track traffic on VLAN1 across diverse servers around the data center is not a problem. For example, tracking VLAN1 traffic across multiple channels and endpoints across the infrastructure is well within its capabilities. However, asking it to track Customer A's traffic, who may be one in a million multitenants, whose traffic may be spread over many VMs around the data center, or even globally, is another thing entirely.

The lack of visibility and control within virtualized networks, of course, raises the question of whether the current network monitoring mechanisms in place today are capable of determining whether an end user is truly getting a good user experience and whether applications are performing as expected.

The problem is that in virtualized networks it is difficult to determine where a potential forwarding problem exists. For example, virtual tunnels may be created within the hypervisor itself, and this results in the physical network having no visibility or no idea of when tunnels are created or torn down. If we want to monitor customer QoE, however, we need to know these things. Furthermore, to be able to access customer QoE requires a means to analyze the traffic flows and optimal paths through the network.

Deep Packet Inspection

So how can SDN or virtualized networks assist in QoE?

There has been a long-sought-after requirement among providers to develop a better insight into IP traffic flows and to be able to correlate them to their customers' behavior, and furthermore to be able to act on that information to improve network performance, reduce the cost of bandwidth, control congestion, and enhance their customers' QoE. This has been the service providers' goal for many years, and SDN and network virtualization promise to fulfill those objectives. In addition, there is the prospect of a collaborative technology: deep packet inspection (DPI). Although the two technologies differ, they can work in harmony because they have similar objectives.

DPI and SDN are very separate technologies, but they seek the same goal, albeit in different ways. DPI seeks to make the network application aware, whereas network virtualization (NV) and SDN try to make the applications network aware.

The driver for deployment of DPI and any associated customer traffic-tracking techniques has been the need among service providers to gain a better insight into IP traffic patterns and user behavior. The wealth of information that can be gleaned from customer traffic usage and behavioral patterns is of immense financial value. To have the capability, through marketing and sales, to act on that information to improve network performance will reduce churn, acquire new acquisitions, reduce the cost of bandwidth, control congestion, and enhance subscriber QoE.

DPI helps service providers regain control over a network that is now primarily an access network for low-revenue customers to connect to the Internet. This is happening as providers are struggling with being relegated to access providers, while carrying competitive third-party applications and services over their networks (to the detriment of their own services and products). By identifying their customers' usage and behavioral patterns by using deep-dive analysis into their customers' data flows and usage patterns, providers can identify those applications in real time. They can then use the data to provide more customer-focused services and products to the customer and personalize the services offerings.

Customer QoE is a major key performance indicator when judging the quality of a network. Virtualization, SDN, and cloud deployments, through elasticity and dynamic provisioning, have delivered the necessary techniques to deliver the flexibility, agility, and multitenant security required by modern web and mobile applications.

CAPEX versus OPEX

WHY IT'S BETTER to RENT WITH the CLOUD

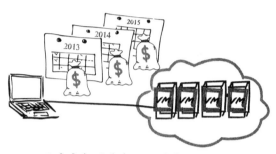

CAPITAL EXPENDITURES
-YOU OWN IT-

PROS:

* You own the equipment and have total control
* Tighter security
* Customized to your needs

CONS:

* You need people to run it
* You are stuck with what you bought for 3+ years
* You use up a lot of cash

OPERATIONAL EXPENDITURES
-PAY AS YOU GO-

PROS:

* You preserve cash
* You get access to the latest technology
* Easy expansion (or contraction)
* Greater flexibility in configurations

CONS:

* You are on a shared infrastructure
* Performance might not be as good due to remote nature of service
* Limited ability to customize environment

Although there are some advantages to owning your own equipment, "renting" is better, because of the flexibility and performance.

* It's the cloud provider's business to have the latest, best performing technology -when you "rent" you get faster access to new technology

* Better networking has eliminated most of the performance tradeoffs.

Monitoring Traffic Between Virtual Switches

In the early days of server virtualization, the proliferation of virtual machines (VMs) in the data center created an extended network access layer. This extension was the result of the hypervisor having its own built in virtual network interface card (vNIC) and a vSwitch. These elements were essential for VM-to-VM communications within the same host server, but they did have some drawbacks such as poor network visibility and management. The original vSwitches were primitive software bridges, which vendors designed to handle communications between locally connected VMs. This was, of course, all that was required from a server and application perspective. The problem was that conventional network management systems (NMSs) were unable to see intra-VM traffic (traffic between VMs on the same vSwitch) because these switches had no advanced traffic management features that would allow flow analysis, remote diagnostics, and traffic statistics. To compound the issue, there was also no method of communication between the hypervisor and the network management system.

In addition to those traffic management deficiencies, there was also the politics of who was responsible for the role of monitoring and management of the VM's applications and their network elements, because these software network switches were under the domain of the server teams, yet were performing a networking function. Therefore, the situation arose whereby the server teams would have to ask network teams to create VLANs, apply a quality of service (QoS) policy, and assign bandwidth for each new VM, which was a bit of a role reversal. However, once these resources were provisioned, the server team had no further role in the monitoring or management of what were effectively network devices.

Getting VM Visibility

Fortunately, VMware came up with the Virtual Distribution Switch (VDS), and Microsoft also released their upgraded Hyper-V Virtual Switch. These upgraded products provided much needed visibility into intra VM-to-VM traffic flows, which had previously been invisible to network management systems (NMSs) due to the traffic never appearing on the physical NIC. There were, however, still some outstanding traffic management issues. These were resolved when Cisco and VMware came up with a much more advanced vSwitch, called the Nexus v1000, which extended the network edge to the hypervisor. The Nexus v1000 provided the functionality that was missing, and as a result, vSwitches could behave similarly to a physical switch. These new breed of vSwitches could now have SPAN ports and could be accessed via NMS, providing networks with the visibility and management tools they required.

Specific advances in technology that mitigated the poor traffic visibility and management issues included the following:

- **Distributed virtual switching:** This technique separated the control plane from the forwarding data plane, and this allowed multiple vSwitches to then be controlled and managed via a centralized NMS, the virtual server management system, or even the control planes of physical access switches.

- **Virtual links between VMs and DVS:** This allows for offloading by the hypervisor of all VM switching to a physical access switch. This gives the NMS full visibility and policy control over traffic flows.

- **vNetwork APIs:** These provided support for other implementations of virtual switches such as the Open vSwitch project, which is compatible with XEN, XEN Server, KVM, and QEMU.

- **Edge virtual bridging:** This technology is based on Virtual Ethernet Port Aggregator (VEPA), and it uses VEPA to forward all VM traffic to the adjacent physical switch. VEPA returns the traffic to the original server if the destination VM is co-resident on the same server. This 180-degree hairpin gives the physical access switch visibility and control of all the VMs traffic flows.

Monitoring VM-to-VM traffic

Today, after a decade of innovation aimed at tacking vSwitch deficiencies with regard to visibility and traffic management, the VM traffic visibility issues are now a thing of the past. However, the same cannot be said about inter VM-to-VM traffic (that is, the traffic that flows across the data center infrastructure).

SDN and NV have brought flexibility and agility to the network by abstracting the complexities of the underlay network appliances Layer 4/7 protocols, services, and applications. By reducing the underlay network to a conceptual Layer 2/3 infrastructure, it makes it much simpler to understand with overlays, and it then confines the configuration complexity to the edge nodes. This is how networks should be: complex at the edge and simple in the middle. Furthermore, as you saw in the preceding chapter, overlays are tunnels that SDN or an administrator manually provision to carry encapsulated traffic through the Layer 3 network using tunnel protocols such as VxLAN, Network Virtualization using Generic Routing Encapsulation (NVGRE), and Secure Socket Tunneling (SST).

What this means is that you do not need to be concerned with the intermediate routers on the path and instead can configure the tunnel's terminating equipment at the overlay's edge. This makes provisioning of tunnels very easy to accomplish. However, this is taking a simplistic view because we are considering one theoretical tunnel with two endpoints. In reality, a data center with 200 or 300 servers and 1000 or more VMs will have a myriad of tunnels. This creates a complex web of overlay tunnels that are crisscrossing through the physical network.

How VxLANs Work

To understand why this is potentially a problem, we have to take a brief look at how these encapsulation protocols such as VxLAN work. The way that VxLAN works is that it encapsulates the data frames within UDP as the transport over the underlay Layer 3 network boundaries. In addition, VxLAN uses UDP source and destination ports to identify the packets associated with each tunnel. The problem with this is that tunnels are transparent to the physical network, so a network management system will only see VxLAN's individual UDP packets flying back and forth across the network seemingly with no correlation to one another. In other words, the tunnels and their data flows are effectively invisible. This is because the network can only see the UDP header and has no visibility into the packet to see the traffic from the VMs inside the VxLAN tunnel. An example of how restrictive this can be is to consider applying a quality of service (QoS) policy per VM. The problem is that the network can only see the UDP outer headers when making QoS policy decisions, so that effectively means that the network can only apply QoS policy to the entire tunnel, and not to the VM or its traffic.

This presents a problem when monitoring and managing virtual networks, for now you effectively have two networks: one the physical underlay, and the other the virtual overlay. This opens up yet another problem, for the physical and the virtual networks are only conceptually separate. As discussed in the preceding chapter, overlays are tunnels through the underlay's physical routers—for the virtual network is reliant on the physical network for IP transport and connectivity. If a physical link fails, a tunnel that uses that link will fail, and its VM's connectivity and its associated traffic will be lost. Furthermore, no obvious correlation exists between the physical and virtual networks other than at the tunnel endpoints. Again, this is viewing things from a simple single-tunnel perspective, but it does not take much imagination to see how the problem scales in a cloud orchestration environment where there may be multivirtual networks with thousands of VMs and their associated traffic flows contained in that single tunnel.

Creating a "Visibility Layer"

It's obviously advantageous to have virtual networks and overlays to provide the abstractions required to simplify the management of inter-VM communications and mobility throughout the data center. Despite this, there is a serious drawback in the lack of visibility that virtual overlays provide into the network and a distinct lack of understanding of the correlation of the physical to virtual network topologies. Therefore, if the promise of automation and orchestration for the provisioning and migration of VMs is to come to fruition, the virtual and physical networks will need to be integrated at the "visibility layer."

Integrating the virtual overlay with the physical network can be done in a variety of ways. One novel approach, which demonstrates the issue and provides a solution, is to use a tool for fast link failure detection from the physical network's existing toolbox. The technique is to have each tunnel endpoint run Bidirection Forwarding Detection (BFD) on the overlay tunnel. At each end of the overlay, the BFD agent (in both hardware and software) monitors the response times through the receipt of the BFD hello messages, and subsequently it is able to determine not only the up/down status of the links but also latency, jitter, and loss by monitoring and recording the time stamps and counters. If you run BFD on the VxLAN tunnel, the evaluation of the virtual and physical networks is conducted simultaneously as an integrated network, which, of course, it is.

Other virtual and physical network integration approaches rely on either out-of-band or in-band monitoring.

- **Out-of-band signaling:** This relies on an external entity, say an SDN controller that somehow knows the tunnel state and can provide some guarantee of the overlay network. The controller will be required to own every node in the underlay physical network and be able to program the tunnel's end-to-end path. Of course, the controller itself has to be informed of any anomalies in network behavior, so it will require that every network device provide feedback of its own current state and network conditions. In SDN, this is a feedback loop, whereby the controller instructs a device to perform an action and subsequently monitors its feedback state to determine whether the action was successful.

- **In-band signaling:** As shown in Figure 39-1, in this method the tunnel endpoints send messages through the tunnel looking for service information. The previous example with BFD is an example of in-band signaling. Furthermore, BFD is a good practical example because the BFD protocol is integrated in both hardware and software in most modern data center class routers. Therefore, with BFD, there are no new protocols or software to implement.

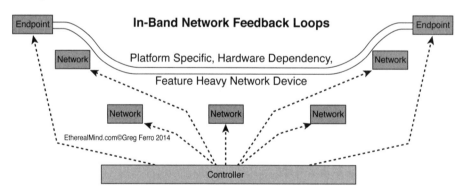

http://etherealmind.com/blessay-overlay-networking-bfd-integration-physical-network/

Figure 39-1 *In-band signaling uses tunnel endpoints to send messages that help determine the health and performance of the tunnel.*

With a solution for monitoring the tunnel state in place, the next consideration is whether you can actually determine which path the physical underlay used to build the tunnel. One way is to run a routing protocol in listening mode to glean from the Open Shortest Path First (OSPF) state database or Border Gateway Protocol (BGP) announcements to construct a representation of the respective routing protocol's network view of the topology. Subsequently, it is a straightforward task for a programmer to map the tunnel endpoint's IP addresses to routing table entries.

The Big Picture

Pulling It All Together

While it worked really well, for a really long time, traditional network designs have turned out to be ill-suited to delivering the application performance and services required by today's enterprises, cloud service providers, and end users—partly the result of the explosion in mobile device traffic traversing the network and the surge in popularity of mobile/web applications, and partly due to server virtualization in the data center (which has enabled cloud service providers to offer compute, storage, and network services on an unprecedented scale). The net result of all of these changes is that the industry has had to rethink networking.

Why the Network Had to Change

Conventional networks in enterprises and data centers were built upon layers of hierarchal switches and routers, in a core, aggregation, and access layer model. This architecture performed well in supporting client/server-style applications, where the traffic flow was predominantly north-south. (That is, the traffic flowed predictively from a client through the network layers to a server.) Modern applications and data flows, however, are no longer so predictive or unidirectional because there is a substantial amount of interserver communications. (That is, a typical web application may require conversations between web servers, other application servers, and several other related database servers.) This predominantly east-west traffic does not perform well under the conventional network topology. Furthermore, server virtualization has also redefined the way that data centers are built; it has had a profound effect on the way compute and storage are provisioned, initiated, managed, and torn down. What enterprises, data centers, cloud, and communication service providers require now are programmable, flexible, and agile networks.

Software-defined networks deliver on that concept of programmability, flexibility, and agility by bringing together, in a symbiotic manner, several of the key virtualization techniques that are either well established or are subjects of intense theoretical and practical study. These key virtualization elements are as follows:

- Server virtualization
- Storage virtualization

- Network virtualization

- Network functions virtualization

- Virtual network management

- Orchestration

SDN brings together all of these virtualization techniques under one umbrella to provide a programmable network that is suited to the demands of modern applications and services. Server and storage virtualization in the enterprise data centers—though not in the SDN architecture—are enablers, because they establish virtualization as not just a credible alternative but a high-performance and cost-effective solution to many data center design issues. Such was the success of server and storage virtualization, insomuch as it delivered on its promise to curb server sprawl, reduce capex and opex expenditure, while reducing server provisioning and application deployment times, that it was almost immediately adopted in enterprise and service providers' data centers.

Although server and storage virtualization are not part of SDN, they played a major role in network virtualization, which is another key SDN technology. Server and storage virtualization became hugely popular with administrators, but they grew frustrated that many of the advanced features of server and storage virtualization went unused due to the static network. Features such as dynamic provisioning and virtual machine (VM) mobility were the desired functions, but this required flexible and dynamic network reconfiguration, which wasn't possible with traditional network design. Network virtualization then became the focus of attention; it was felt that the static network was holding the potential of server and storage virtualization back. Network virtualization, therefore, was developed to support VM mobility and other VM features that typically required them to share a Layer 2 broadcast domain. As you saw previously, this created several issues on a conventional Layer 2/3 hierarchal network, so the proposed solutions concentrated on encapsulation and tunnels or on producing large-scale backbone Layer 2 fabrics. Either way, this presented a problem insomuch as VLANs are required to support multitenancy and provide a (very small) measure of security. The issue here is that manually provisioning, maintaining, and administering thousands of VLANs on a production network isn't feasible.

SDN, though, can provision all those tunnels, either as VLANs or VxLANs, dynamically. In addition, SDN can instantiate, manage, and tear down the tunnels on demand, a thing a network administrator couldn't possibly manage manually.

SDN, therefore, works collaboratively with server, storage, and network virtualization to deliver a programmable, flexible, and agile network for enterprises, data centers, and cloud and communication provider networks. In addition, SDN also leverages another similar conceptual network architecture, that of network functions virtualization (NFV).

How SDN and NFV Tie Together

SDN and NFV have similar purposes—namely to make a network simpler. However, they go about their task in different ways. SDN uses the concept of abstracting the control layer from the forwarding (data) layer of the network appliances, switches, and routers. SDN can then centralize the control and management functions in a dedicated software controller. NFV, in contrast, abstracts the network functions in a network appliance from the underlying hardware and creates software instances of each function that can be used in a VM or as an application on a nonvirtualized server. Therefore, the two methods for simplifying the network are very different, but also very compatible. Consequently, SDN and NFV are often used together to maximize each other's potential in providing a simplified yet programmable network.

Figure 40-1 shows how SDN and NFV compare on a number of fronts. It's important to understand that these two technologies are different and they are used for different things. However, they complement each other.

NFV vs. SDN

Software Defined Networking (SDN)		Network Functions Virtualization (NFV)
Separate control and data, centralize control and programmability of network	**Basic Concept**	Relocate network functions from dedicated appliances to generic servers
Campus, data center/cloud	**Target Location**	Service provider network
Commodity servers and switches	**Target Devices**	Commodity servers and switches
Cloud orchestration and networking	**Initial Applications**	Routers, firewalls, gateways, CDN, WAN accelerators, SLA assurance
OpenFlow	**New Protocols**	None
Open Networking Foundation (ONF)	**Formalization**	ETSI NFV Working Group

Figure 40-1   *How SDN and NFV compare on a number of fronts*

SDN and NFV work well together because although NFV can operate in a totally nonvirtualized environment (for example, by obtaining a software version of a network function such as a firewall and then installing an instance of that firewall onto a commodity server as an application, which is a simple but accurate example of NFV). However, in a virtualized environment, NFV requires that the underlay network be virtualized in order to maximize its own functionality. What this means is that NFV benefits from having a virtual network overlay to work with. By having the concept of customer tunnels to work with, NFV can install instances of network functions within tunnels. This is much more elegant than situating functions centrally or at major traffic aggregation points and massively overprovisioning the bandwidth and network cards to accommodate combined throughput. Instead, a network function can be instantiated and managed per customer on their individual tunnel. Furthermore, if NFV works with SDN in dynamically provisioning those tunnels, SDN can ensure that the customer's traffic is always routed through the network functions regardless of where they are deployed in the network. SDN and NFV can work in close collaboration to provision devices and services to support the appropriate network functions while dynamically controlling and orchestrating network traffic flows per customer/service in a multitenant environment.

SDN's Downside: A Loss of Visibility

Despite all the benefits that SDN brings to a modern network in terms of flexibility and agility, there is one major downside, and that manifests itself through the lack of network management visibility. When conventional networks in data centers rolled out server and storage virtualization using hypervisor and vSwitch technology, there was a gray area created, an invisible extension of the access layer, which prevented traditional network management systems from monitoring intra-VM-to-VM communications and also inter-VM-to-VM communications through tunnels. Improvements to hypervisor and vSwitch technology resolved these issues, but there still remained a problem with visibility across the network. After all, a conventional network management system (NMS) does not have vision into a tunnel, only the tunnel endpoints, so packets encapsulated and traveling through a tunnel look to it as individual packets traversing the network. A tunnel could be passing packets from many customers between the common endpoints. SDN, though, can track individual customer traffic, and it can identify and reroute an individual customer's traffic if it is not receiving the entitled service level agreement (SLA) for resources. Furthermore, SDN, having a global view of the entire network, receives feedback from the SDN-enabled network devices with regard to their state, and it can determine the state of each and every traffic flow, and adjust flows dynamically. Consequently, SDN, although it works to abstract the complexity of the underlay physical network from the software-defined virtual network, does cooperate with modern NMS to provide the required vision into the paths that traffic flows take through the physical network.

SDN Orchestration

The fact that SDN can dynamically adjust traffic flows to meet SLAs or fault conditions requires a high level of control and assurance. For example, an SDN controller is either autonomously controlling each traffic flow, or it is passing the state to a higher application to determine the actions to be taken. This capability to pass relevant network data to a higher application allows for that application to control the delivery of its own SLA requirements in real time. This level of control, called *orchestration*, allows for an application to enforce policy and performance criteria in real time, something that is just not feasible with the conventional network architecture. Orchestration is a crucial element in the SDN architecture because it permits domain-specific policy and rules to be established and suggests ways for the SDN controller to maintain SLA criteria, such as increasing bandwidth, so that it can apply to the underlay network devices.

Orchestration is important if SDN is to have dynamic control and service flexibility over several applications running concurrently that may require quite diverse network conditions. Each application can interface with the orchestrator to request their own environmental conditions, and it is then the job of the orchestrator to manage the controller to fulfill the service requirements through the controller's manipulation of the underlay SDN devices in the physical network. The crucial point here is that the orchestrator can manipulate conditions in the virtual network without making any changes to the physical network topology. Therefore, any changes applied for one application will have no detrimental effect on other applications. In addition, there can be a hierarchy of orchestrators, an orchestrator of orchestrators, which is essential in multidomain networks such as a telecom network that will support many diverse services, fixed-line, mobile data (2G, 3G, 4G), IP TV, VDO, WI-FI, and so on. Each individual service, because of its own complexity, will each require its own specialist orchestrator; it's not practical to consider creating one orchestrator that could feasibly control all those diverse domains. SDN can, however, accommodate each individual orchestrator for each specialist domain, yet have one master orchestrator govern the entire network.

SDN as an architecture is concerned with abstracting the control (intelligence) layer of a network switch or routers from its forwarding layer and centralizing that intelligence so that it can have vision and control over the entire network. However, as you have seen, SDN works with many virtualization technologies to bring utility as well as programmability, flexibility, and agility to the enterprise, data center, or cloud and communication service provider networks.

This chapter focused on how all the virtualization techniques work in conjunction to deliver an SDN network. However, what actual use is this to most enterprises or service providers? Yes, it is clear that SDN provides programmability, but what issues and benefits can that programmability, flexibility, and agility solve or realize in the real world? The following chapter attempts to answer that question.

How SDN and NFV Will Affect You

In just a few short years since their introduction, software-defined networking (SDN) and network functions virtualization (NFV) have managed to obtain almost universal consensus, acclaim, and recognition, as a major theoretical concept for modern network design moving forward. Interestingly, however, the SDN architecture, the actual realistic deployment methodology, does not have that same consensus. Some major network equipment vendors agree with the principles of SDN but want a distributed architecture whereby the intelligence is retained on the network devices and they could be controlled by a centralized orchestrator via vendor application programming interfaces (APIs). Not a surprise given the revenue generated by their intelligent network devices. Others strongly disagree with this approach; they believe it would only compound the risk of vendor lock-in, and consequently they demand that any SDN architecture should be vendor agnostic and network neutral. Subsequently, due to this divergence in opinion, at the time of this writing, there is no roadmap, and no industry consensus of opinion of how to deploy SDN. As a result, although there is near unanimous agreement that SDN is the route to take, adoption of SDN has stalled in the enterprise data centers. However, this is not the case with cloud and communications service providers and their approach to SDN and NFV. In fact, they have been actively researching, piloting, and running proof-of-concept builds, with or without vendor support.

The reasons that cloud and service providers are so energetic and motivated toward deploying SDN and NFV in comparison to their rather hesitant counterparts in the enterprise networks and data centers is not that they are willing to accept risk at a higher level than their enterprise counterparts. Far from it. Cloud and service providers are typically even more risk averse compared to enterprises. The reason they are ahead on this case is that they see tremendous promise and potential in both SDN and NFV to both make and save them money. Lots and lots of money. This is not meant as a bad thing. In fact, it's actually good for everybody. Cloud and service providers have recognized that SDN and NFV can solve many of their longstanding operational issues (which costs everyone more), and the realization that they may finally remedy many of these operational or financial bugbears is too good an opportunity to squander waiting on vendor roadmaps.

It is this difference in the level of motivation driven by the potential realization of a desirable end product that sees SDN and NFV adoption and innovation surging forward in the cloud and service provider networks while stagnating in the enterprise. So, what are these use cases that cloud and service providers are finding so suited to SDN and NFV networks?

Operational Domains

Communication service providers have noted several areas of interest where they believe an SDN network would provide a satisfactory solution to the longstanding operational problem of provisioning. In addition, carriers and service providers saw the possibility for improvements in several of their operational domains, such as new business services and revenue streams, reduced capital expenditure (CAPEX) and operational expenditure (OPEX), and the simplification of increasingly complex layers of networks. These operational domains are as follows.

Mobility Virtualization

Mobile Internet data traffic is growing, and mobile-to-mobile traffic has added unpredictable traffic patterns. Virtualization of the packet core and Gigabit LAN (GiLAN) is currently top of the list for mobile operators who need data networks, which can flex to meet dynamic traffic demands.

Virtual CPE and Service Chaining

Managing customer premises equipment (CPE) is a major operational burden, and truck rolls are a major expense. Both can and do hamper a service provider's ability to roll out new services. Significant OPEX savings are possible if operators can deliver CPE services for a vCPE architecture servicing network functions from the cloud rather than the physical CPE.

NFV and Service Orchestration

Service providers deploying virtual CPE (vCPE) are looking for operational improvements by hosting their services and network functions in a hybrid, physical/virtual environment. Orchestration brings together the virtual and physical networking functions, so that operations can leverage the full benefits of vCPE and improve the quality of experience to end users.

WAN Optimization and Innovation

Operators need a holistic view across the different transport and IP network layers to achieve greater optimization and hence improved traffic engineering. Dynamic bandwidth optimization is more efficient and cheaper than traditional static methods of provisioning WAN links. An SDN controller can apply policy dynamically to improve the customer experience without overprovisioning the bandwidth.

Network Optimization

Networks in operation today are the result of many years of evolution; therefore, they are complex, with multiple layers supporting multiple services and protocols. Furthermore, this complexity comes at a cost. The purpose of SDN and NFV is to create simpler network designs that can bring greater savings and make the WAN more focused on services and customer experience.

Policy-Driven Application Provisioning and Delivery

Successful development and delivery of in-house services and applications is a competitive advantage for modern service provider customers. Adapting the manual and error-prone process of provisioning and delivering services and applications into a dynamic, automated, policy-driven process can result in significant cost savings. Automated provisioning through SDN orchestration leads to faster delivery, more reliable and consistent products, and added improvements in security compliance and end-customer experience.

SDN Use Cases

In contrast to cloud and service providers, enterprise and data centers see much less motivational-inducing promise in the adoption of SDN and NFV. Still there are several use cases for SDN within enterprises and the data center, such as the following.

Network Access Control

NAC follows the user/device as they connect from different areas of the campus and applies the correct policies, service chains, quality of service (QoS), and access control limits.

Network Virtualization

Network virtualization (NV) creates a virtual network overlay on top of a physical network, allowing a large number of multitenant networks to run concurrently and securely over a physical underlay network that can span multiple racks in the data center.

Data Center Optimization

SDN and NFV optimize networks and improve application performance by detecting data traffic affinities or traits, orchestrating workloads with dynamic networking configuration. By adjusting flows according to affinities, data center optimization (DCO) therefore manages and optimizes mice/elephant flows across the network.

Direct Inter-Connects

This application of SDN creates dynamic links between locations, such as enterprise and their Data Centers, or branch locations, as well as dynamically applying appropriate QoS and bandwidth allocation to those links.

Embracing SDN and NFV

Despite these use cases bringing much needed flexibility and operational optimization, especially in these days of big data, they have not been enough to convince enterprise and data centers to adopt SDN en masse. What many enterprises and data center managers do see is a great concept. It's a wonderful idea, but there's not a clear way of safely getting from where they are now (a static network) to where they would like to be (a dynamic, flexible and agile network), and so being risk averse, many businesses think it's more trouble than it's worth—at least for the time being.

In many industries, this is probably a wise decision. (You don't go to all the trouble, cost, and risk of restructuring the network and retraining staff just because it is the latest trend. There has to be a clear end state that makes it all worthwhile.) Therefore, enterprises in either traditional or highly regulated industries such as manufacturing, healthcare, and pharmaceutical that may have service-oriented application (SOA) network infrastructures running bespoke applications that have served them well for decades are unlikely to benefit from SDN and NFV in the short term.

However, industries such as banking, insurance, and financial services are prime candidates for SDN and NFV adoption because they are experiencing huge growth in their data centers to accommodate the explosion in data over the past few years. Consequently, if you are within one of these industries, SDN and NFV will be an item high up on the agenda, and large-scale change is on the horizon. Other small, medium, and large companies may find the motivation to move to SDN an opportunity to skip the trials and tribulations of the re-organization by simply migrating their IT operations and server rooms to the cloud, thereby getting SDN by proxy.

Cloud providers will certainly embrace SDN and NFV innovations because their whole technology approach relies heavily on having elastic networks that are flexible and agile with inherent support for large-scale multitenant domains. SDN and NFV provide the technology to create highly elastic network resources, which facilitates fast service provisioning. By providing the tools, security, and multitenant support required by enterprises, more and more will gain confidence in migrating data to the cloud. Furthermore, cloud providers of infrastructure as a service (IaaS) will benefit as more and more SME (small, medium, and enterprise) customers realize the cost and operational savings that can be made by migrating their traditional data center into the cloud. This change of emphasis toward outsourcing the data center to the cloud will prove to be highly lucrative and cost-effective for all parties concerned. Similarly, software development houses and enterprise development operations will embrace platform as a service (PaaS) because it will be cheaper and more efficient to use cloud platforms, application programming interfaces (APIs), and micro-services than it will be to host their own development platforms, test beds, and tools.

Despite all of these advantages and improvements in service for business, SDN may not be good news for everyone. After all, reductions in OPEX usually point to one thing: creating efficiency, which results in downsizing. This will be one of the key areas of change in the short to mid-term as we see medium and large businesses closing data centers and migrating their applications and data to the cloud. Consequently, there could be network support and data center job losses to follow. However, new opportunities could spring up as jobs shift to other business. (You can expect more cloud and network providers to enter the market, for example.) Similarly, there will be reduced manpower required to maintain the data centers that do survive because skilled vendors' technicians will no longer be required in such numbers, and this will hold true for network administrators and other data center support staff. Consequently, although the future looks very bright for SDN, and the cloud, carrier, and service providers, it might be troubling times ahead for network engineers and administrators, at least in the very near term. In the broader sense, though, the news is quite positive.

Why Cloud Networking Matters

Energy

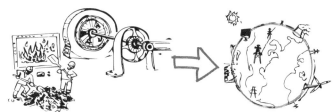

The first light bulb was invented in 1879 marking the dawn of the electric era.

But making your own power was expensive and limited.

It was not until the power grid was established that electricity was broadly used.

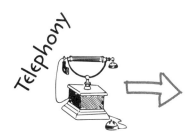

Telephony

A similar thing happened with the telephone, which was invented in 1876.

For years, all calls had to be directly connected, which limited expansion and utility.

Worldwide phone systems and auto switching made broad telephony a reality.

Computing

Virtualized computing is going through a similar evolution. It's been around for a while but its utility was limited in scope and available to large organizations.

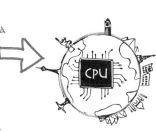

Cloud networking makes this computing capability available to everyone. We think the benefits will be profound!

What's Next in Networking?

The preceding chapter discussed the main use cases for software-defined networking (SDN) and network functions virtualization (NFV) and how they would affect us, whether we are a user, small to medium-size enterprise (SME), enterprise data center, carrier, or cloud service provider. You saw that carriers, cloud, and communication service providers (CSPs) were the ones driving SDN and NFV due to a range of use cases. What is interesting with the carrier, cloud, and CSP perspective is that they are less interested in SDN than they are in NFV. This is noticeable throughout their endeavors to build proof of concepts and run pilot field trials. Presently, industries and the enterprise and data center focus is on SDN, but you will soon see the focus moving more toward NFV because it is providing the motivational drivers to the carrier, cloud, and CSP markets.

Separate but Complementary

SDN and NFV are separate techniques that are often used together because they are such highly complementary technologies. NFV, however, does not require SDN or even a virtualized environment to function; it can operate autonomously. Despite this, NFV is often paired with SDN as if they were tightly coupled or even dependent upon each other. Of course, this isn't true, but the fact remains that NFV must be built upon a dynamic flexible network, such as the type of networks SDN delivers, if it is to operate effectively in any automated system. Therefore, although at present we know SDN and NFV to be separate but complementary concepts, they will grow closer in the future as their activities and goals become inextricably linked.

NVF, which comes under the auspice of the European Telecommunications Standards Institute (ETSI), has received a great deal of attention since 2014 and has probably overtaken SDN and all things cloud as the hottest topic in networking. This can be attributed to three things: the interest and sponsorship of the ETSI, the interest by carriers and service providers in the ETSI-proposed use cases for NFV, and the waning of interest in SDN within the enterprise and data center community. It happened to coincide that as vendors and enterprises continued their struggle for a consensus approach to SDN, NFV was traveling in the opposite direction. Boosted by huge interest from the carrier, cloud, and CSP community, NFV was being tested and trialed around the globe on real-world projects. These trials and proof of concepts where NFV is tested on resolving real issues, which were held between 2014 and the present, will determine the immediate path that networking takes over the coming years.

Virtual Customer Premise Equipment

One important proof of concept was testing the feasibility of virtual customer premises equipment (vCPE). The importance of the vCPE trials was that this was a real test case for how NFV could operate in a large-scale deployment in a heterogeneous network environment. The concepts of vCPE are basic NFV, which makes it an ideal technology to test. Simply put, a vCPE is a virtual instance of the physical CPE that resides at the customer's premises, or in the case of residential customers, in their home. The idea is to virtualize the CPE and remove/bypass the control plane intelligence that contains the integrated network functions on the physical CPE. This would leave only the forwarding plane's mechanisms functional, because they are required to switch packets between the external and internal connection ports. The functions bypassed on the physical CPE are then virtualized as software instances, firewalls, load balancers, Dynamic Host Configuration Protocol (DHCP), Domain Name System (DNS), and so forth on a vCPE residing on a commodity server or virtual machine (VM) on a virtualized server located in the provider's own network.

The advantage of this setup is that by removing all the existing network functions from the customer domain and placing them out of harm's way in the provider domain, the number of service calls and subsequent truck rolls would be dramatically reduced. Bear in mind that each per-subscriber truck roll is estimated to cost the service provider between $200 and $500 per instance. That might not seem a lot, but if you consider a small provider with 2 million subscribers, that will add up to a significant amount in operation expenses per year. In addition, there is also the benefit of lower customer fault calls, increased first-time call resolutions for customer support representatives (CSR), and subsequently higher customer satisfaction and hence reduced churn. Moreover, NFV delivered much more than just a simple reduction in operational expenses; it enabled operations to revolutionize the way they provisioned and delivered services to the customer.

Service deployments and activations that would have taken months were completed in minutes due to NFV. This was accomplished by avoiding the create, test, and deploy cycle required when delivering services to a customer's physical CPE by way of a truck roll and firmware upgrade. Instead, new services could be deployed on the vCPE with a few clicks of the mouse as the operator activated, for example, a new firewall instance for the firewall network function on the customer's centrally located vCPE. Therefore, NFV provided a method for rapid service and application deployment, automated provisioning using service policies, and tight orchestration and integration with the provider's operations systems support/business support system (OSS/BSS) through directly connected application programming interfaces (APIs). For the customer, there were also benefits from vCPE. They not only received better and more timely break/fix resolutions, but they also now had the added benefits of having a centralized self-service portal where they could register devices, order services, configure security, and set parental control policies that followed the device around the network, not just the home.

As a result of the successful trial of NFV as a vCPE and over a range of subsequent use cases, it has become apparent that virtualization is certainly here to stay, and the future strategies being executed look like they are likely to follow a policy of "virtualize everything you can and host it in the cloud."

SDN and NFV Working Together

Despite virtualization's many successes, such as in compute, storage, networks, and now network functions, it is still limited without SDN and orchestration. NFV has its own orchestration module in its architecture, giving it some autonomy, but it still operates better when in conjunction with an elastic, flexible, agile SDN network and a shared orchestrator.

Not everyone agrees that SDN and NFV are equally important; however, they do recognize SDN's important contribution. Some of the ways that ETSI believes that NFV and SDN can complement each other in future deployment scenarios include the following:

- The SDN controller fits well into the broader concept of a network controller in an NFV infrastructure (NFVI) architecture.

- SDN can play a significant role in the orchestration of the NFVI resources, both physical and virtual, enabling functionality such as provisioning, configuration of network connectivity, and bandwidth allocation, and can play an important role in orchestrating the automation of operations, processes, monitoring, security, and policy control.

- SDN can provide the network virtualization required to support multitenant NFVIs.

- NFV forwarding graphs can be implemented by the SDN controller as a means to provide the automated provisioning of service chains.

- The SDN controller could itself be virtualized and run as a virtual network function (VNF), possibly as part of a service chain including other network functions. For example, applications and services originally developed to run on the SDN controller could be implemented as separate network functions within a service chain.

Given the current trajectories of SDN and NFV, it is highly likely that soon the ETSI vision of NFV utilizing and virtualizing the SDN's controller and functions so that they become intertwined into a unified, software-based networking model, will come true. However, by the time this NFV dominant model, which will be based on the ability to abstract and programmatically control network resources (SDN concepts) becomes a reality, we will no longer differentiate between SDN and NFV.

Before we get the impression that SDN is on the wane and NFV will be the new force in networking, perhaps even one day ultimately virtualizing SDN as a network function, we should remember why SDN is so important.

SDN is hugely important because it makes the network programmable, and software control and orchestration is not going to go away. SDN's dynamic programmability and granular control of each lower-layer forwarding device is crucial to building and maintaining vast networks in cloud and web-sized company data centers. These cloud networks need to be programmable, dynamic, elastic, flexible, and agile if they are to be able to meet the vast traffic demands placed on them. The future is SDN. It might not be here yet, and it might not be what we expect it to be based on current architecture, but it will be software-defined networking.

Summary

The big takeaway, however, is this. As a result of virtualization, cloud SDN and NFV networking has changed forever. The networks built on these technologies are more scalable, more agile, faster to build, and easier to manage than anything we dreamed of a decade ago. As is always the case, there will be winners and losers in this. Some leading companies will get overtaken. Some jobs will disappear or get shifted. In aggregate, however, business in general and networking in particular are much better off as a result of these technologies.

INDEX

N

T

W

X-Y-Z

REGISTER YOUR PRODUCT at informit.com/register

Access Additional Benefits and SAVE 35% on Your Next Purchase

- Download available product updates.

- Access bonus material when applicable.

- Receive exclusive offers on new editions and related products.
  (Just check the box to hear from us when setting up your account.)

- Get a coupon for 35% for your next purchase, valid for 30 days. Your code will
  be available in your InformIT cart. (You will also find it in the Manage Codes
  section of your account page.)

Registration benefits vary by product. Benefits will be listed on your account page
under Registered Products.

InformIT.com—The Trusted Technology Learning Source

InformIT is the online home of information technology brands at Pearson, the world's foremost
education company. At InformIT.com you can

- Shop our books, eBooks, software, and video training.
- Take advantage of our special offers and promotions (informit.com/promotions).
- Sign up for special offers and content newsletters (informit.com/newsletters).
- Read free articles and blogs by information technology experts.
- Access thousands of free chapters and video lessons.

Connect with InformIT—Visit informit.com/community

Learn about InformIT community events and programs.

informIT.com
the trusted technology learning source

Addison-Wesley · Cisco Press · IBM Press · Microsoft Press · Pearson IT Certification · Prentice Hall · Que · Sams · VMware Press